A PEDAGOGY OF
POWERFUL COMMUNICATION

CRITICAL ISSUES FOR LEARNING AND TEACHING

Shirley R. Steinberg and Pepi Leistyna
General Editors

Vol. 10

The Minding the Media series is part of both
the Peter Lang Education list and the Media and Communication list.
Every volume is peer reviewed and meets
the highest quality standards for content and production.

PETER LANG
New York • Washington, D.C./Baltimore • Bern
Frankfurt • Berlin • Brussels • Vienna • Oxford

Dana Walker

A PEDAGOGY OF POWERFUL COMMUNICATION

Youth Radio and Radio Arts in the Multilingual Classroom

PETER LANG
New York • Washington, D.C./Baltimore • Bern
Frankfurt • Berlin • Brussels • Vienna • Oxford

Library of Congress Cataloging-in-Publication Data
Walker, Dana.
A pedagogy of powerful communication: youth radio and radio arts
in the multilingual classroom / Dana Walker.
pages cm. — (Minding the media: critical issues for learning
and teaching; vol. 10)
Includes bibliographical references and index.
1. Radio in education. 2. Bilingual education. I. Title.
LB1044.5.W33   371.33'31—dc23   2014000357
ISBN 978-1-4331-1957-6 (hardcover)
ISBN 978-1-4331-1956-9 (paperback)
ISBN 978-1-4539-1321-5 (e-book)
ISSN 2151-2949

Bibliographic information published by **Die Deutsche Nationalbibliothek**.
Die Deutsche Nationalbibliothek lists this publication in the "Deutsche
Nationalbibliografie"; detailed bibliographic data is available
on the Internet at http://dnb.d-nb.de/.

Cover photo by Dana Walker

The paper in this book meets the guidelines for permanence and durability
of the Committee on Production Guidelines for Book Longevity
of the Council of Library Resources.

© 2014 Peter Lang Publishing, Inc., New York
29 Broadway, 18th floor, New York, NY 10006
www.peterlang.com

All rights reserved.
Reprint or reproduction, even partially, in all forms such as microfilm,
xerography, microfiche, microcard, and offset strictly prohibited.

Printed in the United States of America

For the teachers, students, and mentors
of Youth Radio and Radio Arts.
mis compañeros de viaje

Contents

Acknowledgments ix

Chapter One. Introduction 1

Chapter Two. Youth Radio and Radio Arts Curriculum and Pedagogy 19

Chapter Three. Constructing the Observable Curriculum 51

Chapter Four. Constructing Personal Voice 85

Chapter Five. Tania's Story: Constructing a Public Voice 127

Chapter Six. Toward a Pedagogy of Powerful Communication 167

Bibliography 179

Index 187

Acknowledgments

I would like to thank various institutions, colleagues, and friends who have made this work possible. The Spencer Foundation provided generous funding through their Small Grant program to conduct this year-long ethnographic study. The University of Northern Colorado supported my sabbatical leave and graduate research assistants: Madeline Crouse, who helped with data collection and program instruction during the 2010–2011 program, and Megan Edmiston, who edited an early draft of the manuscript. Many thanks to Deborah Romero and Laura Pritchett for reading an early draft of the introduction. I would like to thank Sasha Sidorkin for his encouragement to undertake this project, and Judith Green who took the time to introduce me to her world of interactional ethnography. I am indebted to Tania Zittoun, whose work has been a great inspiration, and who provided guidance, resources, and ultimately feedback on several chapters of this book. Many thanks to Brent and Judy, whose friendship and quiet cabin in the woods allowed me to complete the manuscript. Finally, I would like to thank Mark for his moral support and endless patience.

• CHAPTER ONE •

Introduction

> Democracy will have its consummation when free social inquiry is indissolubly wedded to the art of full and moving communication.
> —John Dewey

In the summer of 2006, a group of teachers and I found ourselves in the city of Oaxaca when the governor sent in troops to violently repress a teachers' strike. Close to a hundred people were killed or disappeared by some reports. Our group was trapped in the mayhem of tear gas, helicopters, streets on fire, and armed police and military, unable to leave the city because the government had shut down the airport and all major highways north to Mexico City.

What caught our attention at the time, in the midst of the conflict, was the key role that community radio played as a lifeline for protesting teachers, opening channels for communication, debate, and expressions of solidarity. As one radio commentator said, "The radio played a determining role in the movement in Oaxaca. The radio opened new spaces for communication and action." Voices that were not normally heard in the mainstream were speaking out, demanding to be heard. As one woman declared, in broken Spanish as she was an indigenous language speaker:

> Queremos también, que nos de este lugar para transmitir lo que queremos y lo que pensimos [sic]. Porque somos humanos. Tenemos derecho también. / We want to have access to this place [the radio station], to transmit what we want and what we think. Because we are humans. We too have the right. (Friedberg, 2007)

As a result of our experience there, Carol, a middle school teacher, and I began a conversation about the lessons we had learned from these courageous Oaxacan teachers and the role that community radio played in the protestors' resistance to the violent government repression. We talked about how we might apply these lessons back home to thinking about how our own community radio could become a partner for developing youth voice, powerful language, civic engagement, and new media literacies to enable second language learners to access channels of communication for greater participation in the public media sphere. Our question was, How can youth radio be used in the United States to address the marginalization and silencing of immigrant students, to revitalize learning, and to create greater equity in second language and literacy education?

We were motivated by our concern with the ways schools in the United States are failing emergent bilingual learners, especially those from working-class Mexican immigrant or Mexican descent families in our region. Alienation and disengagement are enduring problems among urban youth in the U.S. educational system. Researchers (Nieto, 2002; Suárez-Orozco & Suárez-Orozco, 2001; Valencia, 2002; Valenzuela, 1999) and students attribute this phenomenon to a number of factors including lack of caring, under qualified teachers, invalid tests, disabling labels, lack of relevance of curriculum to students' lives, and exclusion of their languages and experiences from the dominant discourse of schools. Carol recounted how, in spite of her efforts to develop a culturally responsive pedagogy and curriculum for her students, her lowest performing students seemed irremediably disengaged from school learning. I, in turn, had seen too many schools with majority low-income English learners where No Child Left Behind and punitive accountability systems were de-professionalizing teachers, dumbing-down the curriculum, and treating young people as mindless automatons; schools where principals expected to see teachers of the same grade teaching from the same scripted literacy page when they walked down the hall; schools where students were not allowed to take science or social studies if they had not achieved a certain score on a commercial oral English fluency test; schools where children and adolescents spent from 30 to 140 minutes a day mechanically repeating mindless phonics formulas using a program originally designed for students with learning disabilities. We were also motivated by concern over the effects of immigration laws that were preventing undocumented students from obtaining in-state tuition, even if they had grown up in the United States. This represents a significant glass ceiling for those students, discouraging them from struggling to graduate from high school when there is no hope of attending college due to prohibition against obtaining federally subsidized loans, which is how the majority of U.S. students go to college (Suárez-Orozco, Yoshikawa, Teranishi, & Suárez-Orozco, 2011). Though the "Deferred Action for Childhood Arrivals" memorandum, signed by President Obama in 2012, has given new hope for a change in the treatment of undocumented children and youth in this country, skepticism remains among many young people and their families about whether the application information will be used for immigration enforcement, how long the policy will remain in place and whether they can trust the Obama administration, which has deported people in record numbers.

Since the summer of 2006 in Oaxaca, with Carol and other teachers and colleagues, I have taken lessons and inspiration from Oaxaca to implement Youth Radio and Radio Arts for emergent bilinguals in middle school and high school classrooms, during and after school (Walker, 2009; Walker & Romero, 2008). We have worked in partnership with a local community radio station, poets, and performing artists in an ecological learning design (Bernstein, 2000; González, Moll, & Amanti, 2005) intended to connect schools to the resources available in the community, and to expand language and literacy practices in schools.

Communication and Education

Thirty years ago, in an incisive exploration of the meanings and purposes of literacy, the North American educational philosopher Maxine Greene (1982) noted the essential relationship between communication and democracy. She wrote, "Only when we have achieved communication will democracy come into its own" (p. 326). Drawing on the work of philosophers Dewey, Arendt, and Habermas, Greene suggested that new modes of communication and new literacies were key to overcoming human beings' alienation, and the "automatism, wordlessness, and passivity" that plagues schools (p. 326). A decade earlier the Brazilian educational philosopher Freire (1970/2000) had begun asserting, similarly, that democracy, education, and communication are inextricably linked, and that to move toward a more just and democratic society of self-actualized human beings, we must take communication seriously. For Freire (2005) the act of knowing is a function of communication. Without communication, the object of knowledge cannot have meaning: the goal of thinking itself is not knowledge, but communication.

Though communication has been at the center of debates about education and democracy, attention to the critical dimensions of communication among teachers of linguistically and culturally diverse students has been missing. In the field of language education, for example, communication has been claimed as both the means and the goal of second and foreign language teaching since the 1980s. Rooted in the work of sociolinguist Dell Hymes (1974), early iterations of Communicative Language Teaching emphasized the social and political dimensions of language as paramount. Over time, however, the social and political dimensions have been left behind and, as Leung (2005) argues, communication has been reduced to a pedagogic technique limited to in-situ activities of the language classroom. Far from the original intent of Hymes, communication has come to be framed in second and foreign language teaching "as a freely engaged, untrammelled and decontextualized human activity in classrooms everywhere" (p. 137).

In the field of ESL and bilingual education in the United States (often called Culturally and Linguistically Diverse [CLD] Education), "communication" has taken center stage in the World-Class Instructional Design & Assessment (WIDA, 2007) and Teaching English as a Second or Other Language (TESOL, 2009) teacher preparation standards (which recently adopted the WIDA standards) as the leading indicator of language proficiency:

> English language learners *communicate* for Social and Instructional purposes within the school setting; English language learners *communicate* information, ideas and concepts necessary for academic success in the content area of Language Arts; . . . English language learners *communicate* information, ideas and concepts necessary for academic success in the content area of Social Studies; etc. (WIDA, 2007)

While this framing of language teaching is an advance over a focus on the language domains (reading, writing, listening, speaking) as independent skills, the new English language proficiency standards are problematic on several fronts. First, the language proficiency standards perpetuate the myth of communication as transmission of information, leaving out important dimensions of language use for constructing identity, proposing new ways of knowing, and challenging social relations. Second, the notion of communication proposed by the WIDA standards limits communication to the use of language within the school setting for schooling purposes, which perpetuates the artificial schism between language used for school and language used for participation in other local/global communities. Finally, the way the WIDA standards frame communication reproduces the ideology of monolingualism and assimiliationism, with the implicit assumption that "communicative competence" refers to conformity to the norms of Standard English and a singular, unchanging set of language practices.

The WIDA position on communication is a fundamentally conservative position that seeks to preserve a false ideal of a uniform language and language practice, and ignores the value for language learners of challenging and transforming language conventions to reshape knowledge and power relations (Horner, Lu, & Royster, 2011). It is also not the way that contemporary multilingual, multidialectal authors and media producers use language, as noted in the National Council of Teachers of English (NCTE) Resolution on the Rights of Students to their Own Language:

> The ability to incorporate both home language and the language of wider communication in writing is a valued skill beyond schools. Well-known authors regularly use these strategies to enrich and extend possibilities for expression in fiction and nonfiction texts (e.g., Alice Walker, Junot Diaz, Gary Soto . . . as well as authors in the fields of science and law). In the same way, students and their audiences can benefit from opportunities and encouragement to draw on varied linguistic and cultural resources in their writing. (NCTE, 2008)

NCTE's position on "The Rights of Students to Incorporate Heritage and Home Languages in their Writing" is shared by the Conference on College Composition and Communication (CCC, 1974), as well as a growing number of educational and professional organizations. However, teacher preparation programs and schools themselves seem to be a long way from embracing these new understandings of language and approaches to language teaching. The "functional turn" in ESL and bilingual education, as currently interpreted in the United States, is important for helping teachers and learners understand what is required to communicate ideas and concepts within particular academic content areas, but it is not enough. Disciplines outside of CLD education, such as applied linguistics, communications, multiliteracies, and New Literacies Studies, offer more expansive and contemporary understandings of communication, to which I turn now.

The field of communication research, for example, goes beyond a notion of communication as unconstrained by sociopolitical factors that shape human interaction. The National Communications Association (NCA, 2001) clearly situates communication within human relations and social and political spheres of life. Communications research focuses on "reviewing specific ways in which communication affects political involvement and shapes civic discourse." In regards to personal and social development, NCA emphasizes that communication research seeks to "understand basic human relationships . . . specific ways in which effective communication affects the quality of family and work affiliations, how interpersonal communication skills impact long term development and adjustment" (p. 3). Communication is, in fact, an integral part of young learners' overall development. Furthermore, communication research addresses the ways that new communication technologies transform communication in personal and professional relationships, as well as how new communication technologies are helping to build new face-to-face and virtual communities. Though TESOL standards require teachers to incorporate technology, it is for instructional purposes only, not for the social, personal, and political development of multilingual learners engaged in multiple communities.

The field of *participatory communication* can provide further direction for language educators seeking to correct the limitations of Communicative Language Teaching. Popular in development organizations since the 1980s, this work centers on the role of communication in social change. While video, theater, and social media have also been used productively to increase participation of marginalized communities, community radio has been the communication tool most widely used in developing countries, now numbering in the thousands (Dagron, 2001). The movement began in the 1940s in Latin America where isolated communities of miners or *campesinos* (poor farmers) began operating their own radio stations to challenge the monopoly of state media, to initiate dialogue, and to broadcast the concerns of the local people. Thousands of independent and community-based radio stations have emerged since the social struggles of the 1960s and 1970s in Latin America, as seen in Oaxaca in 2006, and have since spread throughout the world. Drawing on the work of Freire (1970/2000) development organizations and scholars emphasize the political dimensions of communication and the democratizing potential of participatory communication:

> The main elements that characterise participatory communication are related to its capacity to involve the human subjects of social change in the process of communicating. The theoretical framework for participatory communication owes much to Paulo Freire. His books have not only revolutionised the world of education, but also communication for social change. (Dagron, 2001, p. 25)

While Youth Radio and Radio Arts is a school-based program and the intent is not direct participation in community radio per se, there are dimensions of participatory communication that can help expand our thinking about communication and inform multilingual education.

Reframing Communication within Language and Literacy Education

As communication has taken on new meanings in the postmodern world, language and literacy education need to reflect these changes. Effective citizenship, work, and play now require the ability to produce and consume multiple types of texts (visual, audio, written) and to communicate across cultural and national boundaries. In the context of increasing contact with cultural and linguistic diversity in both private and public spheres, progressive educators argue for language pedagogies that move beyond a rule-based, monolingual, and monocultural framework. The New London Group (TheNewLondonGroup, 1996), which laid the groundwork for a pedagogy of multiliteracies in the 1990s, argued that there needs to be a shift from teaching a standard version of the national language in the form of print literacy to cultivating the skills and orientations necessary for understanding and engaging with linguistic and cultural diversity in multiple media, including resources used for fashioning identities and life trajectories. (p. 64)

At the same time, our notions of traditional literacy—as a mental achievement applicable across disciplines and based largely on print—is being challenged. New Literacies scholars (Barton, Hamilton, & Ivanič, 2000; Street, 2003) have argued that far from being an isolated activity of the individual mind, literacies are associated with particular social practices and identities (doing science, being a poet or a talk-show host) that bring cultural, political, and economic histories to bear on the present. Gee (2003) has further argued that literacies should be viewed as *semiotic domains*, which he characterizes as "any set of practices that recruits one or more modalities (e.g., oral or written language, images, equations, symbols, sounds, gestures, graphs, artifacts, etc.), to communicate distinctive types of meanings" (p. 19). The skills and qualities involved in this type of semiotic work are becoming part of the cultural repertoire and performative competence (Canagarajah, 2013) of young people, which involves active identity work and the projection of shifting personae with changing attributes and achievements (Gee, Hull, & Lankshear, 1996).

It is acknowledged, however, that by and large these new literacies call on different abilities than those currently promoted in the majority of U.S.—with the exception of elite—schools: creativity, flexibility, collaboration, innovation, systems thinking, goal setting, and learning how to learn. Whereas well-resourced schools in a growing number of countries are adopting new technologies and innovative literacy pedagogies, under-resourced U.S. urban high schools have been slow in taking up these innovations (Mahiri, 2004). This is true in spite of emergent efforts to expand teaching practices in urban schools through innovative approaches that draw on research literature on out-of-school settings (Hull & Schultz, 2004; Soep & Chávez, 2010), community literacies (Kinloch, 2010), youth engagements with popular culture (Morrell & Duncan-Andrade, 2006) and social media and other Web-based environments (Lam, 2006). The problem seems particularly acute in under-resourced schools with large numbers of emergent bilinguals, who are pulled out of content-area classes and placed in remedial classes for oral language proficiency, homework help, and low-level reading and writing skills.

The digital divide, in spite of claims that corporate and public investment in school technologies has erased it, persists. Social, economic, and political power continue to shape access to and specific uses of new media technologies in schools, while both first level (affordability and access to technologies) and second level (differences in the purposes and uses of technologies) divides persist among low-socioeconomic status (SES) and high-SES students, reproducing uneven educational development (Hargittai, 2002). Combined with unequal access to the Internet and technology at home, power relations in educational institutions continue to constrain the successful implementation of technological and curricular innovations such as multiliteracies (Mills, 2011).

Taking Youth Media to School

One promising direction for promoting multilingual and multiliteracies pedagogies in schools is the field of youth media: conceived, developed, and produced by young people. Youth media has historically focused on underserved youth populations seeking to support youth's critical engagement with their own social realities (Fisherkeller, 2011; Goodman, 2003).Youth productions in youth media projects tend toward the use of multimedia, blending genres of television and radio journalism, spoken word, music, and visual art (Soep & Chávez, 2010). Youth radio, a subdomain of youth media, helps students develop multimodal literacies through the use of recording and broadcast technology and multimedia movie and audio-editing software. While there is now a large body of research on out-of-school youth media programs, documenting their power to promote youth engagement and critical literacy (Campbell, Hoey, & Perlman, 2001; Chávez & Soep, 2005; Goodman, 2003), scant research has been conducted on school-based youth media (Keenan & Fisherkeller, 2008), and none to date on language and critical literacy development among English learners through youth media.

This study examines a particular kind of youth media project, Youth Radio and Radio Arts for multilingual high school students. I present findings related to the principles of an emerging *pedagogy of powerful communication* that blends practices from youth media, multiliteracies, arts education, and standards-based instruction. My research traces the development of these principles in relation to notions of "voice" and "communication" as they were constructed over the course of the program, and identified by youth in semi-structured interviews at the end of the year.

Theoretical and Methodological Framework

To examine the emergence over time of principles of a *pedagogy of powerful communication* and how notions of "voice" were constructed and understood by participants in relation to communication, this study focuses on the processes of change and continuity at the collective and individual levels. I examine continuity and change across two dimensions of the program as it unfolds over the academic year, considering (a) continuity and change in classroom cultural practices—the reproduction or transformation of local practices and ideologies and how these contributed to developing notions of agentive voice and communication; and (b) continuity and change in socially situated selves across time and spheres of experience, including the personal sense students made of the program, of notions of "voice," and possibilities for powerful communication.

Interactional Ethnography

The method-theory used for this study combines elements of interactional ethnography (Green & Wallat, 1981) and sociocultural psychology with a semiotic focus (Zittoun, 2006). Studies that adopt an interactional ethnographic approach examine how people create meaning through the ways they act and react to each other through the use of language, including verbal and nonverbal semiotic systems with attention to social, cultural, and political processes (Bloome, Carter, Christian, Otto, & Shuart-Faris, 2005). I use this approach to understand how the "observable curriculum" (Castanheira, Crawford, Dixon, & Green, 2001), including language and literacy practices, is constructed and becomes consequential for student learning over time, including the ways in which cultural resources from various media, literary, and artistic domains are introduced, taken up or contested, and transformed by participants in collective activity. To do this I use aspects of the "backward and forward mapping" strategy proposed by Putney and colleagues (Putney, Green, Dixon, Durán, & Yeager, 2000). Following an introduction to the curriculum and the genre approach to instruction in Chapter 2, I analyze the cultural practices set in motion during the first days of the program in Chapter 3, which provides a glimpse of the onset of patterns of language and activity that lay the foundations for the construction of the observable curriculum, cultural practices, and meaning-making processes in Youth Radio and Radio Arts. I then identify segments of narrative discourse from exit interviews in which concepts of "voice" and "communication" are elaborated by focal students Elia (Chapter 4) and Tania (Chapter 5), and trace the "roots and routes" (Castanheira et al., 2001) of development of these concepts and related learning to the onset of patterns in the first days and select subsequent events.

Interactional ethnography contributes to the understanding of change and continuity in the implementation of an educational innovation through its attention to the conflicts and tensions between the tendencies toward the reproduction of existing cultural practices and social structures, and efforts to challenge and transform them. This is particularly relevant for language and literacy alternatives since innovations enacted in a classroom cannot be viewed as "new," but rather must be understood as adaptations of existing classroom practices (Bloome et al., 2005). To examine transformations in classroom practices we must question how literacy and language events transform or reproduce traditional classroom literacy practices (such as read-alouds and the Initate-Response-Evaluate model of questioning).

While interactional ethnography can help the researcher understand continuity and change in group-level cultural practices, ideologies, and social structures, how do we understand the ways that collective processes of continuity and change in the collective come to be understood and lived by the individuals? Sociocultural researchers interested in dialogical processes have shown how analyses of classroom discourses and practices can provide a crucial link between individual psychological processes and their cultural, historical, and institutional contexts (Wertsch, 1991; Zittoun & Grossen, 2013). It is my opinion that the intra-mental and inter-mental processes involved in learning have not received adequate attention in the sociocultural research on classroom practices and learning. Therefore, to understand how cultural resources afforded within the program were appropriated and transformed by the individual-within-the-collective, and how these processes become consequential for individual learning and development, I adopt elements of an approach grounded in sociocultural psychology elaborated by Zittoun and colleagues (Zittoun, 2006; Zittoun & Grossen, 2010).

Adolescence is a period of dynamic change as well as movement through multiple spheres of experience (peer groups, leisure activity, school) that call into play repositioning and shifting performances of identity within divergent systems of meaning and demands of competence. In these processes young people need to forge a sense of continuity across these spheres of experience, such as school, social life, and home. They need to make personal sense of the systems of meaning circulating in these different spheres, define a role for themselves within each, as well as a sense of consistency between their values and actions—a sense of "who they are" across spheres of experience. Zittoun and colleagues (Grossen, Zittoun, & Ros, 2012; Zittoun & Grossen, 2010/2013) have been studying the role of cultural resources used in school, such as philosophical or literary texts, in helping young people bridge the gap between school bodies of knowledge and other, often more important (for youth) spheres of experience such as friendship or romance. These researchers have also examined the ways in which the cultural resources are used by youth to support identity processes, knowledge, and skill acquisition and make personal sense in periods of transition following rupture, such as moving from school to the working world, or moving to a new country. Defined as a break "from customary ways of doing things, taken-for-granted routines and definitions" (Zittoun, 2006, p. 6), the notion of rupture can also be applied to an educational innovation such as Youth Radio in the ESL classroom. Though I do not presume a priori that Youth Radio represented a radical break from the existing ways of doing school, the program did immediately represent a change in terms of the observable curriculum: who was teaching, what was being taught, with what texts and technologies, how people interacted, how space was used, and so on.

Community-Linked Learning Design

A primary interest of this research is to understand what can be learned by connecting students and teachers to community-based media and arts practitioners, and by extending the times and spaces of learning beyond the classroom. The learning design was an attempt to reimagine the classroom, school, and community as a "field of relations" (Nespor, 1997) rather than schools as "spaces of enclosure" within which education takes place (Lankshear, Peters, & Knobel, 1996). As Lemke (2002) states, "Schooling pays too much attention to what we study and not enough to who we become, priding itself on what it brings into the building, but blinding itself to all it shuts out; teaching isolated literacies but not how to make them work together" (p. 35). Youth Radio and Radio Arts was conceived as a networked learning design (NLD), with important implications for learning on the part of students as well as teachers. According to Wenger (1998), a learning design shapes the possibilities for learning across several dimensions. First, a learning design defines the parameters for the kind of person one can become in that community, how competencies will be defined, and the forms of participation that are possible. Second, a learning design embodies the potential for the realignment of "economies of meaning," in which the status quo of power and the legitimization of knowledge and shared meanings are challenged.

Youth Radio represented a systematic effort on the part of researcher and mentors to realign the "economy of meanings" surrounding immigrant—predominately *Mexicana/o*–youth and to provide positive alternatives to the "subtractive" literacy, language, and identity experiences that these students often have in schools (Valenzuela, 1999). The intent of the Youth Radio and Radio Arts design was to create a network of independent media practitioners, educators, and activists, drawing primarily on existing cultural resources within local Latino/Latina communities, to support the literate, artistic, social, and personal development of participating youth. The original goals for creating this network were the following:

(a) To connect students to the lives and work of practitioners in independent media and arts organizations
(b) To provide a culturally responsive, community-linked alternative to the mainstream curriculum that is increasingly test-driven, leaving few opportunities for artistic expression and personal/social development
(c) To promote development of youth agency to deconstruct discriminatory power structures and support teachers and students in developing a discourse that sees multilingual, working-class students as creative, skillful, and smart with important futures to prepare for
(d) To prepare students for participation in their local communities and the global media spheres as critically engaged producers rather than passive consumers.

Social theories of learning support the theoretical underpinnings of the networked learning design. In these frameworks, learning is enhanced when novices are provided broad exposure to ongoing practice that demonstrates the goals toward which newcomers are expected to move—something that does not often happen in schools (Gutierrez & Rogoff, 2003; Lave & Wenger, 1991). Eisenhart and Finkel (1998), for example, in their study of women who work in nonprofit science organizations, found that learning the discipline and becoming a scientist requires that people be connected to—and have opportunities to participate in—larger networks of mature practice, which provides a broad picture of expertise in a given practice. At the cognitive level, networked learning systems support the generalization of knowledge by creating opportunities for people to compare and contrast features of related learning contexts, to interpret new situations in light of concepts they have previously developed, and to deal with counter interpretations (Guile & Young, 2003).

In terms of youth development, collaborative networks that connect young people to community-based media and arts organizations provide opportunities for youth to experience professions and envision careers to which they might not otherwise have access, which enables "imagined futures that go beyond representations of what exists in the present" (Cole, 1996), an important catalyst for youth development. Finally, research has shown that collaborations involving community organizations and agencies that support learning trajectories through these networks have the potential to disrupt patterns of nonparticipation and long-term social exclusion by helping youth develop social capital and a capacity to access resources in distinct sets of social practices (Edwards & Mutton, 2007; Stanton-Salazar, 1997).

In re-conceptualizing the learning context of Youth Radio and Radio Arts as a *field of relations* of multiple intersecting communities and spheres of engagement, we are also forced to take into consideration the presence of transnational youth. As Gutierrez (2005) notes, these students require us to reflect on the effects on learning of crossing borders, and the repertoires of practice that these youth bring to a learning setting. The presence of transnational students and representatives from community-based organizations creates contact zones in which multiple discourses confront each other, and where global, intersecting contexts come into play when young people engage multiple languages and cultural worlds. When communication media and popular culture are added to the mix, as occurred in the program, the researcher-designer must also attend to recruiting youths' engagements with new media and the World Wide Web to their engagements with "literacyscapes" (Leander, 2003) such as transnational dating sites and *narco-corrido* music videos. The networked learning design aims to transform the content and medium of instruction to incorporate the rich and varied experiences of these learners, rather than limit the learner to one language, one history, and one knowledge base (Vásquez, 2003). Numerous sociocultural theorists (Gutierrez, 2008; Moll, Amanti, Neff, & González, 1992) advocate for drawing skills and knowledge from multiple sources beyond the classroom walls and the expertise of the teacher, a strategy that contrasts with the conventional practice of only validating knowledge and expertise associated with mainstream educational structures and personnel. To prepare learners to participate successfully not only in the realm of mainstream institutional culture but also the multiple communities in which they participate and others not yet imagined, the program brought together multiple cultural systems, institutional contexts, and intergenerational groupings for learning both in and outside the classroom.

Participants. This yearlong study took place in a combined multi grade (9–11) class of ESL Studies Skills and Academic Support, with 16–18 students (the number fluctuated) from working-class immigrant families: 15 Latino/Latina, two Nepalese, and one Russian. Liv (this, like all other names in this study, are pseudonyms) is an Anglo, bilingual English-Swedish AVID/Academic Support teacher who worked previously as a district ESL specialist. She is considered an instructional leader in the school and is an active member of the school Culture and Equity Committee. Ray is the bilingual Chicano ESL Study Skills teacher who serves as the faculty sponsor for the Latino Leadership club. I am a teacher educator in Culturally and Linguistically Diverse Education and previously a bilingual elementary teacher. I cotaught the class and collected data, with the help of Milly, a graduate research assistant, four days a week throughout the academic year during a sabbatical leave with a research grant. The paid mentors who participated on a weekly basis included volunteers at the local community radio station, a professional writer, and a university-based theater director, actor, and playwright. Jack, a bilingual radio and print journalist, and Lyle, a radio broadcaster, were with us all year. The hip-hop DJ talk-show host and community-activist, Kareem, mentored as needed. Federico, the professor and theater director originally from Mexico, was our artist-in-residence in the fall, while TZ (Tim) Hernandez (his real name), an award-winning Chicano poet and novelist, served as our writer-in-residence in the spring with support from a state humanities agency. In addition to these paid instructors we had university student volunteers in the spring semester after-school program, and Molly Colburn, professor of educational technology and curriculum studies, frequently instructed the digital story unit.

Data sources generated over the year of study included the following:

- Field notes, conceptual memos, and a reflective researcher journal
- In-depth semistructured audio-recorded exit interviews with focal student participants
- Video and audio recordings of daily whole-group and small-group interactions in the classroom and community settings
- Recorded teacher reflections and staff debriefings
- E-mail communications with staff and school administrators
- Web content coproduced with students for our password-protected website
- Documents from the school and district such as standards, syllabi, and public statements
- Documents and online resources of community-based media and arts organizations, such as a theater playbill and the online radio station mission statement

- Artifacts of teacher work, such as syllabi, poetry, and a digital story
- Artifacts of mentor work, such as radio stories and poetry
- Artifacts of student work, such as drafts of print texts and graphic organizers, drafts of audio recordings and multimedia compositions, and final productions and poetry

Transcriptions of selected video and audio recordings based on analytical need, numbering approximately 250, were created by myself, research assistants, and the bilingual radio mentor.

The original research questions that guided this study were the following: (a) What evidence is there that the social practices introduced by the radio professionals and artists were taken up and became resources for student and teacher learning and development? (b) What kinds of learning and development took place? (c) What evidence can be found of transformation in school discourses and language and literacy practices over time?

Researcher Stance and Subject/Power Positionings

My ontological position in relation to participants in the program was complicated by my position as researcher and co-instructor. Due to my daily presence in the classroom (with the exception of Mondays) throughout the academic year, I became an insider of the Youth Radio and Radio Arts collective to some degree, while still maintaining outsider status—as nonmember of the official school community—capable of perceiving aspects of "the strange" (a requirement for ethnographers) in classroom and school practices. This level of insider status did not in itself accord me access to the *emic* perspective of the group: my attempt to represent the *emic* perspective has been pursued through the analyses and interpretations presented throughout this book.

In addition, since I had become myself a subject of study through the objectification of my person in archived video and audio recordings, transcriptions, and comments by both teachers and students about me and the program, I also found myself in a paradoxical position of having to analyze my linguistic behavior, actions, and subject positionings. I was both outside observing myself as an actor in collective activity and inside engaging in moment-to-moment activity. Yet while I was inside activity my sense making and actions were informed by different timescales of collective activity than the others because I was continuously viewing videos of classroom activity from the past, which positioned me in a particular way. Certain interpretations of interactions and artifact use in different time frames were available to me for analysis, while not to other participants. By virtue of engaging in analysis while the program was ongoing, reviewing and transcribing videos, teacher reflections, and other data sources, I had insights into in-the-moment actions and discourse that other actors in the scene did not: it was like being an actor and a viewer of a movie simultaneously, and the only one allowed to do so. In an effort to reduce the unequal knowledge-power relationship with others, especially the teachers, I often tried to share my privileged insights with the teachers, such as comments made by students about their learning process, or patterns of discourse I was uncovering through discourse analyses. Even so, the distribution of knowledge and perspectives—and therefore power—was always unevenly loaded in my direction.

Finally, I am well aware of my position of privilege and power vis-à-vis the participants in the program—both teachers and students—as a university professor and white, middle-class woman funding the program. I am also aware of the difficulties my social position and the way I am perceived would tend to limit my access to emic perspectives of the student participants, much less understand their psychosocial processes. A few circumstances attenuated the impact of the ontological power distance and my ignorance in regards to the life worlds of the majority Latino/Latina youth I studied. First, I have spent 12 years working and researching in the Spanish-English bilingual population of my community, as a fourth-grade teacher and then as program director and researcher in after-school and during-school arts and youth radio programs. I know many of the families and older siblings of these students. Second, I am bilingual, having lived, worked, and studied in Latin America for six years, which facilitates dialogue with the bilingual students, some of whom preferred to interact in Spanish. Third, as I am a teacher educator in CLD education, I have some knowledge and shared understandings of the professional worlds of the teachers with whom I cotaught, as well as something about second language learners and learning processes more generally.

Structure of the Book

In Chapter 2, I provide an overview of the program design, the genre-based pedagogy, and a sketch of the conditions for learning and youth subject positionings within the school and community to provide context for understanding the dimensions of change and continuity that the program would represent. Chapter 3 examines the first phases of the construction of the "observable curriculum" (Castanheira et al., 2001) and how youth and adult participants began to make sense of the purposes of the program. This includes the introduction of the concepts of "voice" and "communication" by the theater director Federico, who blended languages, cultural memory, emotion, the body, play, and improvisation to build symbolic bridges to student life worlds and develop a sense of *confianza*/trust among youth participants. Chapters 4 and 5 analyze two case studies, focusing on their interview narratives and ethnographic records to trace the "roots and routes" (Putney et al., 2000) of their developing understandings of the social shared meanings of the program, as well as the personal sense (Zittoun, 2006) they made of cultural elements in support of their learning and development. The final chapter summarizes the principles of a pedagogy of powerful communication that emerged from this yearlong study of Youth Radio and Radio Arts.

• CHAPTER TWO •

Youth Radio and Radio Arts Curriculum and Pedagogy

Youth Radio and Radio Arts was conceived as an educational innovation with the goal of transforming remedial ESL language and literacy practices and helping students to "claim and exercise their right to use media to promote justice" (Soep & Chávez, 2010). Adopting concerns of the youth media movement described in Chapter 1, the Youth Radio and Radio Arts program incorporated elements of multiliteracies (TheNewLondon-Group, 1996), critical language teaching (Norton & Toohey, 2004), and community-based arts education (Heath & Smyth, 1999) to promote personal, social, and academic development.

This chapter provides an overview of the program design, the genre-based pedagogical approach, and the radio and radio arts genres that were taught. Following this overview I offer a detailed description of the processes and contexts for production of one specific radio genre, the youth commentary. I discuss the language features of the commentary, the instructional formats (such as instructional conversations), tools, and assessments employed. I analyze how instructional tools such as class readings, production guidelines, and rubrics made visible to students the language and literacy demands of the youth commentary genre. As part of this analysis I examine the "possibilities of selfhood" (Ivanič, 1998) made available through the social practices, texts, languages, ways of talking, and instructional tools used in the teaching and production of a youth commentary. Throughout the chapter I analyze the tendencies within the program toward continuity or change, toward reproducing existing cultural practices and structures, or challenging and transforming the extant cultural ideology (Bloome, Carter, Christian, Otto, & Shuart-Faris, 2005).

Overview of the Program Design

Because Youth Radio and Radio Arts was designed as a community-linked network that connected learning to the work of practitioners in independent media and arts organizations, the program introduced a set of practices and material and conceptual artifacts that were new for both students and teachers. The curricular texts consisted of online multimodal stories taken from the Youth Media International website (2010), mainstream news organizations, the Center for Digital Stories (2009), oral and visual texts, guest speakers, and radio and digital stories created by peers and discussed in class. The practices associated with each genre represented both continuity and change from usual classroom practices. To create youth commentaries, digital stories, vox pops, and feature stories, the students and teachers used audio and video editing software, cameras and audio recording devices, the audio sound board at the radio station, digital cameras, flash drives, the World Wide Web, and iWeb to create content to a program website. They learned how to do background research and evaluate sources on the Web, write a persuasive essay, compose interview and follow-up questions, schedule and conduct interviews, edit their own and others' recorded voices, receive peer and adult critique, and present their work to a larger public. They also drew on existing knowledge from their engagements with online and digital media, such as how to find and download music and find images from Spanish, English, Russian, and Nepalese language websites. Family photos were a rich source for creative materials used in digital stories.

Learning took place during or after school in the classroom or the Mac Lab, the street (for Vox Pops), and the radio station, with field trips to a Chicano theater in a nearby city. The curriculum was co-created by the researcher and teachers with input from mentors and was aligned with standards from social studies (NCSS, 2010), English (NCSS, 2010), Language Arts (NCTE/IRA, 2012), educational technology (ISTE, 2009), multimodal literacies (NCTE, 2007), and English language development (TESOL, 2009; WIDA, 2007, 2012).

Curriculum and instruction were organized around activity cycles and genres, falling within three main domains: radio production and broadcast, multimedia production and digital design, and radio arts. These are presented in Table 2.1.

Table 2.1. Activity Cycles and Genres

Activity Cycles	Genres

Radio production and broadcast	Youth commentaries (Oct.-Dec.)
	Feature story: Our School Community (Jan.-May)
	Work in the KPFW station studios (Oct.-May)
	Vox pops (vox populi) (Dec., April)
	   "If I were mayor of this city I would . . ." (in class)
	   "How can we make this city a better place for youth?" (in the streets)
	Training sessions in the station studios
	Interviews by radio personnel at the station

Multimedia production and digital design	Digital stories: Our Neighborhood Community, personal life stories (Oct.-May) Website content development (Nov.-May) End-of-semester presentations by students of their productions (Dec., June)
Radio arts	Radio skits (Oct.-Nov.) Poetry writing and performance (Mar.-June) Field trips to Chicano theater in a nearby city (Dec., April)

Given that the networked learning design of the program was informed by social theories of learning as situated practice, and apprenticeship into the culture of use as a logical consequence of the situated practice perspective, the program adopted a genre approach to teaching. For each genre taught, we provided overt instruction for developing control of the specific genre focused on (a) the social purpose of the genre, including the kinds of people associated with the genre and how it is used to get something done, such the kinds of tools that are used; (b) the particular structure or organization of the genre; and (c) the language features that are typical of that genre. In a later section of this chapter, I describe in greater detail these aspects of genre instruction using the youth commentary as an example.

A Genre-Based Pedagogy

The goal of genre pedagogies is to guide students toward a conscious understanding of target genres and the ways language creates meanings in context. Hyland (2007) defines genre as the "socially recognized ways of using language. It is a term we all use for grouping texts together and representing how writers typically use language to respond to and construct texts for recurring situations" (p. 237). In this framework, genre has important interpersonal and identity construction functions: composition or multimedia production connects writers or media producers with the value systems and discourses of their audiences. While writing or producing indexes a person's position in relation to social groups, creativity and transformation occur in the rhetorical or design choices that a writer/producer makes as he or she works with the options and constraints of a given genre. Of interest for Youth Radio and Radio Arts is Hyland's argument that teachers of multilingual students should bring the interpersonal features of genres into the center of their teaching from day one, rather than waiting until students have mastered other aspects of communication, such as grammar. He rejects the argument that low proficiency students need to control core forms of language before getting on to more interpersonal aspects of composition "as if these were just dressing on the cake" (p. 238). This was one of the guiding principles behind Youth Radio and Radio Arts: To break the cycle of remedial ESL instruction, the focus of instruction must be on *communication* rather than discrete language skills. This follows from the assumption that the processes and outcomes of communication are meaningful for students, and they will want to learn the tools and practices needed for developing what I call "communication competence."

Critiques and a defense of a genre approach to teaching Youth Radio and Radio Arts. Genre-based pedagogical approaches have been criticized on a number of fronts: for removing genres from the complex sociocultural contexts of their use, for locating the study of genres outside of the lived situations of their use, and in the case of second language learners, for imposing conformity to dominant discourses and enforcing assimilation to standardized dominant language usage, and perpetuating the powerful social relations that genres construct and reinforce (Lemke, 2005). Indeed, due to standardized testing requirements, schools most often attempt to impose rigid genre boundaries and functions on the principle that genre practices can be taught, reproducing existing practices and ideologies in a relatively static way: Schools socialize young people into the dominant culture and society primarily through the uses and meanings of artifacts associated with specific genres.

It could be argued, however, that the networked learning design of Youth Radio and Radio Arts undermined the rigid imposition of genre boundaries, making the multiple interests and practices of genres particularly apparent in this setting. When a media story produced in school is evaluated according to broadcast criteria by the radio station, school and professional media genres are blended, and genre boundaries are blurred. It is true, as Bloome and colleagues (2005) argue, that the "pedagogical situation" of the classroom context powerfully shapes processes, interactions, and outcomes. Yet at the same time, having radio professionals who bring a different set of genre practices and radio audiences as the ultimate arbiters of the quality rather than a single teacher does disrupt the static genre boundaries normally enforced in school. Furthermore, though genre pedagogies have been critiqued for imposing conformity to dominant discourses and language use, the genres taught in Youth Radio and Radio Arts were drawn from *counter-discourses* of youth media sources produced by multilingual urban youth, and could therefore not be seen as reproducing the dominant discourse or monolingual ideologies. The texts—primarily multimodal productions—consisted of the following: (1) recordings and transcriptions of youth radio pieces downloaded from YouthRadio.org; (2) examples from the Center for Digital Storytelling (2009); (3) poetry by published bilingual authors and recent writings by youth; (4) examples of student productions from previous Youth Radio programs; and (5) examples of work created by program staff.

The multiplication of genres and discourses accessed through each genre also led to some genre confusion among participants, making the construction of consensus about "what we are all doing here" (McDermott, Gospodinoff, & Aron, 1978) more challenging. Genre confusion, in turn, made visible—as sometimes acknowledged by participants—internal contradictions arising from the school-community-university collaboration. The audio texts used as models for the commentary genre, for example, often included personal reflections by youth on intimate aspects of their lives. Many of the students took up the personal approach to the commentary. Jack the journalist, on the other hand, felt uncomfortable with the personal angle on the commentary and said so following a "fishbowl" presentation with Delfina on her proposed topic: the injustice of teacher judgments about students based on their "cholo" (Chicano youth) style of dress. It appeared at the time that some students picked up on the contradictory definitions of the youth community genre, as I describe in greater detail later in this chapter. Beto, for example, began his brainstorm session with me talking about his aspirations to become an engineer and the obstacles he might face achieving his goals. After this initial brainstorm, he had extended instructional conversations with Jack, who encouraged Beto to link these anticipated obstacles to larger sociopolitical issues alluded to by Beto, such as drug-related violence. A few days after his conversation with Jack, Beto seemed uncertain about his topic and was becoming frustrated. He turned to me and said, "Does it have to be personal? Can it be more about the world?" Beto's final commentary indeed took up Jack's proposal for the genre: his piece was a powerful indictment of violence in the world, in wars and in their neighborhoods.

The indeterminacy of the youth commentary genre may have caused learning difficulties for some students at certain junctures in the process. For other students, the fluidity of genre boundaries seemed productive. Both Delfina and Tania were able, with the help of Jack, to connect a personal issue to the larger sociocultural context: Delfina, from her teacher's comments about her boyfriend's clothes to the ways adults in general judge youth based on their dress style; and Tania, from her own situation at home to the desires of teens to have a second home in times of need.

The genre confusion that arose in the construction of the Youth Radio curriculum can be explained in part by the fact that genres can incorporate multiple discourses (Ivanič, 1998). We introduced commentaries that drew on the discourses of independent journalism and community histories, public discourses about immigrant rights and youth discourses about heterosexual romance and parent-child relationships. As Lemke (1995) notes, each community and every subcommunity within it has its own system of intertextuality: its own set of important or valued texts, its own preferred discourses, and particularly its own habits of deciding which texts should be read in the context of which others, and why, and how. All of these factors contributed to the complexity of adopting a genre pedagogy in the context of a school-community-university collaboration. At the same time, the learning design helped us avoid the danger of imposing genre conformity and rigid genre boundaries. What we found, in the end, was that youth did creative things with the genre models that adults presented, in some cases taking the genre in new and unanticipated directions that affected the overall development of the collective in interesting ways.

Overview of Genres Taught in Youth Radio and Radio Arts

The radio genres taught in Youth Radio and Radio Arts drew on two genres developed and institutionalized by Youth Radio Oakland (YouthMediaInternational, 2010): the youth commentary and the feature story. In addition, we used the Vox Pop-the "voice of the people"-in which the journalist goes into the streets to gather statements from as many people as possible using a single question. These radio genres were taught in our program, following Freire (2005), to help students become aware of the connections between their own lives and society, rather than personalize their problems as their own. The audio and written texts used to teach each genre were, for the most part, selected to encourage dialogue about generative themes drawn from the students' everyday lives. Investigating issues such as romantic relationships, family life, and immigration from an individual and a sociohistorical perspective allowed students to bring their own knowledge into the classroom and broaden their sense of social context. Youth producers of the pieces selected as models used English, Spanish, and African American Vernacular English. The examples accessed through the Youth Radio Oakland website presented fluid and hybrid genres: Commentaries often included snippets of discourse from a person other than the commentator; feature stories sometimes sounded like mash-ups of commentaries.

Radio genres. In general, the commentary—which will be discussed in detail below—was taught in our program as a kind of audio text of a persuasive essay, drawing on background research and/or personal evidence. We highlighted the structural features of the commentary that were similar or different from a persuasive essay, including the radio discourse genre of the "hook," or lede, and the tag: "For Youth Radio at Beckwourth High, this is [student's name]." Language features included a persuasive personal voice with overtones of youth dialects and tonalities: local language variations were not "whitewashed" out of the youth voices.

The feature story was framed within the general theme of "Our School Community." A feature story uses the recorded voice of the journalist as well as voices of interviewed subjects. As suggested by Jack, the feature story in our program involved interviews with three types of respondents: an expert, a participant, and an affected other. The structural features highlighted for students included an introduction based on background research, interviews, transitions, a wrap-up with "a punch," and the tag. Language features specific to the feature story include different types of questions tailored to different types of interlocutors (an expert is asked different questions than the affected individual), and an authoritative voice in the intro and outro. This genre presented a more formal register than the youth commentary. The audio features highlighted for students included ambient sound designed to "bring the listener into the setting" and the aural balance of voices and sound to create overall cohesion. The technology used included digital voice recorders, audio editing software, Mac and PC computers, and personal flash drives.

Digital story genre. Digital storytelling was included in the Youth Radio and Radio Arts curriculum to provide opportunities for multilingual individuals to represent their meanings and understandings in modes of communication that go beyond spoken or written language. Meaning making, according to Kress (2000) is sensory: Viewing images, touch, taste, and smell give rise to forms of thought and semiotic work as much as reading print text. Stein (2004) reminds us as well that people have different "histories of representation." The ways a person has used modes in the past become part of the fabric of representational resources and emotions that the individual uses in working with different modes. Furthermore, if a person has had a negative association with speech or writing, as several of the students in the program had, this will affect how that person engages with those particular modes; these relations to modes, however, remain fluid and subject to change.

As a multimodal object, a digital story is meant to convey meaning through diverse semiotic modes, such as still or moving images, music, font styles, and spoken narration. The meanings of a digital story are experienced by viewers through the intersection and interrelation among these different semiotic systems. The digital story is thus also a cultural object that, like poetry, enables people to have cultural experiences, as they would watching a film or reading a novel, through the recruitment of imagination and emotion (Zittoun & Grossen, 2010). Yet for a multimodal object to be understood, people must be socialized into their meanings and uses: "One needs to be socialized to thrillers to be able to build up the suspense and anticipate the dangers when watching such a film (one often needs also to know the cultural context of the object to fully understand its meaning)" (p. 176). Digital story instructors (Molly and I) offered explicit instruction in the structure, functions, and rhetorical devices used in digital stories. For example, Molly spoke about the use of metaphor in digital narratives, provided examples, and elicited examples from students to help them understand the concept. My instruction on digital stories focused on the emotional dimension of the genre such as adjusting to life in a new country or sexual identity. We discussed how the images should metaphorically suggest the content the author wanted to convey, how the music could intensify the feeling conveyed by the image, and how the images—including transitions such as fade-ins and fade-outs—and font styles and animation needed to support and sustain the narration. English was the primary language of instruction for the digital story.

The digital story genre as taught in our program was shaped by two sometimes conflicting interpretations of the social purposes of the genre, which in turn were shaped by distinct digital story traditions and practices. One was the genre and workshop practices institutionalized by the influential Center for Digital Storytelling in Berkeley, California, and Denver, Colorado, where I attended a three-day workshop and whose website I used as my primary resource for examples of the genre (CenterforDigitalStorytelling, 2009). The other was the genre practices of digital narratives as taught by Molly within our institution of higher education and her network of practice within the International Society for Technology in Education. The contradictions became apparent through the digital stories we each selected as models for the students: I selected texts that I thought would elicit generative themes for critical reflection and dialogue; Molly selected texts that modeled various subgenres of the digital story and techniques that could be used, such as the avatars and poetry by young children, which I did not always view as being productive of generative themes.

The contradictions that I noted in my reflective journal concerning the digital story instruction, and the curricular goals of Youth Radio more generally, were not limited to the digital story. Ray, at the beginning of the program, expressed concern that the topics we were addressing in the curriculum were "too close to the students" and were "hard for them to take." He felt that the students were not mature enough to handle these subjects, that their concerns were more immediate, not larger sociopolitical issues such as immigration. He did not mention this again after the first few weeks, so I believe he changed his opinion. Some students appeared excited and motivated to be able to explore controversial and emotionally difficult themes through multimodal composition. In addition to the benefits for multilingual learners of engaging multiple senses and modalities beyond reading and writing, of recruiting a broader range of representational repertoires, and the novelty of using image, music, and voice-over for a "class" assignment, I believe that digital stories were of particular interest to these youth for allowing identity explorations as modeled in the examples from the CDS website.

Poetry. The poetry genres used in Radio Arts were selected by the poet TZ (Tim) Hernandez (his real name), whose major influences seem to be multigenerational Chicano poets and the Beat poets associated with his undergraduate creative writing program at Naropa University. Tim is a protégée of Juan Felipe Herrera, poet laureate of California. Many of the genres taught by Tim were inspired by techniques and games used by surreal poets to release the imagination and set in motion a creative process that is free from conscious control. Genres introduced by Tim included *exquisite corpse,* a collectively written poem in which each new line is written without knowledge of the previous line; and *Mistranslations,* which Tim facilitated by providing a poem written in Hmong that the students "translated," having no knowledge of the language, but using recognizable sounds to generate words they knew in English or Spanish. Tim also introduced the publishing genre of the *chapbook;* he published a book of student poetry with a cover designed by him (he is also a visual artist), using a title drawn from a student poem: "Never Unconscious in the Night." English was the primary language of instruction for poetry; however, the poems were written and read using Spanish, English, and code-switching.

Radio improv. The radio improv genres taught by Federico were rooted in a range of historical theater practices shaped by his personal experience and training. These include three summer workshops with Augusto Boal of Brazil, founder of the Theater of the Oppressed. Federico uses exercises and games he learned from Boal:

> Boal uses an exercise so you can see what you can do; What am I comfortable with? What do I need to know to get better at? So that's the purpose of exercise is to confront us with our limitations of what we can't do or what we can do, to get to be where we do know how to do it. (Interview with Federico, 6/18/2013)

Games are centered in the body and the senses and aimed at developing trust and cooperation in the collective, the theatrical "ensemble." These approaches could be seen in Federico's work with the students in Youth Radio and Radio Arts.

Federico also spent several years working with Luis Valdez, founder of the *Teatro Campesino* in California, which has been a major influence on Chicano theater. Federico recounts that Valdez would use the stories of the farmworkers and the actors would get on a flatbed truck and travel around town reenacting these stories. Valdez drew on the tradition of the Mexican *La Carpa*, which were traveling vaudeville shows that traveled from town to town.

In addition to Boal and Luis Valdez, Federico was influenced by British Shakespearean theater, having performed as an actor under the direction of Sir Peter Hall, founder of the Royal Shakespeare Company in Britain. Federico primarily used the exercises and games of Augusto Boal with our students, and participants would have only been aware of the Su Teatro nexus as these were the only intercontextual links made when he was introduced to the class on the first day, and when we took students to theater performances at Su Teatro twice during the academic year.

In his instruction Federico deployed a range of discourse genres (which I will describe in greater detail in Chapter 3) and hybrid language practices, blending English, Spanish, Spanglish, and code-switching.

The next section presents an analysis of one genre, the youth commentary, to exemplify the processes and practices of one production activity in the program.

The Youth Commentary

A youth commentary is a radio opinion piece that draws on elements of persuasive essay, radio opinion piece, and youth media, in which the student defends a position or an idea through research-based or experiential evidence. Persuasive writing is a key genre taught in high school as it is a scaffold to argumentative writing in college and preparation for participation in a democracy (Anderson, 2008). The teachers met the expectations of the language arts teachers for whom they provide second language support by demonstrating that students were learning argumentation writing. However, analysis of the youth commentary texts shows that the commentary as taught in the program was not a genre with rigid boundaries in terms of language features. The texts made available to students shaped the language used, discourses accessed, topics addressed, and identities performed. At the same time the fluidity of the genre, which combined multiple registers and languages, persuasive essay and personal narrative, and sometimes multiple voices, created spaces for transformation and personal sense making. As Anderson argues, hybrid genres seem to generate greater student investment of values and discourses.

The youth commentary as taught in the program was a genre that was reified and circulated in the public media sphere by Youth Media International in Oakland (2010). Soep and Chávez (2010) define youth commentaries in the following manner:

> A commentary is a way for young people to write down their own thoughts and opinions, to explore why the topic interested them in the first place, and to shape something of a narrative arc that may or may not turn out to frame a fuller story with multiple voices and scenes. . . .Commentators share experiences that are personally meaningful, perhaps counterintuitive, and resonate with larger social themes. Commentaries don't have to be objective, but they are reality-based and should take into account opposing points of view. . . . Through commentaries young people articulate perspectives grounded in compelling evidence, which might come in the form of lived experiences, references to research, or bits of dialogue with people they've encountered in their everyday worlds. (p. 115)

It is clear from this description that the youth commentary, as elaborated by Soep and Chávez (2010) and institutionalized at Youth Radio Oakland, is a hybrid genre. The authors state that a commentary can be "objective" narratives based on research or "subjective" narratives drawing on "compelling evidence" from personal experience—of the youth producer or others. Often youth commentaries are a combination of both genres. Examples drawn from the YMI website reveal further hybridity of genres, such as multiple first-person producers using elements of feature stories such as ambient sound and excerpts of speech from people in the context. One example of this is *A Border Story*, in which two female teens present their youth-centered perspectives on living on both sides of the Mexico–U.S. border as well as on either side of the social class "border" within Tijuana, using human and mechanical sounds from the border crossing, audio clips from one mother talking about making tacos, and music from the band Molotov, a song titled "Fijolero (Beaner)," which is a pejorative term used in the United States for Mexicans.

The youth commentary therefore has unique properties that distinguish it both from the schooled persuasive essay and the journalistic commentary: (a) youth commentaries present an authorial voice that represents "youth," speaking in various dialects, accents, and world Englishes; and (b) the ideational content of youth commentaries is always about the life worlds of youth: this can include youth experiences at home, school, other societal institutions, or in the streets of their cities; relationships; presenting family and community forms of knowledge.

In what follows I present an analysis of the contexts, processes, and products of production of multimodal youth commentaries.

Contexts and Processes of Youth Commentary Production

Lyle and I were the principle instructors for the youth commentary. We selected the audio texts used to model the genre, developed handouts, and with feedback from the teachers we created guidelines and rubrics. Jack, who entered the program at week three, acted as a journalistic writing coach, working in small groups or individually to help students elaborate their ideas and language for their commentary writing. Lyle instructed students in the use of audio-editing software Audacity. He did a lesson on Audacity using the LCD projector in the Mac Lab, and worked one-on-one with students in the computer lab as they edited their pieces. He also shared the role of "managing editor" with Jack. The teachers Liv and Ray, and research assistant Milly coached students in the writing and editing processes, helped with the recording, and to some degree with audio editing (Milly much more so than the teachers, who did not feel as comfortable as she did with the technology).

The cycle of instruction and production of the youth commentary encompassed certain interactional genres and instructional formats that were the same across all radio genres and the digital story. The production cycle, which lasted approximately two months with two to three days a week devoted to the activity, included extended instructional conversations and writing coaching with the journalist mentors, who helped students elaborate and refine their ideas and language on their chosen topics while providing guidance on the genre features and approaches to writing and speaking for the radio. This mentoring by journalists in speaking and writing for radio was identified by several students as critical to developing language skills and a public voice for communication in the public media sphere.

The texts used for Youth Radio were selected to promote critical reflection and dialogue among students and teachers around generative themes related to the students' life worlds. My selection of texts was informed by my 12 years of experience working with the Mexican-descent students and families in our area, but not with Nepalese or Russian students, nor did I have access to radio pieces and texts that would have reflected these cultural groups. Table 2.2 presents the titles and descriptions of the instructional texts used for teaching the youth commentary.

Table 2.2 Texts Used for Commentary**

Title	Description
Untitled Personal Account	A personal account about a fallen tree at home, read aloud by Lyle and followed by question and answers to teach the 5 Ws in journalism, written by hand in a journalist's notepad.
"I Thought I Wanted to Join a Gang Until My Cousin Got Killed"	Youth commentary from YMI archives about the lure and danger of belonging to a gang. Recording was not available online so we read the transcript in class, each student with her or his own copy that went into their binders.
"Food and Family"	Youth commentary from YMI archives about the importance of food in one girl's family. Interview clips with her mother in Spanish are embedded in English commentary.
Sonia and Luis from Colorado Immigration Reform Coalition	Spoke to students about the Dream Act and "Dreamers"—youth immigrant rights activists who have "come out," who are "undocumented and unafraid" to tell their stories.
Story about a beaver attacking a trucker	A humorous radio story from Canadian Broadcast Company (CBC), selected by Lyle.
Audacity instructional manual	Projected in the Mac Lab. A copy of an Audacity "cheat sheet" created by Lyle was given to each student.
Text read aloud by Lyle to teach "The 5 Ws"	Text consisted of textbook-like language compiled by Lyle. Written by hand in a journalist's notepad.
"Raids Are Not the Solution"	Youth commentary from YMI archives about Immigration and Customs Enforcement (ICE) raids, deportations, and the separation of families. Audio and downloaded print text copy were given to each student.
"Whoopin"	Youth commentary from YMI archives about the positive effects of belt whippings by a parent.

3-page section on youth commentaries from *Drop That Knowledge* (Soep & Chávez, 2010)	Students were each given a copy to include in their binders. The text was read and discussed as a whole class using AVID reading comprehension strategies: highlighting, writing questions in the margin, etc.
"Students Risk Dreams—and Deportation—in Walk for Recognition" (Nunez, 2010)	CNN online article, projected for reading in class and downloaded to give copies to students for their binders.
"Defying Cops and Clan, Immigrants Trek 1,500 Miles to Washington" (Dwyer, 2010)	ABC online article, projected for reading in class and downloaded to give copies to students for their binders.
"The Personal Side of the Dream Act" (Freed, 2010)	Youthcast.org. Copies of the downloaded text were given to each student.
Outline of Jack's Pitch on Juárez Story	Taken from a professional "pitch" Jack had made to a nationally syndicated radio program. We also listened to the archived feature story as part of the feature story unit.
YRRA student commentaries	Student commentaries were viewed and publicly critiqued in class using a handout to guide discussion. Peer-critique guidelines were based on guidelines used in an undergraduate dance, theater, and music program.

**Because the Youth Radio Oakland educational website is no longer available, it is not possible to correctly cite most of the texts used from that website.

The primary themes addressed in the selected radio pieces included relationships (romantic and familial), parenting (youth positioned as both children and parents), gang-related activity, issues related to school (testing, tracking), and racial profiling. The audio texts selected for modeling the youth commentary were primarily radio productions accessed through the Youth Radio Oakland (YouthMediaInternational, 2010) website, usually played in the classroom using the CLD projector and surround sound system, accompanied by a printed transcription of the oral text when available. In addition to existing youth commentaries, experts from the community provided information—in lieu of the Internet and official news sources—on topics such as the Dream Act and the Dreamers and the dearth of students of color on sports teams in the district. Lyle also provided two texts written by him to teach "the 5 Ws" (Who, What, When, Where, Why—and How) and one radio story for the Canadian Broadcast Corporation. I include the community experts in this list as a kind of text whose embodied signs and discourses can be deciphered and interpreted as performances of social identities, and whose shared information can be used as a legitimate source for research, thereby validating community funds of knowledge.

Language of the commentary. The selection of audio-print curricular texts presented models of communicative practice that included code-switching, variations of English (AAVE, "cholo lango"), and narration in English embedded with extended discourse in Spanish—all heard in the spoken words of youth who produced the pieces. As modeled, dialectal differences from Standard English were allowed in final products of youth commentaries. Language use varied according to the instructor, and interactional format for each phase in the production cycle of the youth commentary is presented in Table 2.3.

Table 2.3 Language and Interactional Formats Used in Youth Commentary

Cycle of Activity		
1. Build background knowledge	(Eng/Span)	Whole class, teacher-led discussion
2. Model genre, play examples	(Eng/Span/AAVE)	
3. Guest speaker on Dream Act	(Eng/Span)	Whole class
4. Brainstorm topics	(English)	Whole class
5. Discuss ideas in small groups	(Eng/Span)	Group discussions mediated by adult
6. Write idea with supporting details	(Eng/Span)	Individual work
7. Pitch story, get feedback	(English)	Mentor-student
8. Write first draft	(Eng/Span)	Individual work
9. Receive adult feedback on draft	(English)	Mentor-student
10. Fishbowl discussion of commentary	(English)	Whole class/mentor-student
11. Do background research and incorporate into draft	(Eng/Span)	Individual/mentor-student
12. Receive editing advice	(English)	Mentor-student
13. Learn recording equipment	(English)	Whole class
14. Record multiple takes	(English)	Mentor-student
15. Upload best recording	(Eng/Span)	Individual
16. Instruction in audio editing	(English)	Whole class
17. Edit audio	(Eng/Span)	Individual/Mentor-student
18. Add ambient sound	(Eng/Span) (Span/Eng)	Individual
19. Save, name, export audio draft	(English)	Mentor-student

20. Public hearing & critique of first audio draft	(English)	Whole class
21. Revise recorded commentary	(Eng/Span)	Mentor-student
22. Get go-ahead from managing editor	(English)	Mentor-student
23. Play final commentary for class	(Eng/Span)	Whole class
24. Receive written peer feedback	(English)	Individual
25. Showcase	(English)	Public viewing
26. Commentaries played on the radio are listened-to in class	(English)	Whole class

In the youth commentary production cycle there was a blending of languages and literacy practices. The dominant language of instruction was English, but Spanish and code-switching were also used depending on the interactional format and who was instructing or mentoring. Both Jack, the bilingual journalist, and I code-switched in our instructional speech and conversations with students. Lyle and Liv used English always. Ray did not teach in whole-class formats but assumed a mentoring role with students in one-on-one and small-group discussions, speaking Spanish especially during informal conversations with them. In small-group work among student peers the dominant language tended to be Spanish, unless one of the non-Spanish-speaking students (two Nepalese and one Russian) or monolingual adults were present.

Language competencies were taught and assessed in the context of the goal-directed activity of producing for broadcast quality. Broadcast quality was defined by rubrics and checklists and in the abstract by the radio station: we never actually learned what criteria they used for selecting youth radio pieces. Though the domains of writing, speaking, reading, and listening were assessed—the latter in the form of reading and listening comprehension of commentary written and spoken texts—the emphasis in teaching youth commentaries was not on academic language related to specific content areas, but rather on the social, compositional, and performative requirements of the genre.

The ways that language domains were taught and assessed in this activity made visible to students the prevailing cultural ideology in the program regarding what constituted language competence and how language was to be used and for what purposes. The intent of the planned curriculum and practices surrounding the youth commentary was to reframe "language" as being used to critically question and investigate issues of concern to youth themselves; to construct a persuasive argument supported by personal or research evidence; to communicate effectively to a general public outside of school; and to use communication technology to amplify one's voice and broadcast one's perspective, thus contributing to the youths' participation in the public discourse.

The assessment of language domains and language features at the vocabulary, sentence, and discourse levels were embedded within these larger goals, and instruction was provided in the form of overt instruction and modeling, instructional conversations around topic development, and coaching in writing for the particular genre of the youth commentary by the journalist mentors. Students were expected to demonstrate their understanding of the youth commentary as both a literacy genre and a discourse genre (Wells, 2007): how a commentary ought to be structured, planning for the opening, the hook, the body of evidence, the closing turn, and the tag: "For Youth Radio at Beckwourth High, this is Delicia Arena."

Learning through instructional conversations. Grant funding obtained for this research allowed me to hire professional writers and artists as mentors for students. The continuity of mentor support allowed for relationships of trust to develop, and for students to benefit from extended exposure and engagement with professionals and their social practices from independent media and the arts. Observations and student and teacher comments confirmed my long-held belief that creating these connections with community-based organizations and active practitioners can greatly benefit young people as well as educators whose teaching practices may be enhanced, and feel reenergized in the process.

Student language and conceptual development benefitted in particular from sustained instructional conversations with Jack the journalist. He took students from a kernel of an idea to expanded, "powerful" essays and radio productions in striking ways. He brought to bear his journalistic writing skills as well as the practices and ways of thinking and talking of the journalist: looking for the controversy, doing targeted research to build background knowledge on a topic for the radio listener, framing questions in a way that will grab the audience's attention. In many ways Jack's mentoring interactions with students mirrored those described by Clark and Fry (1992) in their study of journalistic writing coaches:

> Coaching can happen at different stages of the process. [The coach] intervenes after the reporting, when the reporter is struggling to find a lead. Work at the front end of the process as well as the end and throughout. . . . The coach asks the reporter good questions and listens to the responses. In doing so, he draws upon [the reporter's] experience at the scene milking him for details that may or may not be in the reporter's notebook. He treats the reporter as the expert on this story. [The reporter] does not know what he knows, but [the coach] questions draw the story out of him. The coach is not afraid to tell the reporter what he thinks. The tone of the questions and observations is supportive and collaborative. . . . The coach communicates his values.

> Through his questions and observations the editor lets the writer know what he thinks is important. Information, specific details, telling a good story, the reader. The reporter will hear his editor's questions in his head on the next story. Offering alternative approaches, bouncing back the story to the writer and letting the writer know what you think is most important. (pp. 10-11)

This description mirrors many aspects of the Vygotskian-informed framework and approach of *instructional conversations*—extended and scaffolded conversation about subject matter—which are considered particularly productive for multilingual learners (Goldenberg, 1992; Tharp, 1991). In fact, a number of neo-Vygotskian researchers have argued that teaching and learning should be viewed as an extended conversation. Extended conversational exchanges about academic content with teachers and peers build a shared and deeper understanding of others' ideas and the topics at hand. Furthermore, instructional conversations facilitate the negotiation of the numerous discourses that students bring with them to the classroom from home, peer, and national cultures, and at the same time answer students' need for recognition and differentiation (Rex & McEachen, 1999). Applebee (cited in Rex & McEachen), for example, suggests that literate traditions are "culturally constituted tools" for understanding the world, and that in acquiring these tools,

> students are learning to participate in a variety of socially constituted traditions of meaning-making that are valued in cultures of which they are a part. These traditions include not just concepts and associated vocabulary, but also rhetorical structures, the patterns of action, that are part of any tradition of meaning-making. They include characteristic ways of reaching consensus and expressing disagreement, of formulating arguments, of providing evidence, as well as characteristic genres for organizing thought and conversational action. In mastering such traditions, students learn not only to operate with them, but also how to change them. (p. 9)

Instructional conversations with writing coach Jack and radio mentor Lyle facilitated student access to and participation in the socially constituted traditions of meaning-making and action in independent radio, as well as related literacy genres. In addition to learning the practices of independent journalism, several students reported that what they learned from Jack's coaching helped them to "speak better" ("*hablar major*") and write more clearly with better spelling and grammar. One student, Tania, went so far as to say that after her year in the program she considered herself an expert in writing and could now teach writing to other teens.

Audio editing and learning to "visualize voice." While the different genres taught in the program privileged different modalities, many activities combined multiple modalities and forms of representation. Romero and I (Romero & Walker, 2010) have examined the interplay between speaking, hearing, and seeing—along with reading and writing—that takes place in the audio editing process, and the impact on students' developing understandings of voice. Our analysis focuses on the transformation of the spoken, aural, ephemeral voice, into a physical object that could be seen and acted upon on the computer screen in the editing process:

> In the process of recording, editing, uploading and broadcasting, the *voice* becomes an artifact that mediates interactions in the classroom and among students and mentors gathered around the computer. The attention to voice in the recording and listening process raised challenges for many students who were self-conscious about their spoken English, and who were reluctant to hear themselves or have others listen to them. In the editing process, however, the audio editing software allowed students to hear as well as *see* their voices as a visual representation on the screen. The voice shifted from being a primary object, directly mediating the interactions, to a secondary artifact that became the object of their actions and a tool in subsequent interactions. As students learned to manage the voice editing software, through instruction and collaboration with the radio broadcasters and mentors, they also learned to see, to talk about, and to manipulate the image of their voice on screen. Voice was no longer something personal or intangible, but literally it was transformed into a publicly visual artifact, assuming physical and spatial properties. Consequently, this on screen objectification of voice in the spectrograph image, much like the written drafts on a page, constituted a socially shared object; one which could be located, paused in time and pointed to and, which was available for discussion and deliberate, collaborative activity. (p. 230)

In the audio-editing process, students learned to read the sound waves as symbolic representations of voice and to understand them as visual representations of their own and others' voices. They could see stops and starts, repairs, and longer-than-ordinary pauses (a primary impediment of fluency, I have discovered), in the shape and size of the sound waves: the higher, larger waves represented louder voice, smaller waves the soft voice, and no waves represented silence. Figure 2.1 shows voice waves as represented through Audacity audio editing software.

Figure 2.1 Visualizing Voice

By transposing the sound wave into the "image+sound wave" students were able to edit their voices, and in the case of feature stories, those of the people they interviewed. As students became more proficient in reading and interpreting the sound waves, they also developed an ability to reflect and act upon their own oral production, which gave them a sense of freedom and power in reframing themselves as people who could communicate meaning and be understood. As Tania responded when asked what she had learned about technology that she found most useful:

> I'd say Audacity because that does help you, you know, correct your voice and let people know what you're actually trying to say rather than just like a mumble. You can erase that mumble and actually have the real thing.

"The real thing" I interpret to mean the utterance that carries the intended meaning that others can understand. Elia described a similar sense of empowerment and freedom in being able to delete parts of her speech. When she was first learning Audacity with Lyle she exclaimed, "This is cool" when he showed her how to delete sections of talk she "didn't like."

In the next section I describe how instructional tools such as class readings, production guidelines, and assessments made visible to students the language and literacy demands of the youth commentary genre. As part of this analysis I examine the "possibilities of selfhood" (Ivanič, 1998) established through the social practices, texts, and instructional tools used in the teaching and production of a youth commentary.

Instructional tools and assessments. The youth commentary genre, as presented on the Youth Media International (2010) website, is a subgenre of radio commentary that transforms the radio commentary genre for the purposes of helping youth convey their unique perspectives and experiences. We framed the definition, guidelines, and assessments of the youth commentary in reference to language arts standards for the persuasive essay while adopting a broader notion of the "youth commentary" to include description and emotion in the persuasive argument, and Internet research or personal anecdote as valid forms of evidence. The instructional tools (guidelines, checklists) and assessments used for teaching the youth commentary included those shown in Table 2.4.

Table 2.4 Instructional Tools and Assessments for the Youth Commentary

Checklist for Creating a Youth Commentary
Self-Assessment for Listening to Youth Commentaries
Reading Commentaries Assessment
Guidelines for Pitching a Commentary
Reading and Peer-Critiques of Commentaries
Analyze and Rate Peer Commentaries (Are All Components Included?)
Commentary Writing Rubric final.docx
Commentary Point Scale Final

The Youth Commentary Final Rubric, presented in Figure 2.2, made visible to students the language and literacy demands of this project.

Figure 2.2: Youth Commentary Rubric

Name _____   Total points _____

Youth Commentary Rubric   **100 points total**

Criteria	Exceeds Expectations	Teacher Comments
Title and Tag (Writing) 1 - 5	Title is catchy enough to make a person want to listen, and conveys the content. Your tag at the end includes, "For Youth Radio@ Boulder High, this is ... (real name or pseudonym).	
Choice of Topic (Writing) 1 – 10	Your commentary shows that you wrote about a topic that inspires passion in you.	
Hook (Writing) 1 - 5	You start with a strong hook (or lede) that draws your listener into your commentary. You spent time crafting your opening lines to draw the listener into your commentary	
Evidence (Writing) 1 – 20	You present rich evidence – such as examples from life, images, stories, or research on the topic - that make your commentary come alive in the imagination of the listener.	
Persuasive argument (Writing) 1 -20	You create a convincing argument about your topic. Your position on the topic is clear and persuasive. You found the controversy in the subject. You cause people to have a strong emotional or rational response.	
Conclusion (Writing) 1 – 10	You finish with a bang! Your closing statement is related to your hook, and you tie together the threads of your argument.	
Speaking 1 – 20	Your voice conveys strength and a tone of voice that will convince your listeners of your position on the topic. You speak clearly, fluently, and articulate each word.	
Technology and Research 1 – 10	You used recording equipment and Audacity to create a commentary of broadcast quality, with no errors or background noise.	
Total Points		

While the instructional tools and multiple assessments represented continuity of existing school practices, many dimensions of the project would have represented change from existing school-based literacy experiences. Table 2.5 represents these dimensions of change.

Table 2.5 Ways in which Youth Radio Literacy Practices Differed from Traditional School-Based Literacy Practices

1. The bilingual and multi-dialectal texts used to model the genre
2. The bilingual experts from the community as sources of legitimate knowledge
3. Self-directed internet and community-based research
4. No textbook
5. Being coached by practicing journalists
6. Using recording equipment and audio editing software
7. Opportunities for multiple "takes," rehearsing new language, "fixing" one's oral language production
8. Receiving and giving structured peer critiques
9. Producing to achieve broadcast quality, determined by the radio station
10. The potential of being heard by a radio audience of listeners outside of school

The youth commentary genre and possibilities for selfhood. In addition to establishing the language and literacy demands of the youth commentary project, the instructional tools and assessments, the interactional formats and languages used in youth commentary teaching and learning, represented the "possibilities for selfhood" (Ivanič, 1998) that were available through composition within this genre and related practices. Ivanič argues that possibilities for selfhood and the patterns of privileging among them shape and constrain how people compose texts: "In any institutional contexts there will be several socially available possibilities for selfhood: several ways of doing the same thing. Of these some will be privileged over others in the sense that the institution accords them more status" (p. 27). I will discuss the three possibilities of selfhood as elaborated by Ivanič as they apply to identity processes engaged through youth radio productions, specifically the youth commentary. My interest is in the ways that patterns of privileging shift as the program attends to the heterogeneous interests, values, beliefs, and practices of our diverse community.

First, within a given genre there are conventions for how to establish *authorial presence* that differs from one type of writing to another, and from one social context to another. These conventions influence how (or whether) writers establish themselves as authors in their writing. The Youth Radio and Radio Arts (YRRA) program's modeling of youth commentaries through examples drawn from the YMI.org website and various instructional tools and assessments made visible to students the expectations for authorial presence, as evidenced in the rubric of Figure 2.2: "Your commentary shows that you wrote about a topic that inspires passion in you";

"Your voice conveys strength and a tone of voice that will convince your listeners of your position on the topic."

Second, following Ivanič (1998), a writer's *autobiographical self* develops in the context of socially constrained access to possibilities for selfhood. This means that students are able to identify with different subject positions according to their social group memberships. Whereas students might not yet have been able to identify with the subject position of a white radio broadcaster, the Youth Radio Oakland (YouthMediaInternational, 2010) commentaries provided exemplary texts in which students might see their subject positions reflected and hear youth challenging dominant discourses about Latino/a and other youth of color. For example, in the commentary "Food and Family," the youth producer chose to include untranslated clips of Spanish speech in which the author and her mother discusses the importance of food in their family and her mother's extensive knowledge of edible plants grown in her garden. These discourse segments simultaneously give the listener a glimpse into the soundscape of the author's life and represent Spanish speakers as people of integrity with strong family values, whose knowledge and organic food practices predated the current local food production fad. Spanish language in this youth commentary is represented as a legitimate form of communication on the public airwaves. We discussed with students how the author of this multilingual commentary was engaging in identity work in her piece while challenging the dominant anti-immigrant and English-only ideologies of our country.

Finally, Ivanič (1998) suggests that writers construct a *discoursal self* out of the possibilities for selfhood that are supported by the sociocultural and institutional context in which they are writing or, in our case, producing. A writer's discoursal self is the impression ("often multiple sometimes contradictory") that he or she conveys of himself or herself through composition. Ivanič calls this aspect of identity "discoursal" because it is constructed through the discourse characteristics of a text, which are related to values, beliefs, and ideologies of the social context in which they were written. Whereas the conventions of genres make available certain roles and relationships, which people may conform to or resist, "Discourses, by contrast, are shaped by subject-matters and ideologies such as history, skiing, a feminist perspective. By making particular discourse choices, writers are aligning themselves with particular interests (in terms of subject matter) and ideologies" (p. 46). A number of participants aligned themselves with the subject matter and counterhegemonic discourse of immigration reform proposed within the Youth Radio curriculum through the choice of texts and speakers. Other students chose to avoid political topics and wrote about their friends or the safety of home. Table 2.6 presents the titles and summaries of the youth radio commentaries completed during the fall semester.

Table 2.6 List of Student Commentaries with Summaries

Title	Author/ Producer	Summary
"A World of Violence"	Beto	Beto argues that "peace does not have a chance," and that violence reigns in the world and in his neighborhood.
"My Family in Mexico"	Jesus	Jesus describes his family in Mexico that he can no longer go visit.
"Don't Judge Us by Our Clothes"	Delfina	Delfina argues persuasively that teachers and other adults should not judge youth by their clothing style, using her boyfriend as an example.
"What Are Green Cards?"	Sonia	Sonia poetically describes the pain that can be caused by a card that separates families, and prevents children and families from obtaining their dreams.
"Every Teen Needs a Second Home"	Tania	Tania argues that adolescents should all have access to a second home in case of threats to the teens' safety in their own homes.
"A Near-Death Experience"	Elia	Elia describes her experience of almost drowning, how her mother saved her, and how families should practice water safety.
"Homeless in a Rich Country"	Dipashri	Dipashri describes the shock she experienced upon first arriving in our "country of plenty" and seeing so many homeless people.
"Home Is Where I'm Free"	Nato	Nato describes how he feels safe and free at home, with details about his activities at home.
"When the Love Is Gone"	Sugita	The separation of her parents causes Sugita great pain.
"Weapons Are Dangerous, but Words Can Be Too"	Cipriana	Cipriana argues that words can be as damaging as weapons, focusing on a threat against Latinos written on the boys' bathroom wall.
"Why Are There so Few Students of Color	Raúl	Raúl draws on the knowledge of a community activist and elder in the

in Our High School's Sports Teams?"		Latino community to discuss the underrepresentation of Latinos in school sports at his school.
"Black Magic and My Grandpa"	Delmara	Delmara tells of her grandfather in Mexico who engaged in black magic.
"Losing Can Be Fun When Playing Soccer"	Julio	Julio makes an argument for playing soccer not just to win, but to enjoy the game even when he loses.
"From Worst Enemies to Best Friends"	Maria	Maria describes how her best friend used to be her enemy, and how their friendship made her more reflective about how she perceives people, and the need to get to know others before passing judgment.
"How Do Animals Help Us?"	Josué	Josué describes how his horse helped him stay out of trouble and learn to care for an animal and be safe.

This table presents an introduction to subjects and the construction of discoursal selves that will be analyzed in greater detail in coming chapters. First, I will describe the sociocultural context in which YRRA was implemented.

Context of the Program Implementation

The program design along with the curriculum that was co-constructed over time (Castanheira, Crawford, Dixon, & Green, 2001) represented a rupture for both teachers and students from the normal school routines, norms, purposes, and beliefs about what counts as school learning and teaching. The rupture required change on the part of all participants (including the researcher) and proved to be productive for some students and not for others: Two students were refused admission to the class the second semester due to their disruptive behavior and confrontation with the radio improve mentor. This chapter analyzes student perspectives on the impact of the program and processes that facilitated personal transformation. To understand more specifically the processes involved in the transformations that took place, I use Zittoun's (2006) framework for analyzing transitions through the heuristic of the *semiotic prism*, based on Vygotskian notions of the development of higher mental functions through the mediation of an important "other" that links the object of learning and social mediation in a triangle of mediated cognition. In the framework used here, development is a normative concept that implies preferences for the direction of change: "development is a qualitative change that opens new ranges of possible conduct, that is, it is *generative* for further transitions" (Zittoun, 2005, p. 4). I have described above the developmental preferences that informed the learning design.

At the time of this study, the combined ESL study skills and academic support class was well suited to implementing an alternative curriculum, due to the relative freedom from content-area curricular requirements: ESL and academic support classes at the time were structured as pull-out classes, which meant they were not required to follow a prescribed curriculum. The teachers were open to innovation, were educated in relatively progressive teacher preparation programs, and had 25 years of experience between them working with linguistically and culturally diverse students. They cared for the well-being of their students and held high expectations for them.

Yet in spite of the relative autonomy of the class and the willingness of the teachers to engage in a new approach, the program immediately gave rise to contradictions resulting from student expectations for what counted as learning and being a student in that school. It became evident early on that to study transformation of existing practices, it would be necessary to examine the tension between the forces of continuity and change in this setting. As Bloome and colleagues (2005) argue,

> At any particular moment in the classroom, there are tensions and conflicts between the tendency for continuity (reproduction of extant classroom cultural practices and social structures) and change and, put more grandly, between maintaining a cultural ideology of challenging and transforming it. (p. 52)

Innovation does not occur on a blank slate. Participants bring with them cultural models regarding what it means to be a student or teacher, how a classroom is arranged, and how instruction should proceed. These models are shaped by previous and ongoing schooling experiences, and institutional factors reinforce current teacher and students roles and relationships, and constrain alternatives (Lefstein, 2008).

The Weight of the Past

A great challenge to enacting this innovation at its inception were the general structural and lived conditions of schooling for these working-class emergent bilingual learners, and the weight of the past: "the ways that daily classroom life and years and years of multiple school contexts support and constrain the opportunities students have to learn school content" (Collins & Green, 1992, pp. 59–60). The years and years of a certain way of being a student in this school system, as second language learners and Mexicans, resulted in dispositions described by Ray in the following exchange:

Transcript 2.1

1	Ray	They're all [a group of five girls] failing
2		practically all of their classes.
3	Dana	Really?!
4	Ray	[talks about their grades]
5		Delmara asked, "What good is this [Youth Radio]?
6		How's this gunna help?"
7	Dana	She asked the same thing last semester.
8	Ray	It's good that she's thinking that way
9		'cause you wanna know
10		why you're doin' what you're doin'.
11		When I told her that she's writing and speaking
12		for radio audiences, for more than just the teacher
13		she said, "No, I'd rather have a teacher check me
14		and say 'yes,' 'bad,' or 'good.'"
15	Dana	Really?
16	Ray	But I think it's, it's still wanting that routine
17		where they're just sittin' in a row
18		making themselves invisible.
19		If they can get themselves invisible,
20		they can just get through the day, I think.
21	Dana	That's interesting.
22	Ray	Yeah, I think they wanna fail.
23		I wonder how much it was
24		that they knew what a transition [in the feature story] was
25		or they just wanted to sabotage, or
26		they just didn't want to do it, or
27		how complicated it is and all that.
28		My heart goes out to them because
29		they're at such high risk, the Latinas:
30		their chances are really high
31		of getting pregnant are really high,
32		and dropping out.

Whether Ray's interpretation of reasons for the girls' low grades was correct or not, historical forces were converging to influence their assumptions about what counted as "being a student" and learning in this school and this classroom. As Ray explained in a staff debriefing,

> [Our students] are used to not speaking, [to] sitting in the back of the room in their classes, and not communicating, not participating. And so here they were asked to participate, to communicate, to get out of themselves. They want to, they really want to, but they can't get it out, can't get out. It's been years. It's years and years. They got to that point over years, it's not just overnight. It's going to take a while. I know they feel comfortable enough with, with each other they feel comfortable, nobody is going to hurt them in that group, I think they know that now. (Ray, staff debriefing, 9/23/10)

Exit interviews with students revealed similar perceptions of the silencing process and explicitly linked the development of *voice* to *unsilencing*. Asked about her essay on "invisibility" written at the beginning of the semester, Sonia stated, "I wrote that I feel invisible by some teachers.... Even though I sit in the front they don't ask me if I have questions, or I raise my hand and they just ignore me when I raise my hand." And responding to the question, "Why do you think that, according to your teachers in Youth Radio, that developing voice is important?" Sonia articulated a clear understanding of the ways schools silence students on the margins—linking silence to what Gilligan (1993) describes as a loss of sense of knowing: "High school shuts up a lot of kids. Being a freshman is scary. Once they [students] grow up they don't think they can vote, don't think they know anything" (Sonia, exit interview, 5/1/11).

The students were framed by teachers as "passive learners" who "tend to want to disappear in a class and not participate." Ray explained their passivity in this way: "I think their passiveness comes from years of finding a way to become invisible in their classes." He attributed their silence and feelings of invisibility to their marginal status as racial minorities: "A lot of these kids, they feel like they're minorities and they don't think . . . they're not confident." Being a racial minority in a predominately affluent white high school led to crises of self-confidence, according to him, which in turn led to silence, passivity, and a sense of invisibility. In response to Liv's assertion in a debriefing meeting, "They don't have a voice," Ray replied, "I know they always have to check, even with us: 'Is this okay, am I doing this right,' which is a good thing but also it's more of a simple thing. . . . I have a couple of girls who are really insecure in there" (Staff debriefing, 9/23/10). Sonia confirmed Ray's observation:

> I do raise my hand sometimes, but it depends on the subject. Sometimes I don't feel like answering the questions or saying a comment because I feel like I'm gunna answer it wrong, and I feel like students are going to laugh at me. (Sonia, interview, 6/5/11)

Students, in turn, attributed the process of silencing to the absence of dialogue in classes, to the lecture format that predominated in the school, which prevented interaction and often left emergent bilinguals feeling lost when they could not follow "the big words" of the academic content language, lacking visual supports and other forms of comprehensible input, as described by Delfina above as well as by Sonia in the following excerpt from our interview:

> In this class [Youth Radio] like there's tons where we can talk, I talk more with students. Cuz most of them I talk to them, right? In other classes we have to be most of the time quiet and just take notes. Notes, notes, notes. We never get to express ourselves or make comments because in other classes we just have to take notes and just sit there.

These kinds of statements confirm other studies of multilingual students showing that emergent bilinguals, when included in English-dominant environments, continue to be segregated from native English speakers through limitations in their access to the kinds of interactions and activities that would permit them to develop the body of knowledge necessary for academic success (Gutiérrez, Baquedano-Lopez, & Asato, 2001; Manyak, 2002). Furthermore, students felt evaluated by students and teachers alike, positioned by other students in relation to cultural ideologies that defined academic competence (Bloome et al., 2005, p. 139). Sonia described a situation in a class where, echoing Loli's conclusion about the general perception of *mexicana/o* students in the high school, she was stigmatized and humiliated as an English learner, though in fact English was her dominant language, making this an instance of racial stereotyping and a form of harassment: "Once a girl in my history class said to me, 'Hand this out to the stupid people.' She was talking about the paper for the ESL students." Sonia here is referring to a modification of reading material created by the teacher to reduce the linguistic complexity of text while highlighting the key concepts. This comment was offered in the context of a discussion in Youth Radio about how "ESL students" in the school are treated, and how the students felt their academic needs could be better addressed.

These personal experiences, when discussed as a group, gave a sense of a general positioning of second language learners in the school as separate and unequal. Liv referred to this in speaking of the "structural problems" of the school:

> We've got some serious structural problems in this school, the segregation of the Latino students from the rest of the school up in that other wing, pull-out ESL study skills two times a day, they're missing important content. (Liv staff debriefing, 9/23/10)

> None of the ESL students are in AP [Advanced Placement] classes. When I was new to the school I asked someone in the office about ¡Vámanos! They said ¡Vámanos! was "taking care of Latino kids." It isolates them. The teachers place them there, then they think that's where they belong, not in the AP classes. (Liv interview, 6/2/11)

The geographic segregation Liv refers to in this statement has to do with an after-school tutoring program for Latino students, which is located in a separate wing of the school. When asked their perspectives on the tutoring program, one student reported that she liked going there because her friends were there and she could hang out with them after school. Other students, however, felt that the tutoring program, which I will call ¡Vámanos!, stigmatized Latino students as less-worthy students. When I asked Tatiana if Lesley was in ¡Vámanos!, she said: "Lesley's not in ¡Vámanos! Only stupid kids go to ¡Vámanos! ¡Vámanos! is for Mexicans. So Mexicans are stupid" (Tatiana, personal communication). As Bloome and coauthors (2005) note, social identities are material: they are built into the architecture of buildings, and the literacy tools and practices that predominate for certain groups of students, such as worksheets for second language learners in the lower academic tracks, versus technology-driven inquiry-based research projects in Advanced Placement (AP) classes.

In this and other statements, students appeared to grasp the structural inequities of the school and to recognize the subject positions that young people like them are conventionally afforded. Because these comments were made at the end of the year, it is not possible to know whether these insights were long-held or whether they resulted from critical reflections and discussion engaged in Youth Radio and Radio Arts. It is possible to argue, however, that Youth Radio provided a "thinking space" for reflecting on and representing the young people's questioning and theorizing, for speaking up and acting out against what Freire (1970/2000) has called "the culture of silence."

Living and learning in fear and silence. Students also saw that forces outside school shaped learning within the school. In addition to years of silencing in schools, many of the students—due to their immigration status—lived in daily fear of being separated from their families through deportation proceedings, as expressed by Delfina in the following excerpt from our interview:

> I'm scared that I am going to be separated from my family. Everyone talks about *inmigración*, like we're in a corner—in the news. *Uds nos dicen tengan fe, pero a fuera nos dicen, "Deportaron a tal cual."* [You (program instructors, guest speakers) tell us to have faith, but outside of school they tell us, "So and so was just deported."] We're confused. It's hard. (Delfina interview, 5/14/11)

When the school launched a program to give free laptops to students without computers at home, none of the Mexican students in the Youth Radio class signed up because they were afraid that the documentation process would jeopardize their families' security. One parent told me, when I asked whether the children went to the public library to use the computers since they did not have one at home, that the family never went anywhere but work and school, out of fear of being stopped by police on the road and deported.

Students also experienced threats to their well-being in the form of day-to-day "racial micro-aggressions," defined by Sue and colleagues (2007) "brief and commonplace daily verbal, behavioral, or environmental indignities, whether intentional or unintentional, that communicate hostile, derogatory, or negative racial slights and insults toward people of color" (p. 271). Students reported being the targets of derogatory comments, hostile glances, and white students moving away from a table in the lunchroom when Latino students sat down. There were also overt threats of racial violence, such as graffiti found in the boys' bathroom during the first semester of the program, stating: "All Mexicans will die October 29!" Though most Latino students in the program laughed off the threat as a prank, some students were frightened, and some parents kept their children home from school that week. Cipriana, for example, did a feature story titled "Racial Threats in School."

Finally, students talked about the lack of recognition of their humanity and individuality through the stereotyping process. Delfina spoke to me in her exit interview about her experience:

> Because sometimes, um [because we] don' know they judge us because of, I don' know. Because if one of us is a Mexican, and a Mexican does something bad, they're gunna say it's all of us. So I don't know I don't know how they see us. . . . It may be that they can't see us as someone who, I don' know. (Delfina interview, 5/14/11)

According to the teachers, the cumulative effect of these conditions was to obstruct students' learning and their sense of selves as learners and members of the school community. Most of the students in the program were failing multiple classes. Liv's class was set up for targeted instruction, "for students who are in the achievement gap, in other words, not proficient, not performing up to their potential; who are reading below grade level." These sociocultural conditions and resulting psychological disturbances inhibited their learning and helped explain their poor academic performance, according to the teachers and the students themselves. The teachers, however, stated that for them failure was not an option, and Liv questioned where responsibility for student academic failure begins and ends.

It was against this background that Ray expressed cautious optimism following our first day with the theater director and actor Federico that the Youth Radio program might be the start of a change:

It took some pulling of the teeth, but they participated and I think their passiveness comes from years of finding a way to become invisible in their classes, and, and now hopefully they'll learn that being invisible is not going to help them learn. They have to be more aggressive and alert in, in class. And that they can be confident in that, and, and I think that they got that lesson today. (Ray, recorded personal reflection, 9/23/11)

This introductory sketch of the sociocultural conditions for learning and youth subject positionings within the school and community provides the context within which the Youth Radio and Radio Arts program was introduced. The next chapters address how youth and adult participants constructed over time, through collective activity, their understandings of the purposes of Youth Radio and Radio Arts and the meanings of "voice" and "communication." I begin with a description of the "observed curriculum" (Castanheira et al., 2001) as it was constructed during the first two days of the program.

• CHAPTER THREE •

Constructing the Observable Curriculum

> Language is not simply a tool for communicating information: it is always an act of constructing social relations, identities, and bringing cultural ideology to bear upon an event, a group, or other phenomenon.
>
> —Vera John-Steiner

To examine the emergence over time of principles of a *pedagogy of powerful communication*, this study focuses on the processes of change and continuity at the collective and individual level. As described in Chapter 1, to study change in the context of a literacy-language innovation, the researcher must also examine what remains the same. I therefore examine continuity and change across two dimensions of the program as it unfolds over the academic year: (a) continuity and change in classroom cultural practices—the reproduction or transformation of existing cultural practices and social structures, including power relations; and (b) continuity and change in selves across time and spheres of experience through the mediated use of cultural elements—their take-up and transformation resulting from student *semiosis*, or semiotic work, including identity processes, knowledge and skill acquisition, and personal sense making.

Analysis of the first day provides a glimpse of the onset of patterns of language, actions, and events (Baker 2001), laying the foundations for the construction of the Youth Radio and Radio Arts curriculum. On Day 1 we begin to make visible to the students our relationships with them as their instructors and what counted as Youth Radio. I identify ways in which the teachers and mentors (including myself) shape language and literate practices and how students participated in the co-construction of the "observable curriculum." Through an adaptation of Castanheira, Crawford, Dixon, and Green's (2001) framework, I distinguish between the planned curriculum (that which the teachers and I presented in the syllabus and daily objectives) and the observable curriculum (that which was constructed and observed). In describing the constructed, observable curriculum, the authors write:

> From our perspective, the curriculum is shaped by, and then shapes, what members do and say to and with each other, under particular conditions, for specific purposes, in particular times and spaces, in locally constructed ways. Thus, what members engage in and with becomes the curriculum that is constructed by, and observable to, members (and by extension to researchers), and this curriculum can then be contrasted with the planned curriculum (the curriculum plan of the teacher prior to engaging with the students on a given day or days), and the stated or official curriculum (the curriculum designed by those beyond the classroom walls). (p. 384)

Using elements of an interactional ethnographic approach, which combines discourse analysis with an ethnographic perspective and certain ethnographic methods (Spradley 1979)—I do not claim to offer a full ethnographic account—I reconstruct the observable curriculum from an etic and emic perspective. I interpret what I believe students observed based on my ethnographic records (video and audio recordings, teacher reflections, field notes, interviews), which constitutes the *etic* or outsider's perspective. I also attempt to reconstruct an *emic* perspective, which was acknowledged as having been observed and considered by participants: in Chapters 4 and 5 I explore in greater depth the emic perspective through analyses of student narratives co-constructed with the researcher, myself, during in-depth interviews at the end of the year. In these analyses I take into consideration the experiences of students and teachers both inside and outside of school, as these experiences and their interpretations of them contribute to shaping the contexts for learning. The dimensions of the visible (and interpreted) curriculum that I describe include the following:

1. Audible and visual artifacts and signs (symbols). These include people and their performances, as people can also be considered as texts to be read and interpreted, including the identities they perform and how they position others in the process
2. Student artifacts, including written, visual, and audible texts
3. Technology and media production tools, such as recording and audiovisual editing equipment
4. Languages used (and not used), including the enactment of language ideologies, power relations, and special-temporal and emotional resonances that each language—and languages in interaction—evoke
5. Knowledge and skills that are presented as requirements for successfully completing the class

All of these symbols, artifacts, and performances of selves together contribute to the construction of what counts as Youth Radio, what kind of person one can become in the collective, and what kinds of relations (coercive, collaborative, or both) will be possible. Because the university-school-community collaboration was a key feature of the learning design, I also examine processes set in motion through the collaboration, the challenges and contradictions that arise, as well as contributions to expanding teaching practices and student learning.

In the next section I begin to introduce the actors and preview the practices that will be constructed over the course of the academic year in Youth Radio. I present an analysis of the first days of the program, focusing on elements of continuity, rupture, and change. This analysis, using an interactional ethnographic lens (Putney et al., 2000), examines the developing collective and how patterns of practice were constructed across time and events, as well as how particular practices, people, and cultural elements became cultural resources in subsequent activities for individuals and the collective.

Day One

The first day of the program took place on September 22, five weeks after beginning of the academic year, due to district requirements for when researchers can enter the classroom. The first day consisted of five phases, represented in Table 3.1.

Phases of Activity Day 1

Table 3.1 Overview of Day 1 of Youth Radio

> I. Students' Entrance
> II. Introduction of new instructors
>   a. Liv briefly introduces "Professor Walker"
>   b. Lyle arrives; Dana introduces him as "our radio mentor from KPFB"
> III. Dana does name-adjective activity with students, in English or Spanish
>   a. Passes out name tags and colored markers
>   b. Dana calls on students to give their identifying adjective
> IV. Dana gives overview of program

> V. Lyle does 5 "W" questions activity
>   a. Reads a story he wrote
>   b. Asks students if he covered the 5 Ws
> VI. Dana explains homework: to listen to an interview on the radio; Ray writes homework on the board

Phase 1: Students' Entrance. On the first day of the program I wait with Ray in a room with rows of desks facing a whiteboard. My graduate research assistant, Milly, has a video camera on a tripod set up at the back of the room. There is one teacher, Ray, and Liv's substitute, Julie, present. The students suddenly enter the room noisily, boisterously, most before the bell rings, with Eugenia and Delfina drifting in after the bell. Ray moves to the front of the room, chats amicably with a girl, and then waits while the students settle down.

Phase 2: Introducing New Instructors

Introducing "The Professor." Following these initial movements and self-placements in the classroom space, Liv comes to the front and, once she has gained students' attention, introduces me as "Professor Walker" from the University of Northern Colorado. I feel ambivalent about this appellation, as it is not what I am usually called by youth participants in programs I have directed. I concede to Liv in the name she assigns to me, assuming that the intent is to confer greater status on me and the program to incite greater interest on the part of the students. Liv then walks to the back of the room, while Ray steps to one side of the rows of desks, remaining in the front as though "sharing the stage" with me. In reviewing the video, I appear to have entered the setting with the assumption that I would be "running the show": I take over, as though I were the teacher, and begin to introduce the program. My assumption, my "frame," results from seven years of previous experience directing arts and media programs after school and in classroom settings, in which I directed and co-taught classes in collaboration with middle school teachers. In contrast, the teachers in the current study had a different frame for understanding our respective teaching roles—in spite of several meetings in advance of the onset of the program to discuss this—as they make clear in remarks over the coming weeks. These and other "frame clashes" (Agar, 2006) contributed to the difficulties noted by the teachers and myself during the first few weeks of the program of constructing "thematic coherence" (Bloome et al., 2005; Walker & Romero, 2008) among all participants regarding important aspects of the program, such as the outcomes of instruction and our respective roles as teachers, with the related responsibilities.

• CONSTRUCTING THE OBSERVABLE CURRICULUM • 55

Introducing Lyle, "Our Radio Mentor." When Lyle enters the class, I introduce him as "our radio mentor, Lyle Handy from KPFW radio," gesturing and using a tone of voice that would be used with a media celebrity.

Transcript 3.1

1		[Ray and Dana are in front of the rows of desks on either side of
2		the room when Lyle arrives].
3	Dana:	Hey, Lyle, how are ya? [*smiles broadly at him.*]
4		Okay [*in loud but pleasant voice*]. We just have our [*gesturing with*
5		*arm to Lyle in a welcoming way*] new, our radio mentor just arrived,
6		Lyle Handy, from KPFB radio [*drops arm that was gesturing toward*
7		*Lyle*].
8	Lyle:	[From the back of the room] Hi, guys.
9	Elia:	Hello.
10	Ray:	Do you actually go on the radio?
11	Lyle:	What was that?
12	Ray:	Are you actually on the radio?
13	Lyle:	[*from back of room*] Yes, I do.
14	Ray:	Wow! [*nods his head, smiles*]
15	Dana:	Yeah. And he's also a documentary filmmaker, and a
16		computer expert: he worked at IBM for 20 years? [*looking at Lyle*]
17		Right?
18	Lyle:	Correct.
19	Dana:	[*nodding head*] Right.

In Transcript 3.1, we see how Ray's and my speech help students understand what is academically and socially significant in Youth Radio and Radio Arts, a process of cultural mediation (Vygotsky, 1978). The adults provide explicit support for students to develop their understanding of Youth Radio. Notably, content knowledge and language skills are not highlighted in this introduction; rather, it is professional activity in communities of practice outside of school, and the status attributed to an individual who rises to this level of accomplishment in these fields of activity related to the media (radio and TV) and communication technologies (IBM). Though one person—Lyle—is present in the classroom, multiple worlds are called into being through intercontextual links: IBM (corporate America), radio, and television. However, in making these intercontextual links, the adults are not necessarily successful in constructing thematic coherence and a single shared set of meanings. These intercontextual links may be different for youth and adults, depending on their engagements with mass media and popular culture outside of school: the world of media celebrities (in Spanish, English, Nepalese) and the world of computer experts and powerful U.S. corporations.

In this exchange I assign to Lyle the identity of "our radio man," as well as documentary filmmaker and computer expert. Ray picks up on the celebrity-like status of the introduction, making visible to students that he views Lyle as a media personality and that he is impressed to have him in their class. Ray thus positions himself and others in relation to the media personality, as non-celebrities, lesser beings. This was a position asserted by Ray in front of students on several occasions throughout the year. His comments could also be interpreted as encouraging students to feel "special" that they have a media personality as their mentor: In reviewing video recordings, I interpret my own behavior in a similar way.

Both Ray and I reference a world outside the classroom that is physically embodied in the space in the person of Lyle. Not much more is made visible about this world, except that Ray and I index characters in this world as being celebrities. This is true, even though Lyle was not a celebrity—he was a volunteer at a community radio station—and my intention in bringing him was not because he would represent celebrity media but because, to the contrary, he is a member of an alternative media organization that eschews the norms of commercial radio, including celebrities as centers of value and truth. Nevertheless, from the contextualization cues—tone of voice, arm gestures, signifying smiles—Ray and I make visible our assumption that all participants in the room share the cultural model of attributing value to celebrities and communication media. However, the student Elia challenges this assumption several times during the class, as illustrated in the following transcript.

Transcript 3.2

1	Dana:	=All right. [*Raises voice a notch over the noise, gestures to Lyle*] This is
2		Mr. Handy [*looks toward him*]. What would you like them to call
3		you?
4	Lyle:	Lyle's fine.
5	Raúl:	[*turns around to talk to Silvia*]
6	Elia:	[*Elia and Ray talk about candy*]
7	Dana:	Lyle, and he's the radio man [*makes the gesture used in theater or*
8		*TV, "take it away"*]
9	Elia:	[*Claps slowly, dramatically and makes a sarcastic facial expression; looks*
10		*slightly back at Silvia, her sister*]. Mama! [*short laugh*]

In this we see a clash of cultural models about the media arising from the collaboration. As noted, Lyle was, in fact, not a celebrity—he was a volunteer at a community radio station—and my reasoning for bringing him into the program was not because he would represent celebrity media. The students do not necessarily share our cultural model or acknowledge Lyle's star power. Elia challenges our assumption several times during the class, as illustrated in lines 5, 6-7 of Transcript 3.2. In this exchange, Elia, Raúl, and other students offcamera challenge the authority of the new "teachers" and the celebrity status accorded to Lyle the radio man by rejecting the invitation to be impressed by his proposed celebrity status. In addition, Ray appears to align himself with students—perhaps as result of being repositioned from teacher to lesser status "observer"—in rejecting the assumed authority of the new mentor and instructor by carrying on side conversations with students and passing out candy while Lyle reads his story. So that while I unreflexively take over the role of teacher, the students show solidarity to their original teacher by refusing to ratify the teacherly role that the outsiders presume to take on. This is one of many examples of the challenges we encountered in constructing the Youth Radio program in a class that already existed, and which deviated from the norms of the ESL classroom, as it was historically constructed in the school.

Phase 3: Constructing Student Identities. In the next phase I introduce an activity in which students write their names on a name tag, introduce themselves including an adjective that begins with the first letter of their first name, and share one thing they are good at. The activity thus focuses on identity, on representations of self. Many students appear embarrassed by this activity and being put on the spot to talk about themselves. Many students have trouble thinking of an adjective to describe themselves, so I urged other students to offer assistance, as in the following example.

Transcript 3.3

1	Dana:	Okay, um, so I'd like you to think of an adjective that de-
2		scribes, that starts with the same letter as your first or last
3		name. Well actually, your first, if possible.
4	Girl:	What's an adjective? [*quiet voice*]
5	Dana:	Okay, who knows what an adjective is? [*lacing fingers to-*
6		*gether, licking lips*] (....)
7		*Un adjetivo,* adjective [*nodding head as though encouraging*
8		*them to say what they already know*].
9	Girl 2:	[*Dana puts hand up to ear, nods*]. Describes a noun, right,
10		like smart girl, fast runner, ferocious dog (.) ferocious
11		would be the adjective. (.) So think of a word=(
12	Ray:	[*inaudible, says something to support what Dana is saying*]=
13	Dana:	=that starts with the same letter; it can be in English or

14		Spanish—as your first name=
15	Elia:	=[*interrupting*] Do you know Spanish? [*surprised, intent*
16		*voice*]
17	Dana:	A little bit, I'm, I'm not fluent [*smiles at Elia*]
18		[*students all write quietly for 4 minutes*]
19	Dana:	Okay, put on your thinking cap please [*points with both*
20		*hands to her head*] 10, 9, 8, 7-6-5-4-3-2-1! [*playfully imitating*
21		*pedagogical voice of elementary teacher*]
22	Dana:	[*quickly*] Who has an adjective?
23	Cipriana:	Dancing
24	Dana:	[*walks over to Cipriana's desk, raises eyebrows to elicit a louder*
25		*response, elongates vowels of* dancante, *indicating Cipriana*
26		*did not find an adjective that started with the same letter as*
27		*her name*]
28		[*general pause 5 seconds*]
29	Dana:	¿Cantante?
30	Ray:	!Cariñosa!
31		[*Dana smiles at Cipriana, waiting for her response to these sug-*
32		*gestion by Ray and Dana. When no response comes, she moves*
33		*on to another student, still no response. Modifying the task to*
34		*generate more energy, Dana adds an additional element.*]
35	Dana:	Okay, so let's go around and introduce yourselves, and
36		tell me one thing that you like to do.
37	Ray:	[*Laughs, in side-conversation with a student*]
38		[*Trish can't think of an adjective. Dana asks for assistance from*
39		*other students, girl offers talented.*]
40	Dana:	Okay! Talented Trish, very good.
41	Raúl:	Well, I'm an athlete, so "runner" [*students turn and look at*
42		*him*]
42	Dana:	[*smiles walking toward Elia*]
43	Elia:	Oh my god! [*puts her hand up toward the camera to prevent*
44		*Milly from video recording her*]
45	Dana:	I don't see your name [*Leans to her to see her name tag*].
46		"Elia" [*using Spanish pronunciation for her name*]
47	Dipashri:	Disciplined
48	Dana:	Are you from Nepal?
49	Dipashri:	Yeah.
50	Dana:	Oh cool.
51		[*Dana looks to Eugenia*]
52	Eugenia:	[silence]

53	Ray:	*Elegante.*
54	Eugenia:	[*smiles, bows her head toward the table*]
55	Dana:	Mr. Salinas [*who is in the back of the room*], could you
56		help us with an adjective (..) for Josué?
57	Ray:	Juguetón [*playful, mischievous*]
58	Dana:	Okay! [*Walks toward Jesus, asks him his name, waits*].
59		Do you play basketball? [*to Jesus, gesturing making a bas-*
60		*ket*]?
61	Jesus:	Kind of [*looking down*].
62	Dana:	It's hard with the Spanish [*looks at Ray for help and/or*
63		*agreement, using hands to indicate switching*] the "j"
64		sound in English and
65		the "*jota*" in Spanish.
66	Ray:	[*Nods in agreement*]
67		[*over the next 6 minutes Ray, Dana, and several students*
68		*collectively construct the identifying "Jumping Jesus," "Dancing*
69		*Diana"*]
70	Dana:	[*Gestures toward Beto*]. Beto.
71	Beto:	I don' know.
72		[*general silence of 5 seconds*]
73	Elia:	Brilliant!
74	Ray:	Brilliant
75	Dana:	Brilliant! All right, okay, fantastic.
76	All:	[*laughter*]
77	Beto:	[*smiles shyly, nods a little*]
78		[*Jesus looks at Beto and laughs, boys giggle, squirm in their seats*]

In this phase of the activity, I intentionally introduce hybrid language practices, encouraging the use of Spanish in student responses (lines 7, 13-14, 29, 62-65). In doing so, I am challenging the existing language practices and ideologies of the school, which separate languages and their speakers into separate geographic spaces—the separate wing of the school where the tutoring program for Latino students ¡*Vámanos!* was held, and the separate academic tracks, with the lower, non-AP tracks consisting largely of Latino students. Ray, the ESL teacher, ratified my proposal for introducing hybrid language practice, contributing to the exchange in Spanish.

However, by encouraging bilingual Spanish-English practices and identities to be instantiated in the classroom, I may have also been excluding the non-Spanish-speaking students, two Nepalese and one Russian students, from fully participating in the activity since their languages were not recognized whereas Spanish was. Though I do acknowledge the presence of another language and culture in the class in my interactions with Dipashri about Nepalese residents of the city, these first interactions with students established a pattern of exclusion that would be repeated throughout most of the year by all of the Spanish-bilingual mentors and teachers, in spite of efforts by teacher Liv to disrupt these exclusionary practices.

In this activity I attempt to open a space for students to represent themselves, as well as for others to assist in the representational process, sending into discursive circulation the acknowledged qualities of youth in the room. With the exception of one evaluative, possibly negative label by Ray for Josué, as "juguetón," which means playful but can also mean mischievous or misbehaving, qualifiers were positive and validating. In this interaction on the first day of the program, students and teacher support and scaffold each others' linguistic and creative production (lines 65-67 as well as other segments of this phase of activity), a pattern that would emerge over time as part of the development of trust and community, which students identify as something that had to be constructed, or reconstructed, following rupture represented by the onset of the program.

Yet at the same time that I attempt to create a new space for self-representation, I control the interactions, maintaining power over who can initiate talk and who and how students are to respond: This represents continuity in classroom practices of this school. By requiring students to "capture their essence" in the form of an adjective for their name, I am asserting power over their performances of selves and accompanying language production. Though the activity was intended to be student-centered, the power to elicit speech and disclosure remains in my hands. Students acknowledge this fact, I believe, through their refusal or reticence to respond (lines 1-21). It cannot be known whether failure to respond to this elicitation was a form of resistance or inability to answer due to shyness or lack of linguistic resources. Nevertheless, this tendency to require disclosure and talk when students preferred to remain silent was a tension that remained throughout the first months of the program.

There is a parallel movement, however, of teachers and students wanting to see a shift in existing patterns of what teachers called "passivity" and "invisibility" on the part of students. In his personal reflections and staff debriefings Ray expressed strong support for efforts to ask students to "step up" and "speak out." Responses from students' interviews similarly reveal that many students actually came to value the "sharing of self," the desire to speak and engage in dialogue about personal experiences, but only once trust and a sense of community had been established.

Phase 4: Overview of the Program. The next phase of the first day's activity involved the overview of the program. I frame the program for the students telling them what days they will meet (Tuesday through Friday), with radio on Tuesday and Wednesday. This is the first time the learning network connected to the classroom is introduced, in terms of something that is assumed the students will appreciate.

The next segment follows on the discovery that we have 15 instead of 50 minutes to introduce the program and do two learning activities.

Transcript 3.4

1	Dana:	Okay, so we're gunna quickly, I don' know what we're gunna (.)
2		Well, maybe I should tell you a little about what we're gunna
3		do in this program. We're going to meet Tuesday, Wednesdays,
4		and Thursdays, well—Tuesday, Wednesdays, Thursdays, and
5		Fridays—[*looks toward Lyle*] they gave us another day=
6	Lyle:	=great! [*nodding*]
7	Dana:	=which is fantastic, and we're gunna do radio on Tuesdays and
8		Wednesdays, and that's, we're gunna do interviews, so you're
9		gunna go out and interview people on topics that interest you,
10	Jesus:	[*puts his hand over one eye, smiling mischieviously*]
11	Dana:	(inaudible) write commentaries, learn how to do features where
12		you collect sound and put sound and music and all this stuff to
13		gether. We'll be going to the radio station, we're going to go to
14		PFB and Radio Leyenda in Riverside, and hopefully Univision,
15		if you guys get you your projects finished and everything. You'll
16		be learning how to mix multitrack recordings with music and
17		voice and ambient sound. Wednesdays we've got this professor
18		from Nandigama University coming to help you do theater
19		we'll do a little bit of theater [*gestures with arms to show movement*]
20		and um, *radio novelas* [soap operas in Spanish].
21	Ray:	Thursday
22	Dana:	That's right, Thursday [*nodding head*]. And then Friday another
23		professor from UNC [*points with thumb over her back*], University
24		of Northern Colorado's coming, and she's in educational tech-
25		nology and she knows all about technology [*gestures to indicate*
26		*lots of things*]. She's going to teach you how to do digital narra-
27		tives, which combine video and pictures with narrative and mu-
28		sic and other sound; and blogging online and some Web design
29		for the Internet.
30	Ray:	So Fridays you'll be working a lot on the computer.

62 • A PEDAGOGY OF POWERFUL COMMUNICATION •

In this excerpt I frame the program for the students in terms of which days we will be doing what: this is how I was thinking about the program in the early planning and implementation stages. I also highlight movement from the classroom into the community beyond, introducing the idea that learning will take place in more than the one context and that students' life worlds–such as Spanish-speaking TV–will be incorporated in the curriculum. Finally, I noted at the time Ray's repeating for students, and therefore ratifying his interest, or his perception of students' special interest in, the technology component of the program: "So Fridays you'll be working a lot on the computer." He may have also been translating my academic jargon into language the students could understand.

Phase 5: Introduction to the 5 Ws. In the next phase of instruction Lyle takes over as teacher to conduct the first radio-related activity of the program: introduction to discourse genre of the radio interview. Transcript 3.5 presents his introduction to the radio interview.

Transcript 3.5

1	Lyle:	So, when we're interviewing, guys, we wanna get information, we
2		wanna get views,
3	All:	[*student side-talk*]
4	Lyle:	a lot of views. And what's important when we're doing news is the
5		Ws [*looks down at his notepad*]
6	All:	[*students have quieted down*]
7	Lyle:	W-W-W-What, where, when
8	Girl:	Why
9	Lyle:	(.) and because teachers always throw it in, How is the fifth W.
10		[*takes a few steps to his left*] So you always want those when you do y
11		stories. And you wanna be short (.) and close (.) to the point. [*look*
12		*his notepad, turns the page*] So when we're interviewing, we're gunna
13		trying to do that: Get the 5 Ws in our story. And I wrote really qu
14		a little story about me. See if you can figure out if I have my 5 Ws
15	Ray:	[*comes over to Elia and Silvia with a bag of candy. Girls turn around wh*
16		*Lyle is talking to select their candies, bag rustles. Ray turns to Milly behir*
17		*the camera, says something and laughs: Lyle has begun reading his story*]
18	Lyle:	[*reads from his notepad*] So last Saturday I was taking some trees do
19		in my yard (etc.)
20	Elia:	Ahhh, *queremos los . . .* [*talking to Ray about the candy*]
21	Lyle:	Did I cover all everything? [*to the class*]
22	Ray:	[*smiling, talking to Milly and the camera about the candy*]
23	Lyle:	Could you say it again?=

• CONSTRUCTING THE OBSERVABLE CURRICULUM •   63

24	Raúl:	[quietly] ="Why," you forgot "why."
25	Lyle:	[reads the 2 line story again] [students listening]
26	Girl:	You missed "why."
27	Lyle:	I missed "why?" Why I was cutting down trees or why I had to go to
28		the hospital.
29	Tania:	Who.
30	Lyle:	"Who" is me, wasn't it?
31		[they discuss, Lyle moves back and forth along the lef–from the back-row of
32		seats. No participation from boys' side of the room]
33	Lyle:	That's good.

From this transcript we see that in students' first experience of the actual teaching practices of Youth Radio, much will remain much the same as what they are accustomed to in their high school classes. Lyle reads aloud to them a brief personal account and then uses the Initiation-Response-Evaluation (IRE) discourse pattern that he was probably most familiar with from our own schooling. He asks students to identify whether the Who, What, Where, When, Why (and How) questions had been addressed in his account. He evaluates their responses saying "good" when they answer correctly (line 36), leaving little room for interpretation or student deployment of their own cultural resources. The new instructors (Lyle and I) expect students to focus attention on us and remain silent while we talk, answering questions that we construe: in other words, it is a reenactment of the same practices, roles, and relationships as they are accustomed to encountering in this and other classes throughout the day (as described by Liv and Ray).

Elements of Change and Continuity on the First Day of Class

The first day of the program introduced elements of change and continuity in both classroom practices and selves across time and spheres of experience. As described, classroom practices such as IRE discourse pattern and teacher-centered power relations were reproduced, in spite of the intent of the planned curriculum to offer a critical language and literacies pedagogy, which includes the democratization and decentering of power relations in the classroom (Norton & Toohey 2004). The visible curriculum would have suggested greater sense of change along the dimension of identities and possible selves. The intertextual and intercontextual links[1] made by the new instructors brought multiple worlds into the classroom that were not there before: radio, television, powerful corporations, the university. In addition, the new instructors established links to student life worlds and spheres of experience through the use of hybrid discourse practices that challenged existing language ideologies of school and society, through the elicitation of salient student identities and references to popular music, *telenovelas* (soap operas), and the Spanish language news station. Students heard about new ways of doing academics, such as producing a feature story or a multimodal composition that integrated image and sound. Table 3.2 presents a synthesis of the six phases of activity and the intertextual and intercontextual links made.

Table 3.2 Phases of Activity Day 1

Phase	Activity	Explicit Intertextual/ Contextual Links
1	Introduction of professor (Dana)	University
2	Introduction of radio mentor (Lyle)	Community radio station Documentary film IBM (powerful U.S. corporation)
3	Self-description introduction activity by students, assisted by peers and the teacher	Life worlds of bilingual youth learner or school identities (including "athlete")
4	Overview of program	Local Spanish radio International Spanish TV 2 universities Theater Spanish soap operas (for radio) Interviewing on topics of interest to students Radio feature story Radio commentaries Digital narratives Technology Music, narrative, sound, video
5	The "5 Ws" activity led by Lyle	Radio and television interviews
6	Dana assigns homework	Spanish TV, popular media, as well as school-based practice of homework

Tensions and Contradictions Arising from the Collaboration. Several frame clashes arose on the first day of the program. One of the most obvious was that of shifting roles and assumption of authority among participants. The most obvious to all, it seems, would have been the takeover of the class from a Chicano male teacher by a white female teacher who was not from the school. I ask students not to leave when the bell rings—something that is not done in the world of the high school and these students, I learned. This may be the beginning of an ongoing tension with some of the students, who resist the exertion of control over them by an adult from the outside. I assumed the role of the teacher, with Ray in a supporting role. Ray contributed, perhaps unwittingly, to undermining the assumed instructional roles of the outsiders, by having side conversations with students and handing out candy—an action that was obviously distracting for students—while Lyle was instructing. Another frame clash occurred, this time with teachers, when I asked students to do homework. Later Liv would explain that we should not be asking them to do homework, since this is not a content-area class, but a study skills class: students were to be doing homework for their content classes in this ESL/academic support class.

For teachers and students, frame clashes included the outsiders' lack of knowledge about class norms for study skills class regarding homework and for the unnegotiability of time in class closure routines. In addition, the outsider from the radio station did not match the teachers' expectations for teaching second language learners. Ray and Liv mentioned after this class that students needed more scaffolding for understanding the content and procedures of instruction. Lyle could not have been expected to provide this pedagogical support for the second language learners as he was not, and never had been, a teacher. Ray consequently took on a supporting role to Lyle, writing outlines on the board of Lyle's presentations and vocabulary he thought was new to the students.

In the next section I describe Day 2 when the radio improv mentor Federico enters the scene, introducing several elements of change, making visible to students that this was truly going to be a different kind of class than what they were used to.

Getting Our "Spirits Out," Letting Our Worlds In: Federico and the First Days of Youth Radio

In her exit interview at the end of a year of participating in Youth Radio and Radio Arts, when asked what the goal of Youth Radio was, Tania replies that, in addition to using technology, the goal of Youth Radio was "developing your voice." She attributes the initiation of this process of developing voice to Federico's first days ("when he came in") and links construction of voice to students' overcoming shyness and a sense of isolation, developing a sense of community, and to the ability to communicate with others.

Transcript 3.6

1	Dana:	So, in your opinion, what is the goal of youth radio in school?
2		What do your teachers hope you'll learn?
3	Tania:	Technology for one, just like basically how to use it and then
4		umm, developing your voice. Because at first people are shy.
5		And then the radio drama as well you know people are very shy
6		but like when Federico came in he definitely got like our spirits
7		out and now everyone is like friends with everyone and every-
8		body talks with everyone when before it was just, "I don't know
9		you so let's keep it that way," so (..)
10	Dana:	So you mean like they talked in this class amongst each other?
11	Tania:	Right.

The personal meanings students like Tania attributed to voice, in relation to trust, community, and communication, is a principal theme identified in the data, which I discuss in detail in Chapter 4. In this chapter I describe, through an analysis of ethnographic records and student exit interviews, what cultural practices were set in motion with Federico and how these practices served as resources to mediate students' conceptual understandings of the purposes of Youth Radio and Radio Arts over time, in particular related to voice, community, and communication. I pay particular attention to the opportunities that interactions with Federico provided and how the students' interpretation and take-up of sociocultural resources constructed through these social interactions were consequential for their learning and development over time (Putney et al., 2000).

In addition to spoken and written language, I am interested in the paralinguistic (prosody, timing, intonation) dimensions of discursive practice in the classroom, since it is through their combination with language that context is formed (Schiffrin, 1994) and language ideologies—the naturalized values and beliefs about language use and social interaction—are enacted. Along with contextual affordances of the classroom, I consider the role of relationships among participants as necessary to understanding engagement with language practices. Martin-Beltrán (2010) writes, "if we view language learning as involving participation in a community of speakers, we must attend to discursive patterns and positioning practices that promote participation or act as gatekeepers into these communities" (p. 258). The following description of Federico's first day teaching in the program shows how ideological values embedded in the group's discourse set the stage for the development of community and "voice"—echoing, in part, Federico's definition of it—as well as performances of sophisticated and artistic language use in the context of improvisation, verbal play, and multimodal expression that integrated body with language.

First Encounters with Federico

Excitement and confusion can be heard in the voices of the students as they enter the room on Day 2 of the program. The space has been transformed with desks moved out of the row formation and against the walls, leaving an open space at the center of the classroom. In addition to Lyle and myself, there is now a third adult—Federico—in the mix. I take on the role of teacher, as I did on Day 1, introducing Federico with the grandiloquent tone of someone presenting a very important person, or setting the stage for a theater audience: "This is Federico García Fuentes *de México*, a very famous playwright and actor," enumerating his many achievements, including a production of his play at Su Teatro theater company in Denver, mentioning that we will be going on a field trip there. Federico takes a deep, Shakespearean-style bow. Elia claps—slowly, exaggeratedly, with some sarcasm implied as on Day 1. As I conclude my introduction and leave Federico alone in front of the class, the students are sitting on or leaning against the desks pushed against the wall, facing him. With much authority—though informal, not disciplinarian in tone—Federico asks them to form a circle.

Transcript 3.7

1	Federico:	Let's uh, can you guys do me a	
2		favor; put all your stuff between	
3		the chairs and then come over	
4		here and form a circle.	
5	Delfina:	But like, I don't, I can't [*whiny*	
6		*tone*]	
7	Federico:	!Ay! (..) luego luego. [*with a comic,*	Later, later ("maña-
8		*drawling, nasal tone*]	na," implying lazi-
9	Delfina:	(xxx)	ness on the part of
10	Students:	[*Laughter*]	Delfina)
11	Federico:	Luego luego [*smiling*]	Later, later ("maña-
12	Eugenia:	[*To the girl who says she can't*	na").
13		*move into the circle*] Huevona. [*gi-*	Lazy.
14		*ggles*]	

15	Raúl:	Y tampoco digas cosas feas.	Don't say ugly
16	Eugenia:	¿Cómo le dije?	things (bad words)
17	Students:	(xxx)	What did I say?!
18	Girl:	!Huevona! [giggles]	Lazy!
19	Students:	[Giggling]	
20	Federico:	No digas cosas feas [gentle joking voice, smiling]. Y dejas verte los ojos [gestures taking off glasses– Delmara has sunglasses on]	Don't say ugly things (bad words). And let us see your eyes.
24	SS, Federico:	[lots of overtalk and laughter]	Are we going to
25	Cipriana:	Y vamos a bailar o qué?	dance or what?
26	Federico:	Nooo. Pero un circulo es una forma REDONDA. [speaking as though to young children]. Veo que no entienden que es un circulo [laughs]	But a circle is a round form. I can see that you don't understand what a circle is.
31	Students:	[laughter]	
32	Federico:	¿Nunca has visto un círculo? [smiling]	You've never seen a circle?
34	Cipriana:	No. [Laughs]	

The first student to speak, Delfina, adopts a similarly informal—if not disrespectful—tone in her first interaction with Federico, suggesting half-hearted resistance to the activity and challenging his authority as the new teacher. Federico responds (line 5), joking in Spanish, with an implied "soft" insult—"*Ay, luego, luego*" ("later, later," or "*mañana*")—imputing to Delfina the character of a lazy person. Could he have been playing with—and thereby holding up for scrutiny—the historical U.S. stereotype of the lazy Mexican sitting under a palm tree with a sombrero pulled down over his eyes? (Tania and Yoli, in their coauthored digital story, would use the sombreroed stereotype in representing Mexicans in their neighborhood, in a parodic rhetorical gesture). A number of students acknowledge the cleverness of the playful insult with their laughter (line 7), and Federico repeats the phrase (line 8) to capitalize on their laughter and recognition of his verbal skill. Eugenia takes up Federico's proposition, calling out "*huevona*" (line 7), a common vulgar slang term meaning "lazy," which derives from the Mexican word for *testicles*. Following this defiant challenge to the norms of classroom discourse, Raúl the student sanctions Delfina's use of the vulgarity, (line 9–"*Y tampoco digas cosas feas*/Don't say bad words"), thereby publicly acknowledging Federico's authority and imposing accountability on the group. Federico in turn takes up Raúl's reproach, repeating the phrase gently as a way of reasserting his authority and establishing order (lines 14-15). By this time the students have settled into a circle formation, which can be interpreted as a collective display of recognition of his authority after much effort. Federico continues to poke fun at the students by adopting a preschool teacher tone of voice to describe the shape of a circle and their lack of knowledge about the figure (line 16).

Language Play with Federico. The type of language play that characterizes Federico's interactions with the students has been described by anthropologists—and Federico himself—as the discursive practice of *echando relajo*: joking and teasing in Spanish with undertones of insult (Limón 1994), which seems to have particularly sonorous spatial and temporal resonances for students given how it is taken up and played with. Renato Rosaldo (1989) notes that "culturally distinctive jokes and banter play a significant role in constituting Chicano culture, both as a form of resistance and as a source of positive identity" (p. 150). The edgy humor of these interactions between Federico and the *Mexicana/o* students, with accompanying gestures, postures, and prosody—what Limón calls "speech body play"—demonstrates a multi-semiotic complexity that is difficult to convey in words. What is clear is that this and subsequent exchanges are driven by word games or verbal skirmishes. Like the south Texas *carnales* (close friends) that Limón describes in his ethnography, the youth and the Mexican actor/director in this scene produce language that resembles "playful nips," small insults and humiliations—"*luego, luego*";"*huevona*"; "*Veo que no entienden que es un círculo.*" Limón notes that "this skillful artistic language has the paradoxical effect of interactionally producing solidarity, or as Latin Americans everywhere would say, *confianza*" (p. 133). According to this ethnographer of the borderlands, these forms of verbal art draw upon the domains of language and play explored by Habermas and Marcuse to produce the phenomenon of "human speech play." "Through such speech play the participants produce a world of human value—of *confianza* (solidarity, trust) and *respeto* (respect)" (Limón, 1994, p.35). We will hear more about *confianza* and *respeto* in in Chapter 4.

Federico also seemed (and agreed to this interpretation later) to find pleasure in speaking and joking in Spanish. In subsequent workshops, Federico could be heard engaging in language play with Spanish-speaking students by parodying non-Spanish-speakers' misconjugations and mispronunciations of Spanish, a way of making fun of what Ramon Del Castillo (Del Castillo, 2002) calls "linguistically handicapped" Mexican Americans who speak with the stereotypical *gringo* accent. I overheard a group of boys engaging in the same verbal play with Ray later in the semester; in previous research I had noted a similar practice among Spanish-bilingual middle school students, both Anglo and Latino (Walker, 2003).

At other times Federico simply engages in play with the students, perhaps what Tania remembered when she stated (in Transcript 3.6 from her exit interview) that Federico helped "get [their] spirits out." As can be seen from the extracts and quotes presented thus far, laughter accompanied much of Federico's instruction. In fact provoking laughter, verbal play, and pleasure in the expressiveness and power of the body (speech body play) seem to be a central purpose of Federico's instruction.

Transcript 3.8

1	Federico:	No sabo. Okay= [*joking, uses incorrect Spanish*	I don't
2		*conjugation*]	know?
3	Students:	=(*Laughter*)=	
4	Federico:	(...) ¡Andale! ¡Sápatele un poco!	Go
5			ahead!
6			Let's see
7			a little
8			footwork!
9	Students:	(*Laughter!!!*)	
10	Federico:	Make that foot bigger and these hands big-	
11		ger [*he demonstrates salsa movement with big ges-*	
12		*tures*]	
13	Cipriana:	"Woooooo!!" [*expressively, Federico and she*	
14		*do the salsa dance movement together*]	

In their study of youth engaged in community arts organizations, Heath (2004) and colleagues found that many youth linked their learning in the arts to play: "Much of the learning within the arts is described by young learners as 'play.' 'It's fun, just fun; sure, there's lots of hard work, but we're all in it together'" (p. 340). Like Tania, Elia in her exit interview emphasizes the aspect of play she experienced in Youth Radio: "I think you guys do it to make us have fun and to make like kids, I don't know like, to understand some others things too, to learn some new things."

Building Symbolic Bridges: Language and Cultural Memory

Federico's use of Spanish language, prosody, gestures, and postures in this setting also functions as a performance of his cultural identity as a Mexican, which simultaneously aligns him with the *mexicana/o* students and brings the world of Mexico into the classroom space. In the excerpt above Federico shifts in and out of a conversational style that has deep roots in the Mexican diasporic community, associated with emotions, memories, and imaginations. Federico's and the students' Mexican Spanish transform the temporal and spatial dimensions of the context, which is no longer restricted to an ESL classroom in a city in Colorado, but now includes the reenactment of discursive practices carried out in Mexico, while referencing practices in Nepal and Sweden. As Kramsch and Whiteside (2008) suggest, multilingual discourse practices in the context of globalization disrupt the usual perceptions of time and space. In these exchanges the participants are emotionally occupying several dimensions of space and time that are embodied in their words, gestures, postures, and discourse in the present moment. The indexing of multiple codes by the participants and their associated subjective resonances require taking into account the subjective, embodied time of what the authors term "cultural memory." Describing discursive practices in the context of several multilingual settings, Kramsch and Whitehead write:

> The Maya language is for them embodied memory that, while located in individual bodies, resurrects a collective memory of group practices in the present. DF's voice speaking Maya with a fellow Yucatecan recreates the Yucatan in San Francisco. The Yucatecans in these encounters may be objectively present in a store in San Francisco, but their bodies carry subjective traces of their experiences living in Yucatan, crossing the border, learning to negotiate the vicissitudes of daily life as undocumented residents of the Bay Area. (p. 658)

By performing English and Spanish, the participants signal to each other which symbolic world they identify with at the time of the interaction. Simultaneously, as Federico shifts playfully between Spanish and English in this exchange and subsequent instruction, the discourse shifts validate Spanish as an appropriate form of communication and allow the students to hear Spanish dismantling the deficit beliefs about the people who speak the Spanish language.

These affective and subjective dimensions of language prove significant both for the construction of meanings in the present moment and for developing the personal meanings that are necessary for learning over time.

Letting in emotion. The subjective resonances of Federico's and the students' artistic use of Spanish and English appear to have been consequential in the short and the long term, for teachers as well as students. Ray, during a debriefing on the day of Federico's first class, refers to the subjective resonances of Federico's body speech, highlighting a gentler, more intimate side of

Federico's language:

> So being a majority and a minority are all the things you are fed all day long, all the little messages, maybe all the stuff over a lifetime that you have to kind of recheck yourself and train yourself to trust people, and just the language too, just the rhythm of the language. in the morning sometimes, I like to hear the Spanish news, even though it's not local just cause the rhythm is softer and more acceptable in the morning when you're still, when you're sensitive to everything, when the lady is talking all rough [example] ahhh, oh ok, I need something softer right now. The speed of the English language, and all that. I'm not a psychiatrist, but a lot of it is psychological. You know, all those little things, "Andale, ah come on." He [Federico] really tapped into their culture, the culture of the language too. (Ray, staff debriefing, 9/23/10)

Ray experiences Federico's Spanish and body speech as the language of intimacy used with family and friends. His observations are reminiscent of Tannen, Kendall, and Gordon (2007), who suggest that the subject of the talk with children in family contexts is often less significant than the *sound* of the talk, "with all its paralinguistic and prosodic richness provides an occasion to express the positive emotion, such as fondness or attachment, that the speaker feels toward the child" (p. 64). In her ethnography of the discourses of women and children living on the U.S.-Mexico border region, González (2001) described the emotional resonances of Spanish:

> Ineffably, I knew that the dimensions of Spanish were far different from the dimensions of English. They did not feel the same, taste the same, or sound the same. Spanish was the language of family, of food, of music, or ritual—in short, of identity. It was the language of endearments to children. . . . English was for arithmetic, for the doctor's office, for the teacher. English was for the newspaper and television. (p. 50)

This depiction parallels Ray's description of the emotional and psychological resonances of Spanish versus English for him and the second language learners in the class.

Getting Spirits Out through Play and Improvisation

In addition to the theatrical influences of Boal, Valdez, and Shakespeare, Federico's repertoire draws on martial arts, which emphasizes the development of the human body's power, agility, and grace, and the *La Carpa* theater tradition that perfected the vaudevillian comic style of exaggerated facial gestures and body postures.

Federico was not alone in drawing on this cultural repertoire of Mexican theatrical performance. Eugenia was the student who expertly built on Federico's introduction of the cultural and artistic practices of improvisation and

• CONSTRUCTING THE OBSERVABLE CURRICULUM • 73

Mexican/Chicano theater, and she most benefitted from his building this symbolic bridge to her own cultural practices and talents. In preparation for the radio show, Federico facilitated improvised radio skits in which groups of students created radio commercials based on randomly selected and paired words resulting in products they had to sell, such as "Strong Penguin" deodorant and "Yummy Revolution" candy. Eugenia, who was failing most of her classes and missed several sessions with Federico due to appearances in truancy court, was one of these students who found the opportunity to "shine," as Liv said, in this alternative space. On the first day she refused to participate in Federico's workshop and initially remained at her desk while the other students stood in a circle. This did not last long, however. Her improvised Mexican market vendor scene in which she hawks "Strong Penguin" deodorant to the customer Raúl, who smells badly, is done completely in Spanish. When Eugenia employs the discourse genre of the Mexican market vendor, Mexico suddenly appears in the classroom.

Transcript 3.9

1		[Eugenia is standing alone behind a podium at the front of the classroom, with an open space in front of her. Raúl enters from stage left after 10 seconds].	
2			
3			
4			
5	Eugenia:	*Pásale, pásale,* (.) [*speaks in strong, lilting voice, using immediately recognizable Mexican market vendor tonalities, gesturing for customers to come in*], *lo dan en lo lo barato, el desodorante STRONG PENGUIN* [*strong nasal uplift in voice on "Strong Penguin"*]=	Come right in, come right in! We're selling it cheap, the deodorant Strong Penguin for sale.
6			
7			
8			
9			
10			
11			
12	Federico:	=[*Gestures to Raúl to come "on stage"*]=	
13	Raúl:	=[*Playing the customer, comes on stage laughing*]	
14			
15	Eugenia:	= *Pásale, pásale* [*does a vague gesture of applying deodorant under her arm*]=	Come in, come in!
16			
17	Raúl:	=[*Gestures to Eugenia with his thumb, then doubles over laughing while she continues hawking the deodorant, pretending to apply deodorant*]=	
18			
19			
20			
21	Eugenia:	=[*Laughs out loud, shaking her shoulders and head*]	
22			
23	Federico:	=¿*Un desodorante de qué?* [*Approaches the podium behind which Eugenia stands, leans*	A what kind of deodorant?
24			

25		*his body sideways toward her with his hand*
26		*cupped to his ear, the other arm outstretched*
27		*to the "audience"]*
28	Eugenia:	*de Strong Penguin [doesn't miss a beat, con-* Strong Penguin!
29		*tinues lilting voice of market vendor]*
30	Raúl:	*[stands upright to listen to Federico, looks at*
31		*Eugénia, points at her and doubles over*
32		*laughing again]*

In this improv, Eugenia and Raúl take the slightest bit of structure—"Strong Penguin"—combine this structure with the everyday communicative genre of the Mexican market vending, and transform these into produce a powerful theatrical moment. Liv's personal reflection gives a sense of the effect of Eugenia's performance:

> I think Eugenia, I mean, it was so wonderful to see when she was working with Federico and they were doing their commercial things, and also that she got Raúl involved and that group was just like, so it's great cause I think some kids have that voice naturally and some. . . . Now we just present them with different situations and they can do this. (Liv, personal reflection, 9/28/10)

Federico's work with students, based in improvisational theater, encourages participants to play and share themselves in a way that draws out students' creativity and builds self-confidence. The improv experience is powerful because it challenges the participant to take risks and helps the young people overcome their fears and inhibitions in creating a comic skit that is as much a pleasure to perform as it is to view, as seen in the unhinged laughter among participants. For the group, the process was transformative, as it revealed to the students and adults the richness of their imagination and the power of their creations. Vygotsky (cited in Zittoun, 2005) wrote that play opens up an imaginary zone for children that allows them to "explore and rehearse new possibilities, and engage emotion without the risks involved in real experience" (p. 116). Grounding improvisational play in the animated body with Federico also contributes to releasing the imagination and opening the door to other ways of knowing through improvisation.

An important outcome of the Radio Arts curriculum with Federico and later with the poet Tim Hernandez were changes in participant perspectives about themselves and others through the recognition of each other's creative capacities and the extent of their linguistic and cultural repertoires. This was particularly important for teachers who reported that they rarely had a chance to see these hidden artistic capacities of students. For students who were experiencing new forms of recognition, these activities must have been consequential as well. Deficit views of students from nondominant cultural groups may be in part shaped by skills-based definitions of language and literacy, and perceptions of learners who are not proficient in English as lacking intelligence. The Radio Arts component of the program created an alternative space of expertise for some students, in which they could refigure their roles as poets, writers, and performers with talent and a larger communicative repertoire that even they themselves were aware.

Federico Introduces the Concepts of "Voice" and "Communication"

In the final analysis of Federico's first day I present his introduction of the polysemous concepts of "voice" and "communication," and subsequently show the intertextual links and "revoicing," or take up of these concepts by students in their exit interviews.

Federico Introduces the Concept of "Voice"

Federico was the first to introduce the concept of "voice" in relation to Youth Radio. In Transcript 3.11, Federico offers a polysemic notion of "voice" as part of his introduction of the "radio show" that he will be teaching, structured in two parts. The first has to do with the physical, sonic qualities of the voice symbolically and physically located within the body. The second is framing of "voice" in terms of what people do with their voices: the communicative and social purposes of voice, along with its existential implications.

Transcript 3.10

1	Federico:	What we're gunna do, is we're gunna come up with a radio
2		show, right? Now, meaning that, we're gunna be using our
3		voices.
4		But there's something about using your voice.
5		And that means that a voice is not disembodied.
6		Do you understand what I mean by that?
7		*Voice cannot happen unless you have a body.* (…)
8		There's no voices that come out of nowhere. Right? (..)
9		They come out of a body. Even things that make a noise.
10		[*bangs once on the table to make a noise*]. To make that noise

11		I need to bang this.
12		I can't [*makes silly gesture in the air*]
13	Students:	=Laughter=
14	Federico:	=Laughs. Right? There's no body there to make sound to
15		[*continues beating the air*].
16	Students:	=Laughter=
17	Federico:	Right? So you need to work [*gestures to his upper body*] in
18		order to
19	Students:	be able to produce your voice. [*He stops moving suddenly*] [*Students now completely silent, watching him curiously*]

In this introduction to the "radio show," Federico emphasizes the performative aspect of voice, and makes explicit semantic links among *voice*, *Radio Show*, and *the body*. Schools for the most part tend to treat the learner as though their heads were severed from their bodies. Federico introduces the idea that we know through and express our knowledge and emotion through the body. This is contrary to what most often happens in school as Darder (2010) writes,

> Many classrooms and community settings exist as arenas where knowledge is objectified and abstracted from its concrete reality. Youth are then expected to acquiesce to an alienating function, which artificially severs their body from its role in the construction of knowledge. (p. xiv)

In this exchange Federico presents the argument to the students that without body there is no voice. Through his voice tone, gestures, and the sound of his fist banging on the table, he stresses that voice is connected to the body and that the real-world, embodied voice will be the core of the radio show. Freire (1995) wrote, "I know with my entire body, with feelings, with passion and also with reason" (p. 50). Federico's work with Augusto Boal in Los Angeles influenced his teaching from the body, as the entry and exit point of liberation. With the students he began with movement in play, through what Boal called "exercises and games," to free up the energy and begin the transformation process. However, not only is the body the foundation of individual voice, it is also the sense-based way of knowing and connecting to others, a form of communication that subverts enacted social hierarchies and opens the door for more horizontal relations.

Toohey (2000; Birdwhistell, 1977) uses Bourdieu's notion that the body is implicated in power relations to show how physicality can be another kind of "discourse" in students' struggle for identity. But power is not necessarily always "coersive," as Cummins (2000) points out. Bloome et al. (2005), drawing on feminist theorists, similarly encourage researchers of language and literacy to think not just in terms of power "over" but also power "with" others; of caring relations that increase the power of many, rather than simply convey power to the few. In this line of thinking, Birdwhistell (1977) in a study of body motion and communication (kinesics), points out that conversation can be like a dance. In Federico's teaching on the first day, nonverbal communication between him and the students looked pleasurable and coordinated. (See Photo 3.1.)

Photo 3.1 Federico and Cipriana acting out a part

Ray noted that Federico and the students' body motions, gestures, and spatial distribution contributed to creating a sense of community:

> And he talked about the body, the words coming out of a body, and that's so true. And being in a circle, they're like spokes, they're like the body, and there's no barriers in between them, like a desk or something. So all of a sudden, that was kind of like a trust exercise, all of the nonverbal that come with the body. When you don't speak the language that well, you pick on that really quickly. That's probably why they felt comfortable right off the bat cause they saw a lot of nonverbal, or stuff that they are familiar with, gestures that they are familiar with, that they have at home, so they felt safer or something. (Ray, staff debriefing, 9/23/10)

Later in the lesson, Federico asks the students to create movement to accompany an adjective that describes them and begins with the first letter of their first name, and all students are invited to mirror the movement. Many students have difficulty with this task, either due to inhibition or in opposition to a requirement that represents a radical break from normal ways body and space are used during class time. Federico amplifies the gesture or dance step of each participant and encourages everyone to mirror the movement. The body in motion becomes simultaneously an instrument for communicating "who we are" and a kind of text to decipher to know the other. Breaking from the traditional desk-based task, Federico opens the door for other modes of communication that go beyond language and for embodied identity work—linked to the self-describing adjective—that is not often available to students who know and express themselves kinesthetically, such as athletes and dancers. Dipashri, who is new to the country, shows herself to be a beautifully expert Nepalese dancer in this activity. Later in the year she will be a featured dancer in the annual schoolwide carnival, which surprised the program staff given her reserve and shyness. For this activity, Delfina, who is from Mexico, also chooses to do a movement from the popular Mexican *cumbia* dance style.

While eliciting culturally specific forms of expression in dance, improvisation, and language to allow students' life worlds to enter the classroom and engage them in learning, Federico submits youth cultural practices to the same critical scrutiny that he does the dominant language ideology and traditional forms of knowing and learning. In the self-describing adjective and movement activity, Federico makes clear that all students are expected to mimic student representations, male or female. When Josué refuses to mirror "Dancing Dipashri's" Nepalese dance movement, Federico calls out, laughing, "She did Hopping Josué!" He expects the boys to do the girls' moves, just as the girls are expected to do the boys' moves. This was an apparently hilarious, carnavalesque, turning the status quo on its head situation, judging by the uproarious laughter on the part of the boys as well as girls. To further emphasize the point that expressive movement is not gender specific, following Delfina's swiveling *cumbia* step, Federico states that the hips are a source of strength and moves to the center of the circle to execute a powerful judo kick-punch that leaves him face-to-face with Josué in martial arts position, and for a dramatic moment he holds this pose, then relaxes his warrior stance, stating, "What do you think football players do? They gotta use their hips!" In this performance of masculinity and power he at once makes public one of his many other identities as a black belt in judo, and he suggests to the male students the futility of challenging his authority. To save face for Josué, Federico ends the exchange by joking with him in Spanish.

Challenging traditional gender roles, identities, and culturally specific ways of moving and being in the body was a pattern seen in the analysis of Federico's teaching over time. Whereas other mentors and teachers treaded softly in this domain, seeking not to upset fragile adolescent gender identities and behaviors, Federico was unafraid to enter this loaded terrain. His fearlessness over time would lead to frame clashes, seen on his first day in Transcript 3.7, and increasing in intensity until they erupted in a verbal altercation between Federico and Maria during Week 10 of the program. Once again the collaboration led to conflict and tensions: contradictions emerge in the enactment of Federico's pedagogy in the context of this classroom and high school, where the practices of professional theater meet the culture of school and youth. On the one hand, his pedagogy helped build symbolic bridges from students' cultural and linguistic repertoires to the curriculum, and this contributed to the development of a sense of community and trust. On the other hand, his college-level expectations for embodied self-expression and challenges to traditional gender roles appeared to present too much risk too fast for some youth who may never have experienced this type of approach before.

Federico on Voice and Communication

At this point in his instruction, which precedes the extract below, Federico treats voice in terms of its physical, sonic, and performative properties. In Transcript 3.13, together with Elia and Delfina, he adds another layer of meaning to the notion of voice. The students hear that in addition to being connected to the body and used for radio performances, voice is used more generally for *communicating*: (a) communicating to know others and oneself and to share oneself with others; and (b) communicating to express who we are and what we stand for. Significantly, he concludes his speech on communicating stating, "Communicate! Someday, your life may depend on it."

Transcript 3.11 Federico, Delfina, and Elia co-construct a theory of communication and language

1	Federico:	And there's also something very important to think
2		about. What do we use our voices for? What do we
3		use our voices for? [*gesturing toward his chest*]
4	Elia:	[*quietly*] to speak
5	Federico:	To speak? And why do you, why would you say we need to
6		speak? [*gesturing from his mouth outward*]
7	Delfina:	To communicate.
8	Federico:	To communicate? Communicate what? What are you=
9	Delfina:	=To other people like how you, like yeah
10	Federico:	Like to other people, how do you, like yeah?
11	Students:	*Laughter*

12	Federico:	Well what would you wanna say? I mean why . . . ? What
13		would you wanna . . . ? I mean I'm, I'm . . . Have you ev-
14		er thought about it? Wouldn't it be all better if we didn't
15		say a lot, just like= [*arms outstretched sideways*]
16	Elia:	=laughs=
17	Federico:	=stay quiet?
18	Delfina:	No!!
19	Federico:	No? [*Federico raises eyebrows as gestures upward toward girl*
20		*with palm upraised, inviting her to continue*]
21	Delfina:	No, I mean cuz (.) how're you gunna know everyone else.
22	Federico:	Ahhhh, interesting! [*gestures to her acknowledging her com-*
23		*ment*]. How're you gunna know EV-ER-Y ONE ELSE [*in-*
24		*dicates other students in the circle with arm gesture as he*
25		*speaks*]. Right? How're you gunna know (.) who you ARE.
26		How're you gunna say, 'Hey wait a second, I'm this...
27		Wait a second, I stand for this?' What a second I (.) be-
28		lieve in this. Right? Like well, we, how would you know
29		where I'm from if I don't say to you I'm from Mm . . .
30		Mm . . . Mm . . . Meh [*hitting the back of his head, other arm*
31		*stretched out to the front, comic gesture*] Meh . . . [*sputtering*]
32		Meh . . . He . . . He. Co! Eh México [*hitting his head comical-*
33		*ly*]. ¿Verdad? That's where I'm from, right? I have to get it
34		out. So I have to speak=
35	Students:	=*Laughter*
36	Federico:	=And (.) your voice is used for many things, for many,
37		many things and we'll have a discussion about this, uh
38		but mostly is to get to know ourselves, to communicate.
39		... [*Federico talks to Eugenia in Spanish. He asks the class to re-*
40		*member what adjectives qualify nouns. Eugenia speaks quietly,*
41		*and thinks about what adjective she should use. Federico asks the*
42		*class to offer suggestions. They are quiet. Dana and Federico both*
43		*offer suggestions. Federico starts listing 'E' adjectives*].
44	Eugenia:	Elegante.
45	Federico:	Was she communicating to us?
46	Eugenia:	Elegante. [*more slowly and loudly, making a clear gesture*]
47		You have to make sure that we GET it. So communicate to
48	Federico:	us. I know you're a great communicator because I've seen
49		you communicate. Now you guys have to communicate!
50		Someday your life is going to depend on that, on
51		communicating.

In lines 30–33, Federico does a comical improvisational skit in which he seems to be making fun of the shame and fear some people may have of being Mexican, hitting himself on the side of the head as he sputters and stutters out the syllabated word "Mm . . . Mm . . . Mm . . . Mé-xi-co." He seems to be conveying that "We Mexicans need to communicate who we are and where we're from, and show that we are not afraid or ashamed to be Mexican in the United States." This is part of letting people know who you are, performing your ethnic/national identity: "I'm this." In this way Federico is addressing Ray's and Liv's concern regarding the students' debilitating lack of self-confidence, or sense of self-worth. As Liv noted in her exit interview, developing voice for these students is important

> so they have a sense of self-worth, so they know who they are and can begin to accept themselves, and can see that they have value and meaning. Self-esteem, it's huge: it's going to impact both their personal and their academic life. (Liv, exit interview, 06/05/11)

In the weeks following, Federico continues to build on these themes, emphasizing the need to develop one's voice to defend and advocate for oneself, themes that are frequently echoed in student exit interviews.

While he continues to tease students (making fun of Delfina's "Valley Girl" talk) and engage in verbal play, Federico manages to weave in serious commentary and *consejos* (advice) on the meanings of communication, including existential questions about how we know who we are, how we come to know others, social identities (being Mexican), and the role of communication in being human. This is a key event in which themes related to voice and communication are addressed that will be taken up and echoed in later discourse, student work, and interview responses. The main themes introduced in this segment are the following:

Theme 1: Communication is necessary for knowing oneself and others.
Theme 2: Communication is necessary for making oneself understood.
Theme 3: Communicating means sharing one's values and beliefs: taking a public stand.
Theme 4: Communication is necessary for accessing the knowledge we don't yet have: communication is needed for learning.
Theme 5: Communication happens with the body as well as the voice.
Theme 6: Communication can be fun.

Learning the Rules of Youth Radio during the First Days of the Program

On the first full class period of the new program, students begin to learn "how to do" Youth Radio, to learn the rules and norms of the program. As students make sense of the program rules, they begin to understand what is possible to do and become in this particular educational setting, and—for some of them—to make it their own (Evaldsson and Corsaro, 1998). During the second class, Federico's language use and student take up of his Mexican linguistic and paralinguistic resources represented discourse that was available to be appropriated and used by students (Putney et al., 2000). The Mexican discourse practices that erupted in the classroom on the second day of the program can be viewed as one *cultural element* that becomes a resource for the development of social relationships over time. Zittoun and Grossen (2013) suggest that by giving a semiotic form to a personal experience—such as being a speaker of Mexican Spanish in a monolingual school—the person makes it accessible for oneself as well as for others. The cultural element is turned into an object of joint action, shared emotions and ideas. Furthermore, the transformation of a cultural element into an object of joint action creates shared meanings that are a first step toward the construction of personal sense (Zittoun & Grossen 2010), which is required for learning and development. The shared meanings are what we see expressed by Tania and other students regarding the purpose of Youth Radio. The personal sense, in this case, is the individual meaningfulness that each attributes to concepts of voice and communication.

During his first day of teaching in Youth Radio, Federico introduces a new set of resources for the expressive repertoire of the youth. He states and demonstrates explicitly that the body can be a tool for communication and encourages students to explore who they are, and to communicate to others who they are through expressive means centered in the moving body. Federico embeds Mexican Spanish in his communicative discourse, using it to connect to students, extending their linguistic resources, and engaging them in verbal and embodied play. He seamlessly shifts between Mexican Spanish (*chilango* Spanish from the capital) and more academic discourse. The discourse shifts validate Spanish language as an appropriate and valued form of communication. Yet in asserting the rights of the majority Spanish speakers to use more than English in the classroom, Federico also excludes the three non-Spanish-speaking students. The discomfort expressed by Liv regarding their exclusion was a sign of tension arising from the collaboration, and the enactment of instructional practices over which she and Ray had little control.

The analyses of discourse and ethnographic data presented in this section on Day 2 signal how participation in group activities with Federico was consequential for students along dimensions of both continuity and change. To further examine how this history shaped their subsequent understandings and actions I devote the next two chapters to analyzing two case studies, focusing on their interview narratives and ethnographic records to trace the "roots and routes" (Putney et al., 2000) of their developing understandings of the social shared meanings of the program, as well as the personal sense they made of cultural elements in support of their own learning and development.

Note

1. *Intertextuality*, the juxtaposition or relationship among texts (which can include conversational, electronic, and nonverbal texts), contributes to the construction of meanings and values attributed to a given text, such as a feature story discussed in class. The related concept of *intercontextuality* (Bloome et al., 2005), refers to the social construction of relationships among contexts and social events, both spatially and temporally, such as when the journalist mentors says, "Remember when we practiced Vox Pops in the classroom? Now we're going to do the same thing, interviewing people on the mall."

• CHAPTER FOUR •

Constructing Personal Voice

> Aprendí que puedo hablar. (I learned I could speak.)
> —Elia

At the end of the school year, as students were wrapping up their projects and preparing a showcase of their work for family members and the broader public, I conducted hourlong interviews with students in Liv's office, over coffee or lunch. The interviews were designed to access students' understandings of the notion of "voice," "communication," and the people and cultural elements that facilitated their learning in the program.

For these long interviews I used a semistructured format, which allowed me to pursue some established general questions and to explore emergent themes in addition to concepts and questions defined in advance of the interviews. In addition, I included questions designed to explore themes identified through analyses of ethnographic data.

The interview protocol was adapted from a protocol used in Zittoun and Grossen's (2010) longitudinal study of the use of cultural elements—such as philosophical and literary texts—by high school students and teachers to bridge the contexts of school and life outside of school. The interview protocol for the Youth Radio Program was organized around nodes of Zittoun's (2006) the semiotic prism, shown in Figure 4.1.

Figure 4.1 Semiotic Prism (Zittoun, 2006)

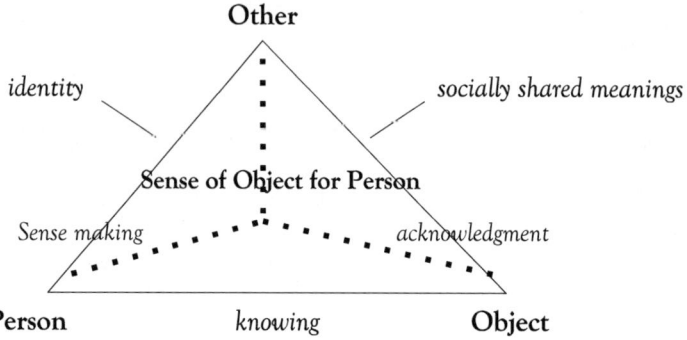

Zittoun's (2006) representation of processes of change and development in the form of a semiotic prism expands Vygotsky's triangle of the *person*, the *object*, and the *other* who mediates thinking about the object, to include a fourth node of *personal sense* of the object for the *person*. Zittoun adds the fourth node for the purposes of studying transitions in adolescence as well as development processes in childhood. Zittoun's semiotic prism is a useful heuristic for examining the dynamics of continuity and change in young people, as it allows for analyses of mediating elements that result in new states of thinking, being, and acting during periods of change. Development in this framework implies three interdependent processes of change involving the use of cultural, cognitive, and social resources: identity processes, knowledge and skill acquisition, and personal sense (Zittoun, 2006, 2008). First, transitions sets in motion identity processes of repositioning the person "in her social and symbolic fields" (Zittoun, 2008, p. 166). This suggests the redefinition of identities, involving new representations of past and possible future selves. Second, relocations, such as transitioning from a student in a remedial ESL class to a participant in a Youth Radio program, require new forms of knowledge and skills as in learning new communication technology and radio discourse genres. Third, to be successful in these identity repositionings, new relations and new learning, the person must make sense of the socially shared meanings of the communities in which he or she participates, as well as the changes he or she experiences. Adolescents often use cultural elements for these purposes.

Cultural elements are *semiotic devices* made out of signs in a material, perceptible form that carry meaning that is socially shared. A digital story is made out of semiotic units (music, images, narration, text) to which other people attach meanings that come to be shared through cultural processes such as viewing and discussing model digital stories in the classroom. When someone creates a new digital story, he or she uses the existing genre rules of multimodal composition through processes of *internalization*, while adding new elements or new translations of existing forms through processes of *externalization*.

Zittoun (2006) defines two types of cultural elements. First—and the primary focus of her research—are cultural elements with a discrete, physical presence, such as a novel or film, which enable cultural experiences involving the imagination, which allows people to inhabit other worlds or spheres of experience. Second are less concrete cultural elements, such as linguistic practices of a specific group: "Both of these cultural elements are part of a defined symbolic system that encompasses clearly identifiable objects, rules, and actors" (2006, pp. 34–35). In this study, I present findings related to both types of cultural elements. In Chapter 3, I discussed the Mexican and American discursive practices enacted in the classroom by Federico and the students. In this chapter and Chapter 5, I explore the uses of radio genres, poetry, and digital stories as cultural elements that become symbolic resources when the young people use them as tools for thinking, feeling, or defining new identities. I explore these processes related to the development of the concepts of *personal voice* and *public voice*, using case studies of two participants in the program, Elia and Tania.

Following Rupture, Reconstructing Community

In the previous chapter, I described how Federico began to build a sense of community through culturally specific discourse practices, trust-building exercises, laughter, play, embodied expression, and comic improvisation. Building a sense of community and dialogical relations appears to have been a prerequisite for developing a sense of voice following the rupture represented by the implementation of the new program the sixth week into the school year.

The timing and design of Youth Radio and Radio Arts forced people to experience rupture as they entered the program. The school district did not allow researchers to begin research projects until the school year was well underway. This meant that the onset of the program caused an interruption of already established routines, practices, and expectations. The learning design itself represented a break from the known way of "doing school," such that cohesion and consensus about what we were all doing there took time to reconstruct: Liv and Ray reported that neither they nor the students were completely clear during the first few weeks about their roles or the learning outcomes, and noted that the number of new adult mentors may have been confusing for students.

The teachers explained that they had spent the first five weeks of the semester prior to the program "building community": community-building activities prior to the program included an essay on students' feelings of "invisibility," responses to the Luis Rodriquez poem "Sí se puede," and class inclusion in activities surrounding the visit of Chicano author and activist Victor Villaseñor, a visit organized by Liv. For Liv, developing community meant creating a strong symbolic structure of routines, norms, and rules. The class norms, generated with input from students the first week of the semester, were posted on chart paper and referred to regularly by her.

Ray shared similar views on the importance of community. Though his instruction surrounding community-building was less explicit than Liv's, his interactions with students, staff, and in recorded personal reflections made his position clear. From the beginning of the program, Ray urged us to spend more time trying to get to know students as individuals and "try to build community":

> I don't think they're lost or anything. I think they just . . . it would be nice to create community with the adults. . . . Talk to them just as you would children, then they'll build trust with the adults. (Ray, after-class debriefing, 9/23/10)

Later in the year, Ray stated, "It's really important to feel like they belong to have voice" (Ray and Dana, personal conversation, 4/13/11).

Though it took time to reconstruct a sense of community following rupture, over time students and teachers reported feeling trust and a sense of a protected space in which they could share themselves, communicate, and learn. As Elia stated in her exit interview, echoing Tania's remarks discussed in Chapter 2,

> The class got really close, everyone was really friendly: there was trust. That is how we began to speak to everyone. . . . I didn't have low self-esteem, I felt confident about myself. You guys, the teachers and everything, they knew how to get our *confianza*, our trust and everything, they got pretty close with each other, you know? It wasn't just about that class, "oh do this and that." It was like getting to know people, not just as students, getting to know students, their personal lives, not just as students, but like how we are outside of school too. (Elia, exit interview, 6/01/11)

In this excerpt, Elia points to two elements that were critical, in her mind, for developing interpersonal communication and personal voice: (1) the need for teachers to get to know youth as people and their lives outside of school, to make the curriculum more relevant; and (2) trust and the willingness to talk and share oneself with others.

Overcoming the Divided Classroom

Students in Youth Radio reported feeling intragroup tensions that impeded intersubjectivity and communication. Replicating findings from other studies of urban classrooms (Camangian, 2010; Hill, 2009), this study revealed that many students experienced a sense of isolation and mistrust of each other in their classrooms, which inhibited their learning. Tania's previously discussed statement is particularly relevant this point:

> [A]t first people are shy. And then the radio drama as well you know people are very shy but like when Federico came in he definitely got like our spirits out and now everyone is like friends with everyone and everybody talks with everyone when before it was just, "I don't know you so let's keep it that way."

Several students interviewed noted that in other classes they never spoke, and they expressed a sense of invisibility and voicelessness in the midst of people in these classes. When asked, "How would you describe yourself as a student in this class [Youth Radio]? Is it different from how you were in other classes?" Dipashri remarked, "I don't know most of my [classmates in other classes], they don't know me."

Sharing self with others. In this segment, Dipashri contrasts Youth Radio with her other classes as being *known* and *not known*, which could be understood as *seen* and *not seen*, or not "recognized." The transcript of her extended remarks read, "I have shown myself more in this class: this a good thing." This statement mirrors similar comments by other students, and suggests that sharing self within community were elements of a dynamic, recursive process with important implications for learning. Tania, Dipashri, Beto, and Elia all spoke to this point.

For Beto, showing oneself, or sharing oneself with others, was the most crucial learning outcome of the program for him: he mentioned this three times in his exit interview. In response to the exit interview question, "Did you ever take that idea as inspiration for a story about your own life?" Beto responded, "Yes, it made me think I should, inspired me to be more open in my life, to share my life with others, see if they can compare my life to theirs." In related statements Beto expresses the desire not only to share himself with others for his own needs but also to "show others how to share themselves." This theme of social responsibility felt by youth participants, the need to use their new understandings, skills, and knowledge in the service of others, will be explored further through Tania's case in Chapter 5.

Sharing oneself in community was a core principle of learning and development in the program. Jean-Luc Nancy (1988), reminiscent of Hannah Arendt, writes that "freedom appears as precisely the internal exteriority of the community; existence as the sharing of being" (p. 75). Arendt (1958) described the "public realm" (closer to what we call "community" today) as one in which individuals acted in such a manner that they disclosed themselves to others and were, in turn, acknowledged by others. The sharing of self in the program was predicated upon trust, and trust was a result of creating a sense of community. Freire (1970/2000) wrote that in problem-posing education, which is found in "love, humility, and faith," dialogue "becomes a horizontal relationship of which *mutual trust* between the dialoguers is a logical consequence" (pp. 77–78, italics added). Though it is not clear whether trust was a consequence or a cause, *confianza* (trust) was at the core of the sense of community students experienced.

How did students develop an understanding of the value the program placed on sharing of self in community? This core idea was promoted through values and rules that came to organize the social group across time. The principles of creating *confianza* and sharing of self were not explicitly identified as goals of the program, and yet exit interviews and other ethnographic data reveal that it was a key learning outcome for students. Students perceived this implicit aspect of the curriculum that was made available through the kinds of texts, talk, and relationships that evolved over time, as expressed by Elia in her interview.

Transcript 4.1

1	Elia:	It's just like we got really close with each other like everyone just
2		talked with each other and there were no problems there? Like
3		everyone was really friendly and that make me like, um, get like,
4		*come se dice, 'confianza'?*
5	Dana:	(.) trust
6	Elia:	Yeah, like trust everyone and then, well, that's how we started to
7		SPEAK for each other, you know, like, everyone expressed how
8		THEY felt and everything. Yeah, it was really, everyone got to
9		express their feelings, you know, like, to SPEAK for themselves.
10		And the commentaries, they were about their lives, like the one
11		I did about drowning? Yeah, a lot of them talk about, like, their
12		personal lives? The (.) like Eli and Lizzy, she talked about her
13		grandma, how, like, she died or something? They were like really
14		personal stories, you know? And they shared with the class
15		cause, like, they had confidence=with the whole class=

The fact that several students independently presented this perspective—that they were able to share with others because there was trust in the group—

is evidence of emerging, shared values, norms, and beliefs that were not explicitly taught but were co-constructed among participants. The attribution of importance to openness, connection, and sharing of self appears to have been a joint accomplishment of this particular collective. In this extended response, Elia highlights the interrelated meanings among community, dialogism, and voice. Starting to speak "for" or with each other, expressing their feelings, sharing stories about their lives and their families: these were core principles of communication in the class.

The sharing of selves was facilitated on a number of levels. One had to do with co-constructing a learning environment in which students' bicultural and bilingual identities were valued and viewed as worthy of representation. This required the construction of a "protected" or "safe space" for interdiscursivity. The following is an excerpt of a discussion in which Ray noted the need for creating a protected space in face of the general lack of safety experienced by the students in their everyday lives:

Transcript 4.2

1	Dana:	Tania's attitude is improving too, have you noticed?
2	Ray:	Part of that is the community they're in, like that after school
3		[component of the program]. 'Cuz they all need something to
4		where they can feel a little safe? If they're undocumented,
5		they're all unsafe. Stuff like what's happened to Tania. If she's
6		behaving, they're going along, that means something's happen-
7		ing, something right's happening.

Ray's remarks reflect findings by a number of authors who have written about the need for creating "safe spaces" in schools for urban youth living in poverty (Camangian, 2010; Nieto, 2010).

Building Community after School

Extending the program to one day after school a week contributed to building community among participants in the program. In these after-school sessions, held in the school Mac Lab beginning in the spring semester, students worked on editing radio and digital stories and learning the basics of Web content development for the program website we used to present student work at the final showcase. They also learned how to use a "beat machine," to create basic music loops, and search for and download images, ambient sound, and music in the correct digital format from the Web.

Computer play and mediating talk. Seeing that students were choosing to use the computers in ways not anticipated by adults, we allowed a certain amount of time for "play" on the computers: most of the students did not have computers at home, and we believed this affected their use of the computers available in school. Students accessed their favorite sites (limited by the school Internet firewalls), which were viewed in peer-only groups with lots of laughter and commentary or critically analyzed with mentors. While some educators might consider this a waste of on-task time, based on my research in after-school programs (Walker, 2003, 2009), I have concluded that this sort of time may be a critical to the recruitment and retention of youth who are giving up their free time to stay after school in adult-controlled spaces. By allowing youth to connect their out-of-school interests and identity work through youth culture to school-sponsored learning activities, we were tacitly building bridges between the two domains. We hoped that, through the use of new media technologies and popular culture genres (spoken word, rap, *norteña* music, video clips from the Internet), we were able to develop students' embodied and reflective awareness of the possible connections between the in- and out-of-school spheres of experience, in this way making school more relevant to their everyday lives.

An example of the ways that mentors mediated continuity between spheres of experience of youth peer culture and Youth Radio can be seen in an ongoing conversation that occurred between the KPFW mentor Kareem and a student who was interested in *"narco corridos"*—a Mexican form of musical ballad in which drug traffickers are portrayed as heroes. Kareem expressed an interest in the student's passion for *narco corridos* and engaged him in animated dialogue over several weeks about what fascinated the young man about this music and what it meant to him, especially the violence. This led to a larger group discussion about the situation in the Mexico–U.S. border regions and how the drug violence had directly affected the lives of families of some youth in the group.

I came to see this computer "play" as a productive time for having engaging interactions among youth as well as thoughtful interactions (scaffolding language and conceptual development) with professional media mentors. I believe that being allowed to have fun as well as doing the expected program work was a draw for the students who brought in friends who were not part of the sixth-period ESL class. I overheard Beto describing to a friend the digital story he was creating about his neighborhood. The "outsider" student was shocked that Beto was allowed to discuss such things as gang activity in a school assignment and joked that Beto should include bandanas among his images—a common symbol of gang membership. Beto laughed and said yes, he could, if he wanted. I did not interpret this to mean that Beto and his friend were members of a gang: over the years I have heard many such references to gang activity among Latino youth in Beckwourth City who are not gang members. Rather, I interpreted this exchange as evidence that students felt comfortable incorporating into their projects representations of their lifeworlds that were normally excluded from school work and the school discourse.

After-school sessions also provided opportunities for practice with technology and new language. This was critical for students who did not have computers at home and those needing time to develop confidence in their oral language production. Ray encouraged students to come after school in this way:

> The group, our group, the radio group meets today after school today. This is really important. Because I'm doing an iMovie too, I know this hard. It is challenging to get the words right, to get the words matched up with the pictures; then you gotta get the pictures in there. So after school is a perfect time: you get help, you get tutors. It seems like you get more help there than here [during class time]: there's no talking, no teachers talk to you like this, like I'm doing now. You just go in there and get to work. So use that time. (Ray, addressing the class, recorded 3/10/11)

Liv expressed a similar opinion:

> What a difference it made in the spring when we able to do the after school. They're talked at so much, but it is not scaffolded. It was a real eye-opener, seeing what we teachers took for granted in terms of technology skills for these students who don't have computers at home. (Liv, interview, 06/05/11)

By providing youth the space to express themselves through divergent means and share their lives and interests in a safe, supportive environment, they became invested in their projects and in participation in the community itself. As several youth and adult members of the program noted, participation in the community was a prerequisite to learning and to the emerging constructions of voice.

Food and community after school. Several factors in the after-school program contributed to developing a sense of community. One important factor, I believe, was informal interactions and food. The hot, home-cooked, and healthful snacks we provided each week became both a draw (Julio: "We're having tamales? I'll be there!") and a facilitator of trusting relationships. Over food, adults and youth shared stories, joked around, and talked about nonschool-related topics. Power relations shifted, if only for the time that we were together in that environment. We got to know each other as people with stories and lives outside of school.

Because I had noted the sense of isolation students felt in the school building, I encouraged members from the larger school community to join us in eating and socializing in the hallway, including the janitors and a security guard. These adults expressed interest in and support for what the youth were doing in the Mac Lab, as shown in the following excerpts from field notes:

> Craig the janitor sticks his head in the door. I call across the room, "Do you want us to clean up out there?" He said, "No, I just wanted to know what project they were working on." Turns out Craig was involved in his college radio for eight years. He asks the kids about the specifics of their projects—what editing software they're using, what audio board they used at the radio station. These informal exchanges provide external input that reinforces the significance of the students' work, and positions them as emerging experts in the domains of communication technology and alternative media. (Field note, 3/10/11)
>
> I invited José, the janitor, to have a burrito. He talked to the kids about his degree in business from Mexico. Oscar said they might like to interview him some day. The security guard, whom the kids like a lot and call "Batman," also joined us to eat today. (Field note, 4/4/11)
>
> In response to our invitation, José the janitor attended the students' final showcase and gave positive feedback to them afterwards. (Field note, 5/24/11)

The participation and interest expressed by these members of the school community expanded the boundaries of the program and permitted valued interactions with nonteaching school staff, in addition to program mentors.

Building and expanding community through field trips. Field trips were conceived as opportunities for enrichment, fun, relationship building, and boundary-crossing learning, in the sense of youth participating in new contexts with people different from themselves, often strangers. During the "Vox Pops on 5th Street" field trip, for instance, students interviewed strangers on the street with the question, "How can we make Beckwourth a better place for youth?" Individually they interviewed a police officer, two young saleswomen, a Latina mother and educator, and had casual, laughter-filled interactions with various passers-by including a visiting speaker from Uganda and a youth group from New York.

As noted earlier, one of the reasons for seeking funding for this after-school program was to expand the contexts of learning in school to include the wider community, in particular, community-based media and arts organizations: it was not possible for students to visit the radio station during the 50-minute school period. We made five trips during the year to the radio station where students learned the basics of DJing, audio board use, and station identification. They met the staff, were given a tour of the station, and learned about the organization's mission, all of which gave them a frame of reference for understanding where and how their radio pieces were being broadcast when they were aired on the station's Morning Show at various times throughout the semester. Also at the station the group did a prerecorded interview with Kareem for his weekly Urban Radio Show. The local newspaper sent a photographer to cover this group interview for an article published in the spring. As shown in excerpt below, Ray, like the students, valued opportunities provided after school to get to know each other as people outside of the teacher–student dynamic:

> The field trip went really well yesterday. I took the four boys in my car it was a good time to bond with them to understand them better, to kind of hear them, because the idea of the class is to have voice and it seems like, of the class, those boys have the least voice, because they're the quietest. They seem to have nothing to say. Everything's neutral, everything.... They're not outspoken about anything.
>
> So it was nice to hear them in the car as we drove, and it kind of let them be themselves and see them in a different light. I thought that was one of the highlights of the field trips, driving them there. Because they're the group that kind of is a lot more distant, as far as, I never get a chance to interact with them because when I do, they don't interact much with me. I think that was beneficial to bond a little bit more with them in that setting. (Ray's recorded personal reflection, 10/29/10)

The Youth Radio and Radio Arts after-school program was designed to extend and enrich the student learning taking place in a regular sixth-period class that combined an ESL study skills and academic support class. The program provided the time and space to accomplish our larger goals. We found that the students' after-school time with mentors and each other in the Mac Lab, at the radio station, and on field trips greatly extended the in-school learning. Informal interactions and new experiences in new settings contributed to promoting trust between adults and youth, which helped develop a greater sense of belonging to the YRRA community and the broader civic community. In Chapter 5, I return to this topic of feeling a sense of belonging to the larger civic community in the context of analyses of the construction of *public voice*.

Constructing Personal Voice: Echoes of Federico's Teachings

In the next section, I introduce findings regarding communication and personal voice. I examine the "echoes" heard in exit interviews of discourse and new practices launched during the first days of the Youth Radio program, drawing on Bakhtin's (1986) dialogical notion of "delay." In this framework, "delay" seems particularly apt for explaining student use of language and concepts introduced early on in the program in their articulation of understanding concepts of voice, communication, and the purposes of Youth Radio and Radio Arts. Castanheira, Crawford, Dixon, and Green (2001) call attention to Bakhtin's argument that sooner or later, what is heard and actively understood will find its response in the subsequent speech or behavior of the listener: "In most cases, genres of complex cultural communication are intended precisely for this kind of actively responsive understanding with delayed action" (p. 176). The researchers go on to argue that each action of the teacher, whether in spoken discourse or visual action, can be seen as "proposing to students actions to take, positions to take up, and information that is a potential resource for future action and identity formulation" (p. 60).

Student interview responses show evidence of Federico's words and concepts as having been heard and actively understood by students, from the time of their introduction early in the year through subsequent, supporting instruction by mentors and teachers. The clear presence of his words and concepts in student narratives, as shown below, leads me to believe that there was something about the way Federico communicated—the way he drew out students' ideas and experiences, the embodiment of his *consejos* (elder advice) in familiar gestures and discursive practices, and pointedly encouraging students to use their bodies to internalize the concepts presented—that made a mark. We hear echoes of his discourse and key themes in student narratives regarding their understanding of *personal voice* articulated in their exit interviews. The themes related to personal voice that I will explore include (a) advocating for self, (b) speaking out, (c) having and expressing an opinion, and (d) developing voice to know others and self.

Echoes of Federico's words in Elia's construction of "voice." As Tania did in her exit interview, Elia—though without mentioning him directly—references Federico's discourse on communication made the first weeks of the fall semester in response to questions regarding voice.

Transcript 4.3

1	Dana:	For you what does that mean, to develop your voice?
2	Elia:	To (..) like, be able to talk, like to speak for yourself or some-
3		thing like (.) to stand up if you're sick, you say you're sick, if
4		you're you know=
5	Dana:	=mm hmm=
6	Elia:	=not just be in a quiet place not talking, you know=
7	Dana:	=uh huh=
8	Elia:	=like defend yourself. Trying to be with other people to get to
9		know new people, and everything? Yeah. Just not a lonely per-
10		son to talk, *speak for yourself.*

• CONSTRUCTING PERSONAL VOICE •

11	Dana:	Why do you think teachers think that's important, and the
12		mentors?
13	Elia:	Well I think that like cause like when a kid needs help or
14		something, some kids just say they're quiet. They don't even
15		talk, you know like they don't say anything. Or they don't ex-
16		press the way they feel sometimes. They're having problems
17		with their life outside of school, and then they come to school
18		and then there are things like, oh like you have to learn this or
19		that and they can't even think about learning right now be-
20		cause they're having problems rights now or in their house-
21		hold. They have to like, be able to tell someone, to like talk to
22		their counselor, to like express it in poems or like just get eve-
23		rything out, and yeah you know not just stay quiet when you
24		need to speak up for yourself. You can do that you know and
25		not just stay there and be quiet. Not do anything about it.

In this excerpt, Elia expressed the idea of the importance of being "able to talk" and "to speak for yourself," which echoes Federico's *consejos* (advice) on self-advocacy. In Transcript 4.4, an excerpt of class interactions on September 30, 2010, Federico's second class, we hear the discursive roots of some of concepts and language used by Elia to talk about "voice" and the personal meanings she made of people and objects in the program. In this excerpt, Federico, Ray, and students co-construct the notion of self-advocacy and the continuity of self in discussing situations in which one would need to communicate one's needs, one's values, and one's "self."

Transcript 4.4

1	Federico:	So we wanna make sure that the per-
2		son receiving the communication
3		receives the communication (.) Right?
4	Ray:	You said, "Gets it."
5	Federico:	[Looks at Ray eyebrows raised in question]
6		Yeah! "Gets it!" [emphasizes point with
7		his head] (.) You gotta GET it [in gravelly
8		New Yorker voice] Right? Now.
9		We were talking about communication
10		about getting who you are [reaches arm
11		out to boys]. In what situations would
12		that be important? [puts hand up to face]
13		(..) Most of the time we have to be at-

14		tending to, and listening to what other	
15		people's needs are [*stretches out both*	
16		*arms*] That's what makes human beings	
17		great, when they're not selfish and they	
18		think about the concerns of others. Do	
19		you follow me? (.) But every now and	
20		then it's important for us to say, "Wait	
21		a second. This is who I am" [*pointing to*	
22		*self*] [*Looks at boys, who shuffle their feet*	
23		*and look down*] What are situations	
24		where you have to say, "This is who I	
25		am?" [*Looking at Juan Carlos, gesturing*	
26		*toward him inviting a response*] ¿En qué	What are situa-
27		*situación te encuentras cuando tienes que*	tions where you
28		*decir, "Un momento. Yo soy quien soy,*	have to say, "Just
29		*Y no me parezco* (inaudible) [*moving arm*	a minute. I am
30		*up and down, he looks to the rest of the*	who I am, and
31		*class half-smiling*]	it's not right . . .
32	Juan	(inaudible)	
33	Carlos:		
34	Federico:	[*repeating what Juan Carlos said*] ¿Cuando	When they say
35		*te dicen cosas?* So when people say	things to you?
36		things to you, you have to be able to	
37		stake and say, "No!" (..) Right? ...	
38		I am not unfair, I stand for justice,	
39		right? [*Federico continues eliciting exam-*	
40		*ples from students*]	
41	Dipashri:	(inaudible)	
42	Federico:	[*Repeating her words*] You're trying to	
43		meet someone and they don't know	
44		who you are, right? ...	
45	Junior:	(inaudible)	
46	Federico:	When they're name calling! [*nods head*	
47		*vigorously*] I'm not bla bla bla. Blue blue	
48		blue. ... I know there's one you en-	
49		counter every day because I did when I	
50		was a kid ... [*continues on to discussion*	
51		*about a situation in baseball which Raul*	
52		*plays, of pitcher needing to disagree with*	
53		*the catcher who is communicating via non-*	

54		*verbal signals with fingers, fists, gestures]* I
55		want one more, then we're gunna
56		move on. I want one from you *[indi-*
57		*cates Delfina]*
58	Delfina:	*[smiling, swinging her legs]* (inaudible)
59	Federico:	Huh?
60	Delfina:	(inaudible)
61	Federico:	How about that? How about that situa-
62		tion? Just say, "I'm sick." *[speaking*
63		*slowly]* So when you are not feeling
64		well, you have to communicate it, "I'm
65		not feeling well." *[walks toward boy,*
66		*shakes*
67		*his hand]* Oww! Ow! *[screams, grabs his*
68		*hand]* Why'd you do that?! *[glowering at*
69		*Noel]* I'm cut in the hand! Right? I had
70		to tell him, "We're gunna shake like
71		this today *[reaches out to Noel with his*
		elbow] because
72	Noel:	*[touches Federico's elbow with his elbow]*
73	Federico:	I got a cut in my hand *[nurses his hand,*
74		*then walks back to his original spot]* (..)
75		Sometimes when you have a disability,
76		or you have a problem, you have some-
77		thing that needs to be attended, you
78		need to communicate, right? Yes or no?
79		*[Walks over to Juan Carlos and does a*
80		*mimed comic gesture toward him, smiles,*
81		*looks at Juan Carlos who smiles slightly]*. ...
82		Communicate! Someday your life is
83		going to depend on it.

Elia's narrative echoes both concepts and language introduced by Federico, especially in regards to the theme of self-advocacy and the importance of communicating one's needs, one's sense of self, and values:

> Elia: Be able to talk, like to speak for yourself, or something like (.) to stand up if you're sick, you say you're sick.

> Federico: Just say, "I'm sick." So when you are not feeling well you have to communicate it, "I'm not feeling well."

Yet at the same time that Elia shows evidence of taking up Federico's notion of communication and voice, she asserts her personal sense or understanding of voice. Developing voice for Elia meant overcoming a debilitating shyness and sense of isolation from others (echoing Dipashri's offering on this topic). Developing voice meant developing the ability to connect with others, share one's inner life and objective life conditions with others: "Trying to be with other people to get to know new people, and everything? Yeah. Just not a lonely person to talk, speak for yourself."

Another co-constructed meaning of voice, echoing Federico's words—"Some day your life may depend on it"—was linking communication to the question of survival, when an adolescent is experiencing serious emotional or mental trouble, as her sister was that year. When asked, "Why do you think teachers and the mentors think that [speaking up for others] is important?" Elia responded, "If kids need help they don't say anything. If they're having problems outside the house they can't learn anything. When you need to stick up for yourself, you can do that, you know?" Here Elia expands on Federico's (and others') discourse about "voice" as meaning speaking up and advocating for oneself, saying you are sick when you are sick, seeking help if you need it because it affects what goes on in school as well as home or among peers. Federico's declaration in September that "Someday your life may depend on it" may have had a particular resonance for Elia and her sister, who attempted suicide that year, but who was also observed by many as being unusually happy and engaged when in the presence of Federico. The cultural resource introduced by Federico, his concept of communication and the necessity of advocating for oneself, became a symbolic resource for Elia as she appropriated this concept, in the process transforming the shared collective meaning of communication introduced by Federico into her personal sense regarding the importance of voice and of youth radio for her own development.

In general, the related concepts of *self-advocacy* and *speaking out* were introduced in Federico's classroom discourse that appeared to be salient for both students and teachers: Seven of the nine students interviewed mentioned aspects of self-advocacy first introduced by Federico. Ray revoiced Federico's teachings in this way:

> Hopefully this will trigger something that they'll realize that things apply that they can, they can apply a lot of things, not just this class, to their, and practice it, and be able to acquire, acquire the type of character that it takes to be a good student. In this case, I think what [Federico] was saying was advocate, and speak: you're sick, so you're sick. You don't understand so you don't understand. So hopefully they understood that and they can start speaking up for themselves, defending themselves if they're communicating more.

The second language part: learners need to learn to advocate for themselves cuz their parents aren't advocating for them. Parents in the meantime don't come to the school, so this will help the second language learners in that way. What they're learning is the need to communicate, not to be reserved. (Personal reflection, 9/23/10)

Student constructions of "voice" in terms of self-advocacy and speaking up for yourself were articulated in the following ways:

[In Youth Radio] you learn to speak up for yourself. (Yoli)

[Developing voice means] to be able to speak for yourself. (Eugenia)

[The purpose of Youth Radio is] inspiring people to speak out. (Beto)

If you don't know how to develop your voice nobody is really going to listen to you. (Sonia)

The construct of voice as speaking out, having the right to speak, and advocating for self was closely related to the notion of having and expressing an opinion, of "knowing what you know" (Gilligan, 1993):

You need to let other people hear your voice, because you matter too, and your opinion matters. (Sugita)

In this class you say what you're thinking, not just like answering teachers question. In other classes you only talk about the subject, not your opinion. (Sonia)

In most of classes we never learn of these things. There might be lot of opinions in certain topics that we can express. (Dipashri)

[Instructors in Youth Radio are hoping you will learn] that you have the right to speak up, you're opinion is never wrong or right. (Sugita)

If a teacher says something and I don't agree with it I can say I don't agree; in group discussion I can point out my view on it. (Delfina)

You will learn how to express yourself and how to let people know what you think and talk for yourself, but also for other people, to express your opinions. (Sonia)

Student Constructions of Personal "Voice"

In addition to the importance of developing voice to participate in community and speak out or advocate for self, students in their exit interviews elaborated the following meanings related to personal voice. Developing voice is important for self-confidence:

[Developing voice is important] so not to be scared [sic]. (Elia)

Hablar mejor, tener mas confianza / To speak better, have more confidence. (Delfina)

Being more confident. (Sugita)

[I have been able to develop my voice through Youth Radio] because it gave me the courage to speak with others. (Eugenia)

Developing voice means expressing your feelings:

Think more deeply about a certain topic. Talk about what you feel. (Sugita)

Give us a chance to express what we feel and let others know what we think about topics. (Yoli)

Sometimes when you feel sad or have something going on in your life, you have words coming out of your mind. It's nice to share your feelings. (Masha)

Developing voice means knowing how to use language in socially appropriate ways, developing "communication competence":

[Developing voice means] different ways of expressing what you think, and also how you use your language, and where you use it. Like in your house you just talk like, you don't even say the words how you're supposed to say them, and in school sometimes if you're looking for job or something on your future, you have to talk, not proficiently, but like uh, like using the correct language. (Sonia)

After the interview with my counselor I [realized that I] need to practice more. It helped me but I still need more work. They are *muy educados*/very proper, polite. You need to be really polite with them, you are thinking about how you act in front of them. (Elia)

Like my interview with Mrs. Masters—it was fun. We have a lot of respect for her. It was kind of weird, like *solo quieres hablar bien con ella decir bien las cosas*/it's like, you only want to speak well with her, speak correctly. (Delfina)

Developing voice is important for success in school:

[Teachers] want the kids to achieve voice, *que no se quedan caiados*/so they don't remain silent. *Los maestros quieren entenderlos pero si no hablan, no pueden*/Teachers want to understand them, but if they don't speak, they can't. (Delfina)

Because teachers like it when you talk in class, when you ask questions if you don't understand something. I understand that teachers get frustrated if you don't talk, when you don't understand something and later fail a test. Then they will feel like they aren't doing their job right or something. (Yoli)

Doing presentations in class. (Dipashri)

Now I can speak better in other classes—you have to speak better. (Tania)

Speaking in public, in world history, I can speak. *Antes temblada/*before I shook with fear. *Las computadores, puedo usar lo que aprendi/* computers, I can use what I learned. (Delfina)

Developing voice is important for success in future careers:

Cuz when you grow up get a job you would have to speak a lot and present something, not to be scared. (Tania)

Cuz when you grow up get a job, you have to speak out and be more comfortable to speak and share you voice. (Yoli)

[Developing voice means] learning how to speak; knowing how to talk when going into an interview, how to present your voice, show who you are. So I think Youth Radio prepares you for the future. (Tania)

[Developing voice is important] for job interviews, people like people who are talkative and stuff, especially in a job you have to deal with the public. They like people who can talk and are easy to talk to. (Yaire)

Interview responses from the nine focal students revealed complex understandings of their own learning, personal transformation, and deep insight into the underlying goals and constructed curriculum of the program. These responses suggest that for the students interviewed—not all of whom are represented above—Youth Radio and Radio Arts helped them develop confidence and the *courage* to speak and have their opinions heard. They indicate an awareness of the ways power operates to reinforce inequalities in classrooms and schools for culturally and linguistically diverse learners. Whereas students had expressed a sense of exclusion in English-only classes, either due to the shame at their "non-native like" pronunciation or their inability to follow the uninterrupted stream of academic English words in the pure lecture format of many classes, in Youth Radio and Radio Arts, students were able to develop a sense of belonging and connectedness to the group, the ability to participate and to learn. Whereas students reported not feeling valued for the linguistic and cultural richness they brought to school, Youth Radio asked them to "show where you live, how you live...show people what you're made of." Whereas most print-based academic assessments prevent students from negotiating forms of representation and favorable identities, the multimodal and multidisciplinary projects in Youth Radio allowed for a broader range of expression, interests, and talents, and more opportunities to rehearse alternate identities.

In the next section I examine processes of continuity, change, and emergent understandings of personal voice in the case study of Elia, using a semiotic prism analysis to elucidate changes that occur in the "architecture of the self" (Zittoun, 2006) through the appropriation and elaboration of cultural resources made available in the program.

Elia's Story

At the end of a year spent together in Youth Radio and Radio Arts program, Elia and I sat down over lunch for a long interview. We talked of many things as side conversations to the interview questions. She was animated in the conversation and seemed excited that an adult—a co-teacher in the class—was interested in what she had to say. Toward the end of the interview when asked, "What have you learned about yourself in this program?" she responded, "*Aprendí que puedo hablar*/I learned I could speak."

Having seen Elia's efforts throughout the year to do well in this class, her struggles with the technology, her reply gave me pause: How was I to interpret her meaning? What meaning(s) did she attribute to the word "*hablar*/to speak" in the context of the interview studded with questions about the meanings of "voice"? If she learned that she could speak in this program, what were her schooling experiences like outside of the program? What meanings did she make of the program itself? What were the implications for a powerful statement about self-transformation?

The significance of Elia's remarks can only be appreciated in the context of the multiple overlapping sociocultural contexts of her life and learning. One is the larger sociocultural context of Elia's life in the United States and her schooling experience here. Like most of her classmates, she is an emergent bilingual who has been placed in a remedial ESL Study Skills course, within a tracked high school with AP and non-AP classes and a separate wing for english learners, mostly Latino students, that divide students along economic and ethnolinguistic lines. She and her classmates report varying degrees of feeling invisible and silenced for much of the school day. In spite of teachers' encouragements, these students have little hope of going to college due to the current immigration law. Though she is a bright, hardworking, and engaging young woman, Elia is failing three classes, and for this reason has been placed in this remedial study skills class.

Elia lives with her older sister, toddler brother, mother, stepfather, and occasionally extended family members in a single-wide trailer on a dirt road alongside other trailers behind a strip mall. In one of her poems, Elia writes about the semi-feral dogs that wander around the neighborhood and wake her up at night. Ray told me that the family is very poor: he bought lunch for Cipriana, Elia's sister, in the early fall because she did not get her free and reduced-price lunch set up correctly. Elia keeps a change of clothes in her school locker to have clean clothes for school after nights she spends babysitting at the home of a mother's friend who works the night shift at Target. She and her sister trade off taking care of her little brother and do all the cleaning and cooking since her mother sleeps in the day after working from the afternoon until early morning at Target. She rarely goes out with friends, and when she does, her mother requires that she be home by 9:00 p.m. Elia and her family live in circumstances of vulnerability and fear due to their undocumented status. Her mother brought Elia and her sister to the United States with her sister as a young child to escape domestic violence. Ray thinks the girls should be receiving counseling for posttraumatic stress.

The Context of Elia's Development

Elia was described at the beginning of the year by Ray as being "excruciatingly shy" and insecure. Ray observed on the first day of Lorenzo's teaching that students lacked self-confidence due to their status as racial/ethnic minorities: "A lot of these kids, they feel like they're minorities and they don't think ...they're not confident." When Liv asserted in the same debriefing meeting that "[The students] don't have a voice," Ray included Elia in his response referring to students experiencing extreme lack of confidence:

> I know they always have to check, even with us: "Is this OK, am I doing this right," which is a good thing but also it's more of a simple thing.... I have a couple of girls who are really insecure in there, Elia is in there and she is really insecure.

Ray attributed many of their learning difficulties and poor academic performance to lack of confidence, which Elia confirmed in her feature story titled "Extreme Presentation Anxiety." Elia had Ds and Fs in all of her classes during the first half of the fall semester. Her lack of self-confidence also seemed to contribute to what Ray called her "language barrier" and vice versa. She spoke of not understanding lectures, reading content, and instructions in class. Like Delfina, Elia described shutting down and "losing interest" in class when she was pushed off track by a teacher's "big word." Feelings of insecurity and inadequacy ensued, which led her to stop listening and trying to follow the thread of instruction.

> Sometimes like, or like subjects that I don't really understand like Biology, or those subjects Literature, History; it's not that I don't care, it's just that I'm not interested in that, like (.) Yeah, it's my interest is not in that, you know? So that's why I just give

up like really fast. It's just like: I don't understand this, I'm not going to do it, I don't care. (Elia, interview audio recording, 6/1/11)

On several occasions, including an important interview where she represented the program for fund-raising purposes, I noticed Elia appear to lose her memory of events or subject matter—such as projects she had completed in the program—when placed under pressure to "perform" her knowledge. In the spring Ray said of her, "She's like the cowardly lion, who thinks he doesn't have the courage. She always second-guesses herself even though she is usually correct."

A sophomore during the year of her participation in the program, Elia was the student who, in Transcript 2.1, responded less than enthusiastically to the introduction of the program on the first day. She was in fact quite disruptive of classroom activities during the first several weeks of the program. I attribute this to the fact that the program represented both too much change—from what she knew and expected from her ESL study skills class—and too much continuity with what she didn't like about school (see Chapter 2 discussion of Day 1). Both aspects had to do with relations of power and the lack of connection among people in school. Elia was very close to Ray (and as a result of participation in the program, to Liv) and may have felt she owed loyalty to him when the new "teachers" appeared and "usurped" his authority as the teacher. Her sarcastic, theatrical clapping during the introductions of Lyle and myself on Day 1 (Transcript 3.2) could be interpreted as a rejection of the new teachers.

At the same time, Youth Radio at first seemed to Elia to be "more of the same": "I thought it was going to be so boring and all we would do is homework," she wrote in her digital story narrative about the program at its inception. Elia found school in general to be coercive and lacking in interest. Contrasting projects in Youth Radio with work in school, she states,

> And you get excited because you're going to get to do something YOU want, you like, not *what teachers make you do*, or like "You guys have to do how this says," you know? And you don't even want to, or something you know?
>
> Cuz you didn't really see [the mentors] every day. And they didn't even like, like when they came *they weren't like telling you what to do*, or like, you know, like the teacher: "Okay, class, we're going to do this and that and everything."

As a sophomore when she began the program, she had learned the routines and expectations for ways of being an "ESL student" versus "*gueritos*" or "Americans" (i.e., white) students in the school, from whom she felt a distinct separation. As expressed by other students in the class, she felt a sense of "invisibility" when among the affluent white students, the majority social group in the school. She wrote in an essay on invisibility assigned by the teachers prior to the onset of the program:

> I think some people are invisible to others because they think they are better than others. If a person is different than other by culture or just don't have any money then they just don't talk to them or even look at them. The other people feel ignored because of that.

Elia's sister Cipriana wrote her commentary about the racial threats against Latinos scrawled in the boys' bathroom that fall: "All Mexicans will die Oct. 29." We discussed the threat and community responses to the threat in the context of a structured "public (class) critique" (similar to a studio critique in art) of Cipriana's commentary: the racial aggression was therefore present for Elia and the rest of us as part of the larger discourse on *mexicana/o* students in the school.

Elia knew how to do school at Beckwourth High, and she knew what to expect from her remedial ESL study skills class with Mr. Ramirez. However, instead of Mr. Ramirez's ESL class, she found herself in a combined ESL/Academic Support class with *three* teachers (including me) and various other mentor-instructors. The lack of continuity and the sense of uncertainty this entailed may have been difficult to navigate given the many economic, legal, and relational challenges Elia was facing outside of school.

Living undocumented in the United States means coping with fear and stress on a daily basis (Suárez-Orozco, Yoshikawa, Teranishi, & Suárez-Orozco, 2011). As Ray noted, "They all need something to where they can, to feel a little safe, right? If they're undocumented, they're all unsafe." This makes it hard to focus on learning, as Elia pointed out: "[Y]ou have to learn this or that and they can't even think about learning right now because they're having problems right now or in their household."

Elia also endeavored to create continuity across the spheres of experience of her peer group, work and educational expectations for youth in the United States. She struggled with the culture of romance (Holland, Eisenhart, & Conell, 1990) among her peers, and by her senior year in high school she had no friends left in school because, as she reports, they had all gotten pregnant and left. She did not have a boyfriend like most of her friends, because she felt that young men her age were too jealous and possessive.

Elia's most immediate, pressing concern was the depression and attempted suicide by her sister Cipriana. If death of a close relative can be felt as a major rupture during adolescence (Bagnoli, cited in Zittoun, 2006), then attempted suicide of a close sister—and continuing instability and worry related to her condition—could have similar effects. Zittoun suggests that the specter of death can trigger conscious and unconscious questions, which require emotional elaboration and meaning making. The threat of death in her family may have contributed to Elia's strong response both to dialogical relations that developed in the program—the close connection to others and sharing of self and personal stories—and projects that afforded opportunities for the elaboration of emotion and the reflection upon difficult existential questions such as the meaning of life and death.

> And the stories and the commentaries. They were about their lives, like the one I did about drowning? A lot of them talk about, like, their personal lives? The, (.) like Alicia, and Eugenia. She talked about her grandma, how like, she died or something? They were like really personal stories, you know? And they shared with the class cuz like, they had confidence (*confianza*/trust) with the whole class.

Elia's Work with Symbolic Resources

For her commentary (written after viewing my digital story) Elia composed a piece about a near-death experience. For her first digital story, she created a multimodal story about her sister Cipriana:

> Have you ever had a near death experience?
>
> Have you ever been at death's door?
>
> I have! My family took a trip to the ocean when I was a child. I was with my mom and sister in the ocean. My mom was holding all three of us together in the water. She could only touch the bottom by the tips of her toes. I could feel the ocean moving around us. All of a sudden I could see an immense wave coming towards us. It was coming so fast that I panicked and started crying. I was only 5 years old, and I felt like a little pebble in the deepest part of the ocean. I looked for my mom but I couldn't see her. I yelled but then I started sinking. I couldn't think of anything, just how scared I was. My mom got close to me and grabbed me by the hair and pulled me up to the surface. At that point I held tighter to my mom than I ever had before. Holding on to my mom I felt so safe and protected.
>
> It all happened so fast, no one else in my family had time to react. They were all sitting at on the beach. When my mom and I told everyone else what happened, they just laughed. They thought that my experience was a normal part of swimming in the ocean. Even so, I still remember this experience as a teenager.
>
> How fragile our lives are.
>
> Life and the people around us are very precious.
>
> Do we need to nearly drown before we remember how important these people are? Our loved ones and our friends are important all the time, not just after a near death

experience. You should hold on to them and tell them how much you love them every day.

For Youth Radio at Beckwourth High, this is Elia Anguiano.

In this personal narrative, Elia is able to express her appreciation for life and loved ones, while externalizing her fear of death, perhaps both for herself and her sister. This commentary could also be an expression of her identification with her sister through their shared near-death experiences. Through Jack's prompting, Elia transformed her personal story into what he called a "kind of public safety announcement." The conclusion could also be read/heard as a kind of "*consejo*," or advice, a pattern seen in youth productions in the program about the value of life and loved ones. In giving *consejos* against the backdrop of a childhood event, Elia is repositioning herself from a child to a wiser, older youth. The process of creating the commentary gave Elia the thinking and feeling space for beginning a process of self-transformation.

Elia's entrance into meaning-making processes in the program began with our public (class) viewing of my digital story about my son, according to the narration in her digital story "The Unexpected Woman":

> At the start of my sophomore year I was signed up for a study skillclass. I thought it was going to be so boring and all we would do is homework. But instead, when I walked into the class, I saw an unexpected woman who was not a teacher at the high school. Standing in front of the room. Her name was Dana Walker. She looked interesting and got my attention right away. She told us that our studies skills class was going to do a youth radio project, and even though I didn't know what she was talking about, she sounded enthusiastic. I wasn't that excited until I saw Dana's digital story about her son. I connected with her digital story because I was touched by how deeply she cared about her son. Her example made me energized to do my own digital story.

As she states in her narration, Youth Radio held no interest for her as an alternative to regular classroom practices—that is, until she saw my digital story about my son. My digital story was not presented until Week 2, so the students had already been introduced to digital story production with viewings of several examples facilitated by another instructor, Molly. It was therefore not the genre itself, or the excitement of composing multimodally, that caught Elia's attention: it was specifically my digital story, according to her narrative, that set in motion the semiotic processes that led to her transition from nonparticipation to participation in the program. Zittoun (2006) notes that cultural elements (the "object" in her semiotic prism) become meaningful for people when they touch on personal experiences and mingle with memories and embodied representing, and when they are in the presence of others. When a cultural element such as a digital story or a poem becomes a symbolic resource—that is, it becomes an instrument for psychosocial processes—it can be used to think about the past, discover alternative possibilities, or define future pathways. "When used in this way a cultural element can play a key role in the reconfiguration of a person's life narrative, and may therefore contribute to enhancing the person's agency in her own life trajectory" (Zittoun & Grossen, 2013, p. 105).

For Elia, cultural elements afforded in Youth Radio became meaningful for her when they helped her make sense of her life experience, and when her life experiences could be explored in reflective spaces, emotionally elaborated, and acknowledged by another or others in the group setting. My digital story about my son, titled "I Think He's Going to Make It," was a representation of my fear and hope for the survival of my son, who had experienced depression and various forms of self-destructive behavior. The story included a song that I sang to my son as a child (sung by me), images of him as a child and young adult, a narrative segment on the near-death of a friend who had a bicycle crash at night while riding drunk, music created by my husband with *shakuhachi* (Japanese bamboo flute), and sounds of nature. Several students and Ray told me at the end of the viewing that they had been moved by the digital story. Elia came to me with tears in her eyes to tell me how much she liked it and began to speak excitedly about doing a digital story about her father in Mexico, but said that she had no photographs of him. My digital story was viewed several times over the course of the fall semester in response to requests by students.

The digital story, I believe, provided an experience that "echoed" or "mirrored" an emotional or embodied experience for Elia, or even perhaps facilitated a more complex experience, such as lending imagery or content to help her verbalize something that was previously unformulated (Zittoun, 2006). In the following excerpt Elia presents her interpretation of my digital story and its personal sense for her:

Transcript 4.5

1	Dana:	Is there anything you read, viewed, or listened to in class that
2		affected you in any way? Is there anything you saw or heard in
3		class that affected you in any way?
4	Elia:	Your story.
5	Dana:	My story? About my son?
6	Elia:	Yeah, it was really like, wow. It left me speechless [laughs]. It
7		was really cute.
8	Dana:	So, what was it that affected you?
9	Elia:	About the story?

10	Dana:	Um-huh.
11	Elia:	Well, for someone that's like already in a gang and ever
12		thing, it's like really hard to change for them, and like in
13		drugs or anything. So it's like pretty much your hopes are
14		down for them you know like you're just thinking like you
15		lost your son and everything and then how like time passes
16		and then it everything changed and everything. It's like a mir-
17		acle like how he changed like that. Cuz no one could like (.)
18		It's not easy to stop doing that and like become like a good
19		person or something like you know? So that's why I like, I was
20		really thrilled with that story. Cuz it was like really sad and, I
21		don't know, it was happy how he, I liked how he changed and
22		everything. It's like you couldn't believe that you know. It's
23		like hard to believe. That's why I was like amazed with that
24		story?
25	Dana:	That's nice.

Elia's narratives from her exit interview and her digital story "The Unexpected Woman" position me (*the other*) as the catalyst for her appropriation of the digital story and its transformation into a *symbolic resource* for mediating identity processes (new identities as a student and creative person, a person who is able to speak in public and with strangers); knowledge and skill development (new interest in computers, poetry, and creating movies); and making new connections between life and learning in school. I believe, however, that the process was actually the reverse: the object (my digital story) mediated the person–other (Elia–myself) relationship. Or perhaps the digital story *was* me, a symbolic representation of someone who had suddenly become significant for her. Over time our relationship mediated her relationship to Youth Radio curricular objects (the person-object relationship) such as the commentary and feature story, which allowed her to appropriate these objects for her own personal meaning-making. As Zittoun and Grossen (2013) write,

> Research has suggested that . . . the function of this other person is to give legitimacy to the "personal sense" that the cultural element has for the person herself. Thus, personal sense can be seen as the dynamic outcome of significant relationships with others. Put differently, the transformation of a cultural element into both an object of transaction and a transactional object creates shared meanings that are a first step toward the construction of personal sense. (p. 9)

Extending out further across time, our relationship and the person-object relationship (Elia–digital story) associated with me continued to play an important role in Elia's conduct on two fronts. First, it facilitated the development of another *person-other* relationship with the poet Tim Hernandez that mediated Elia's relationship with poetry and the personal sense she made of a poet's way of seeing the world: "Timmy showed us, you know, like to put more meanings to things you see in life." In her exit interview, poetry and Tim were the most salient elements mediating meaning-making for her over the year. Second, it could be said that Tim and I (the specific *others*) became "internalized" or abstract/imaginary others that mediated the furtherance of *person-object* relationships and meaning-making that reverberated in her school, home, social life, and future orientations. She began to demonstrate greater agency, to trust her thinking abilities and her voice, and to reposition herself as a capable student and person. Zittoun (2006) writes,

> Thinking is a fragile mechanism that requires complex and good-enough conditions to occur. The most favorable situations for development are of a social and interactive nature. The emotional, embodied meanings the child attributes to a given situation, marked by these relationships, are deeply connected with the development of new relationships, are deeply connected with the development of new understandings, the construction of new skills and new identity definitions. (p. 21)

At the end of the year, Elia recounts that she had begun to try harder in her other classes and was not giving up so easily. She said that she had an easier time doing oral presentations in other classes. And though it is impossible to attribute causal effects to her participation in the program, Elia stated during the year that she did not see herself attending college and never checked her GPA; in 2013, she graduated from high school, obtained a scholarship, and will be attending a community college.

As stated earlier, I believe that it was the digital story about my son that first opened the door for her, that encouraged her to engage her emotions and creativity, to trust others and share herself, and to allow others to mediate her relationship to cultural resources afforded in the program and school. As Elia and the other students began to create and share their digital stories in the group, these in turn became resources for the development of more distributed social relationships and understandings, lending to a broadening sense of community and intercultural understanding.

In her digital story about her sister, which she did not complete because it was not good enough in her estimation, Elia used the digital story as a thinking and feeling space (Zittoun, 2006) through distanciation that allowed for the naming of, and giving aesthetic expression to, her deep feelings for her sister. The story shows pictures of the sisters together, of Cipriana in many settings, while the narrative speaks to her extraordinary beauty, wisdom, and compassion and tells how important her sister is to her. It is interesting to note that Elia chose not to use this digital story as her final submission. Nevertheless, the digital story was a creative space that allowed for the elaboration of her emotions in a multimodal composition (including images, music, voice-over, and written text) that would later, in the exit interviews, be linked semiotically to her concept of voice and its importance for individual and interpersonal use. Her use of her "voice" as a symbolic resource mediated a link to personal sense and identity work of another individual, in addition to the shared meanings already developed by Elia in relationship with others, such as Federico, in the program. This connection adds yet another dimension of the social, that of intersubjectivity.

Developing continuity across spheres of experience. How does this process work? When adolescents, who already engage in a plurality of spheres of experience, are faced with rupture or critical moments in their lives that threaten their sense of who they are, they may seek to create a sense of continuity across these spheres and to establish a coherent system of values and actions. This is a particularly daunting task for adolescents who experience daily microaggressions of racism and culture clash between their home communities and the dominant social-class group of school, where cultural elements (such as a history textbook that leaves out their histories) and segregating spatial arrangements may be experienced as "symbolic violence" toward their personal and social identities (Zittoun & Grossen, 2013). Immigrant youth located (by schools) at the intersection of multiple worlds and ideological systems such as language and gender may find learning contexts that allow explorations of identity and elaboration of emotion of greater interest than test-driven school subjects that leave no time for these considerations.

In her exit interview, Elia demonstrated unusual self-awareness about aspects of school that promoted her engagement in learning processes and those that inhibited her learning. At the end of her sophomore year when the interview was conducted, the determining factor in her learning was *interest* in a topic. Interest in turn depended on two subfactors, both related to power, agency, and identity: being positioned in the classroom by the teacher as having the agency to select topics of inquiry, and to bring her understandings from her life experience to bear on new learning in school. It seems that she had lost interest in school from spending too many years subjected to what Freire (1970/2000) called "banking education," "being *talked at* all day long," as Ray said, being forced to do academic work that seemed irrelevant to her, in conditions that were often alienating: no connection to others, sitting in the classroom and never speaking, never expressing her opinions, as Sonia stated in her exit interview:

> In other classes we have to be most of the time quiet and just take notes. Notes, notes, notes. We never get to express ourselves or make comments because in other classes we just have to take notes and just sit there.

Ray confirmed this perception on several occasions. In a staff debriefing he explains,

> I don't want to offend anybody, but if all day long they've been sitting and listening to someone talk all the time. (Ray, staff debriefing, 4/13/11)

And in a personal reflection he noted, referring to a class with Federico:

> They're accountable to use the things they're learning, and to follow through and apply it to their lives, and . . . many teachers have them fill out homework and do work that doesn't apply to them.

Elia's digital story narration and her exit interview both reveal that curricular elements and "school work" became interesting to her when they involved relationships with significant others or cultural elements that allowed her to make connections to life and elaborate troubling emotions and difficult existential questions.

Transcript 4.6
```
1  Dana:  So what percentage of your classes are meaningful to your life?
2  Elia:  None...I think you guys do it to make us have fun and to make
3         like kids, I don't know like, to understand some other things
4         too, to learn some new things...just having classes like to study
5         or do tests on.
```

Table 4.1 presents a schematic analysis of Elia's representations of her experience in Youth Radio and Radio Arts in contrast to school with a focus on the theme of making connections between life and school, and being able to pursue topics of interest in school work.

Table 4.1 Contrasts in Elia's Perceptions of Her Experience in Youth Radio versus Other Classes

Youth Radio and Radio Arts	Other Classes
Elia: It wasn't just about that class, "Oh do this and that." It was like getting to know people, not just as students getting to know their personal lives, not just as students, but like how we are outside of school too. It was really easy	. . . just about that class 'oh do this and that' It was like getting to know people, not just as students getting to know their personal lives

• CONSTRUCTING PERSONAL VOICE •

for us to tell you about our lives. It was really to fix stuff, you know? It was easy to go into deep stuff because with some of my teachers I would never say anything about my personal life.	. . . with some of my teachers I would never say anything about my personal life.
Elia: It depends on what I'm interested in you know? Like in that radio class. You know I like the digital story: so I'm like really into it, try my best. Like I have problems sometimes but I keep trying. I want to get to the point that I finished and say, "Oh yeah! I'm finished!" and I'm really proud of my work.	Sometimes, like subjects that I don't really understand, like Biology, or those subjects Literature, History. It's not that I don't care, it's just that I'm not interested in that, like (..) Yeah, it's (.) my interest is not in that, you know? So that's why I just give up like really fast. It's just like: I don't understand this, I'm not going to do it, I don't care.
Dana: And what makes you interested in something? Like with the digital stories? **Elia:** Well you could do a story and like show it to other people, like a story about every which subject you want, like about your family about anything you want and like you get to choose and then you're like: "What am I gonna do the story about?" or like, "What's gonna be the music? And you just keep thinking about it. And you get excited because you're going to get to do something you want, you like, not what teachers make you do, or like "you guys have to do how this says" you know?" And you don't even want to, or something you know? So it's something that you want to do and however you want to do it. And so it's like pretty much yeah. That's why I like it. It's like *it's our choice* to do it, like anything we want.	. . . not what teachers make you do, or like "you guys have to do how this says" you know? And you don't even want to, or something you know?

Though school does not seem to offer much of interest to Elia, she nevertheless values academic-related knowledge and skills gained in Youth Radio and Radio Arts. This is true in spite of the fact that much of work in the program—writing and editing drafts, reading and evaluating sources, being assessed and graded—was perceived by some students as "too much like school."

Knowledge and Skills Acquisition

Language development. Language development was an area of knowledge and skill acquisition processes that was explicitly targeted in the exit interview protocol. Elia's response to my question regarding how Youth Radio and Radio Arts might have supported her second language development focused on the rehearsal and practice required for achieving fluency in narrated text in recordings for radio pieces and digital story narratives, as shown in Transcript 4.7.

Transcript 4.7

1	Dana:	So one of the reasons we developed this
2		program was to help, um, students
3		learning English develop their language.
4	Elia:	Hm hmm
5	Dana:	In what ways has youth radio helped
6		you develop your language skills?
7	Elia:	Language skills [*said reflectively*]
8	Dana:	And it could be English or bilingual,
9		because we spoke English and Spanish=
10	Elia:	=yeah=
11	Dana:	=in the class=
12	Elia:	And did my English kind of improve?
13	Dana:	Do you think it did?
14	Elia:	Um, a little.
15	Dana:	In what ways did it help you develop
16		your language skills?
17	Elia:	Well by (.) talking a lot, you know? Like
18		recording your voice, you practice and
19		practice and read like three times, or
20		many times the things that you were
21		gunna say?
22	Dana:	Hm hmm
23	Elia:	The (..) narration? Or whatever you say?

24	Dana:	Uh huh.
25	Elia:	So that way you practice a lot? How to
26		like, say it right and everything?
27	Dana:	Uh huh.
28	Elia:	And then you record it. You're like try-
29		ing your best to like, record it right so
30		people can like, understand? And that's
31		like a way that my English kind of im-
32		proved.
33	Dana:	Uh huh. You did, I think of almost any-
34		body in the class, you practiced the
35		most.
36	Elia:	Yeah?=
37	Dana:	=cause I found like ten recordings of
38		Elia's [*laughs*]=
39	Elia:	=Oh! [*laughs*]=
40	Dana:	=[laughs]= (..) But that's good! That's
41		really good, cuz it does help, cuz like uh
42		(..) I used to play the flute? (..) And
43		when you, to become really good, you
44		have to practice=
45	Elia:	=a lot=
46	Dana:	=everyday=
47	Elia:	=yeah=
48	Dana:	=do the same thing over and over=
49	Elia:	=over again=
50	Dana:	=it kind of seems boring, but it feels
51		good
52	Elia:	Like once you have it done, you feel
53		good about it.
54	Dana:	Yeah.
55	Elia:	By yourself and everything, cuz like the
56		first (.) recording I did was really (.)
57		BAD, and I couldn't really understand
58		myself.
59	Dana:	Uh huh.
60	Elia:	But the second got kind of better and
61		then the third was better and the
62		fourth, maybe it was *la vencida*, you	The charm.
63		know? It was (.) *la buena!* [*laughs out loud*]	The good one.

64	Dana:	Uh huh. So what does that mean, "*la*	
65		*vencida*"?	
66	Elia:	Like *la*, like *ya bien asi*, like, you know,	It's finally correct.
67		have you heard that *dicho en español?*	Saying in Spanish?
68		Like, *la tercera es la vencida?*	The third one's the
69	Dana:	Ha no!=	charm?
70	Elia:	=No?!=	
71	Dana:	=I don't get it	
72	Elia:	It's like, the third one, *Ya va a ser*, like	The third one is going
73		the good one, the best, yeah	to be the good one.
74	Dana:	Oh, okay great. Well, thank you for (..)	
75		telling me that (.) I didn't know that *di*	Saying the third one
76		*cho la tercera es la=*	is going to be the
77	Elia:	=*vencida*=	charm
78	Dana:	=like the winner?	
79	Elia:	Uh huh.	

Elia viewed YRRA as providing important opportunities for her to develop her English. In Transcript 4.7, Elia emphasizes the importance for developing her English fluency through *practice*, in preparing to record her spoken texts for a radio and digital story audiences. In recording her narration the first time she perceived her narration as "bad...I couldn't really understand myself." By the third or fourth (or 10th, according to the number of attempts I have on file) recording, she felt she had developed enough fluency and confidence in her reading and speaking to do a final recording. Elia's remarks recall findings from Heath (2004) who found striking advances in language development among second language learners engaged in community arts organizations: "Writers and dancers, like all artists, segment into bits and pieces components of the coming whole. They think into a future that is bodily and mentally engaged in casting forward in time, and they practice, practice, practice to build habits mental and physical" (p. 339).

The greater language fluency Elia developed may have contributed to reducing what she called "extreme presentation anxiety" in her coauthored feature story on the topic. She reported being able to speak with confidence in the class, partly because she trusted the members of the group but also because she felt confident in her speaking: "It was really easy for me to talk in front of that class you know how like, sure, *segura* I was *de mi misma*. I didn't have low self-esteem, I felt confident about myself." She felt this was a new competency that she could apply in other classes.

Communication technologies. Other knowledge-skills acquired that Elia saw as applicable in other classes or life included technology skills: she considered herself an expert in the audio editing application Audacity—thanks in large part to the one-on-one mentoring she received from Lyle, the KPFW volunteer and occasional news director. In fact, Elia was asked to do a presentation for the other students on how to use Audacity, which she conducted in the Mac Lab. Like Tania who appreciated "getting rid of the mumble" for the real thing (her real thoughts), Elia felt empowered being able to delete parts of her speech: Working with Lyle in the Mac Lab in October when she was first learning Audacity she exclaimed, "This is cool" when he was showing her how to use the application to delete sections of talk she "didn't like." She also said that she would like to continue to learn more about iMovie.

Given that she did not have access to computers at home and therefore was not able to practice and play around with new digital technologies in her leisure time, Elia showed great persistence and resilience, as well as self-advocacy and skill in drawing on the social resources made available in the program. She came to the after-school component of Youth Radio every week during the spring to work with Milly, myself, and student volunteers from a local university. She was frustrated often, losing or erasing files, or the software or recording equipment did not work. One of the difficulties working with digital files is that they need to be carefully named, organized, and managed. Elia and her sister had great challenges in this area, losing their work time after time. In fact, during the final showcase of student productions for a general audience including community members, Elia's digital story "Unexpected Woman" was not viewed because the voice narration could barely be heard. But she did not complain, pout, or express frustration. She carried through with her responsibilities as presenter and member of her group with grace and presence. This, I believe, is testament to her great resiliency and sense of hope, which helped get her through high school—in spite of numerous obstacles—and into college.

Writing. Though Elia did not talk about the development of her expository and narrative writing in her exit interview, Liv noted a significant change in Elia's identity as a writer from the year before. Elia was able to write: she would say her ideas, and then write them. As a freshman she would always say, "Tell me what to write, Miss." This is also significant in terms of identity processes, in her relocation from a dependent nonwriter without agency, to a writer who composed "powerful" stories, in her words, about topics of abiding concern to her. Ray noted in November a sense of excitement and pride in Elia's completion of the full cycle of production, a commentary:

> The kids did a great job on their commentaries, recording them. I think they really, um, when they read them into the recorder, that they were very proud of them and

felt ownership over them. Especially Elia. When she was sharing it with me the excitement she had about it (inaudible), so that's a really important. A crucial part of learning is if you find it's not work, if it's something you love. And so right now a lot of them, they view school as work-and hard. But if they can find things that make them love it, then, work turns to something they enjoy and it seems like maybe they're are enjoying seeing that the process, the writing process, is worth it as they come to the finished product.

More generally, Ray believed that students were truly *learning* because they felt this same sense of ownership in their work, which was no longer a chore but rather something they enjoyed doing because they could see all their hard work coming to fruition in the final product that would be heard, possibly (if it achieved "broadcast quality"), by radio and Internet audiences across the world (like most radio stations today, KPFW has an Internet presence and frequent call-ins from listeners in other countries).

Despite her debilitating shyness and lack of self-confidence, Elia capitalized on the social resources made available in the program. She asked for help from all mentors, male and female, as when Jack the journalist was helping her consolidate an idea for her feature story.

Transcript 4.8

1	Jack:	Okay, Elia, do you have any ideas?
2	Elia:	No, I don't. I think you should help me think of something.
3	Jack:	Okay, let's see. Let's go around the room. Eugenia, what do you got working on?
4	Eugenia:	[inaudible]
5	Jack:	What?
6	Eugenia:	I don't know yet.
7	Jack:	[*To Elia*] Something related to school.
8	Elia:	Give us some examples.
9	Jack:	All right, obviously I'm gunna see if there are any existing ideas.

Elia came after school every week during the spring and stayed until 5:00 p.m. She asked questions and, as can be seen in transcripts of her interactions, asked clarification of English she did not understand, and often repeated phrases that she either did not understand or that she wanted to learn the meaning of and memorize through reiteration (this was a strategy used by Delfina as well).

Identity Processes

In her feature story titled "Presentation Anxiety," Elia confronted head-on her anxiety about public speaking. She interviewed students and staff members in the school, did background research on the topic, and pushed through difficult pronunciation in the introduction in which she talks about her own struggles:

> Like many people throughout the world
> I have extreme presentation anxiety.
> The last time I did a presentation in my world history class
>
> I felt like my heart was going to burst out of my chest.
>
> My heart beat was so powerful, I could barely keep my body from shaking
> And instead of thinking about the presentation
> I was focused on how nervous I was.
> As a second language student,
> My stress over presenting in front of a group
> is exacerbated by the fact that I am also struggling to express my thoughts
> in an unfamiliar language.
>
> Presentation anxiety is a response to fear
> That causes us to blush, shake, stutter, sweat
> And be tongue tied...
> (*continues into background information and interviews for feature story*)

In this feature story, Elia finds ways to reposition herself from someone incapable and humiliated by speaking in public, to someone who could interview other people and speak in an informed and articulate way about her difficulty. Though she represents herself in the feature story as someone who still suffers from public speaking, in doing so, in the act of re-presentation and enactment of her problem, she transforms herself. Through her feature story, Elia makes herself understood: she communicates. Through this externalization she translates into a semiotic form what occurs within her in social situations in which she is expected to speak publicly. She is also able to translate into action the transformation from a person who cannot speak publicly to someone who can: She reports that she has more facility with public speaking in her other classes toward the end of the year.

This is an example of a young person's use of a symbolic resource to relocate herself symbolically in relation to a given position, which calls for a redefinition of the status attributed by others: "if a 'bad' student is seen by his or her teacher reading a 'good' book, he or she may be symbolically legitimized and relocated" (Zittoun, Duveen, Gillespie, Ivinson, & Psaltis, 2003, p. 8).

In this we see the identity and object-relation processes that Zittoun (2006) calls "acknowledgment." Acknowledgment involves in the *person-other-personal sense* axis and requires two forms of acknowledgment: recognition by others of the legitimacy of the person's new actions or thought "work" and acknowledgment by oneself. Elia received recognition from instructors and other students in the class during the public critique of her piece for her accomplishment both in addressing the psychosomatic problem she has with public speaking and in producing a high-quality feature story of broad interest. She was acknowledged as having achieved a degree of control over the genre conventions of the feature story, projecting an authorial voice appropriate to the genre and establishing a position of authority on the topic through background research and multiple perspectives.

In her exit interview, Elia presents other facets of identity repositioning, which—through joint activity—she accomplished during the year. Elia discusses the opinion teachers have of her as a "lazy student." She agrees that she can be lazy but asserts that she is someone who works hard if she cares about what she's doing, and she reports that she has been trying harder in her other classes than she used to. She also resists the positioning by teachers who say she is someone who gives up too easily. Elia explains that her difficulties have to do with language, not a lack of desire to learn and produce: "Like in some classes I just don't understand, and then I give up because I think I can't do it."

The Significance of Personal Sense Making

In undertaking this study, I was particularly interested in the question of how educators can make learning meaningful and promote youth development to combat long-term trends of alienation, nonparticipation, and academic underachievement. Developmental psychologists such as Zittoun (2006) have shown that for learning to take place and new learner identities to emerge, people must elaborate personal meaning and emotional responses to new situations: meaning making is central to learning and development. When a person is not able to make sense of a task one is required to do or the situation one finds oneself in, one's thinking abilities can be inhibited: "Learning difficulties can often be analyzed in terms of the task lacking sense or of conflicting identities" (p. 167). Sociocultural psychology studies the dynamics of meaning-making in which groups and individuals engage as part of larger processes of human development. Sociocultural theorists of learning similarly focus on the individual-collective processes of meaning making. Wenger (1998), for example, argues that identities of long-term nonparticipation, such as academic disengagement, develop when individuals feel powerless to negotiate meanings within communities to which they belong.

Making personal sense, the fourth element in Zittoun's (2006) semiotic prism, involves making sense of socially shared meanings and what is happening in one's life. People do this through semiotic work involving cultural elements (*objects*) and people (*others*). In this closing section about Elia's coming to voice and personal sense making in the program, I focus on sense making that involved the mediation of an important other in her thinking and feeling processes. Vygotsky (1978) wrote that the emotional meanings that the child attributes to a given situation are marked by relationships with important others. Building on Vygotsky, Zittoun (2006) argues that these early, embodied meanings become deeply connected with the development of new relationships, the development of new understandings, and the construction of new skills and new identity definitions. Elia's case in many ways confirms these theoretical insights as applied to the symbolic work engaged by adolescents through cultural elements mediated by significant others, as I discuss in this closing section.

Tim and Elia's Personal Sense Making

Tim—or "Timmy" as she called him—was a central person in Elia's narrative about her sense-making experience in the program. Tim was a writer in residence in YRRA, funded by a state agency supporting the humanities. He had already received the American Book Award for his first published book of poetry, and he received the Premio Aztlan Prize in Fiction for his first novel, *Breathing, in Dust*, while in residence in the program. The son of migrant farmworkers from the Central Valley of California, Tim connected immediately with the students who asked him about his tattoos, his family, his birthplace. He told them the story of how poetry saved his life, helping him channel his anger over the death of his uncle who lived with his family at the time.

Tim made identities available to the youth that they did not find in their other classes: young, Latino, from a working-class background, successful, artistic, creative, and not afraid of being so. Tim also embodied an important component of the learning design, which was to provide opportunities for students to develop a personal, expressive voice through creative writing and performance. Based on my experience codirecting an after-school poetry and arts program, I have found that Latino/a students learning English responded favorably to poets and to writing poetry, perhaps due to the oral traditions and the important role of the public poet in Mexican society. I found in previous studies that many boys and male youth, as well as girls and female youth (which would be more expected), responded with enthusiasm to opportunities for self-expression—especially about love and personal struggles—through poetry.

At the end of the six-week Friday workshops, Tim published a professional-looking "chapbook," the cover designed by him (he is a visual artist as well), with individual and collective poems by the students. In addition, he signed a personal copy of his award-winning novel *Breathing, in Dust* for each student at the end of our final showcase in May 2010. Elia did not mention either artifact, though her poem appeared in the chapbook. What she did mention was the change brought about in her way of thinking or seeing, due to Tim's presence in the program, as demonstrated in the following series of responses from her exit interview.

Transcript 4.9

1	Dana:	Was there a speaker, a book, a digital story, a radio story that
2		changed your way of seeing things?
3	Elia:	Timmy. Yeah. He sees things, like, in a different way. I like how
4		he expresses himself and how he like tells us to look at things
5		in a different way or like in a really unique way like I don't real-
6		ly know how to explain it, you know? Like about our names,
7		umm, the poems that we were going to do about our names.
8		Like: "Think about your names, think about what it means,
9		think about how it sounds," or you know, like (.) I've never
10		thought about that, or like I never would've thought about
11		that, you know? And so he said that I was like, "Oh, I really, my
12		name? I don't really know what my name sounds like to me or
13		what's the meaning of my name." So, I never really thought
14		about that until he said that. And I think it's going to be inter-
15		esting to do that poem—call my name.
16	Dana:	Do you think that what you've learned in youth radio can be
17		used in everyday life? Can you think of an example?
18	Elia:	Well, yeah, I think, to try and like (.) just try, to look at things
19		in a different way (..) How do I tell you this? Like how Timmy
20		showed us, you know, like to put more meanings to things you
21		see in life.
22	Dana:	Do you think it helped to have mentors who are professionals
23		in journalism, radio, poetry, theater? In what way?

24	Elia:	They weren't your own teachers. And they were just new peo-
25		ple and everything and how they were and what they do, and
26		they come and teach you what they know and everything so
27		you, it's interesting and you learn from them. See like Timmy.
28		He came and he taught us that, and like I didn't even know
29		that. I didn't even really pay attention to my life until, or pay
30		attention to the things that surrounded me, you know?

In these excerpts, Elia clearly highlights how Tim mediated her thinking, feeling, and creative processes, helping her arrive at new understandings. Given the manner in which this mediation is presented, we might consider them life transforming as a critical moment in the life course of this young person. Tim showed her how to pay attention to her life and to "put more meanings to the things you see in life." Given Elia's close experiences with death, and the possibility of her sister taking her own life, one might contrast this new sense of meaning with the *meaninglessness* of life represented by her sister's attempted suicide.

Elia also signals the importance of Tim's forms of expression and creativity. His teaching seemed to open new doors for her, perhaps to her own creativity, to trying out new ways of seeing, speaking, and being, which is the purview of the artist alone. In this way Tim also mediates identity processes: the "construction and mobilization of representation of oneself in the past, and of possible selves in a future at a given socio-cultural location" (Erikson, cited in Zittoun, 2004). This is accomplished in part through a poetry exercise that focuses on one's name, its meaning and sonic qualities. There is a sense, in Elia's words, of an augmented sense of agency and power in the world.

Art, mediated by the poet, may have been the key that opened the door to new worlds for Elia, new understandings, new ways of seeing, and new imagined communities in which to participate. As Moran (2010), building on Vygotsky, writes,

> Art is important for individuals to connect with their communities. It is a mediator and organizer of the interaction between the individual and the social, between one person and her community. Art provides, "the social technique of emotion, a tool of society which brings the most intimate and personal aspects of our being into the circle of social life." (p. 249)

I believe that Tim, as artist, did this for Elia, bringing "the most intimate and personal aspects of our being into the circle of social life." Elia linked her developing sense of personal voice to the Youth Radio and Radio Arts community and trust; she linked her new understandings and ways of seeing the world, and possibilities for expression, to Tim, his poetry, and life teachings.

Due to a confluence of factors, no doubt, Elia changed significantly over the year and subsequent years as I followed her development through high school and into her summer before college, the time of completing this book. From a sardonic, disruptive observer, Elia became an enthusiastic participant whose externalizations caused change in the program itself. It was due to Elia's stated desire to have more time working on her digital story, another tool for artistic expression "which brings the most intimate and personal aspects of our being into the circle of social life," that we created the after-school component of the program. In my field note I wrote,

> We are trying to get two periods next semester, with the help of [the assistant principal]. Not enough time to get into and complete work. Elia asked for time during 8th period to work on digital story. Principal was open to the idea, though it is complicated. (Field notes, 11/10/10)

She came every week to the after-school sessions. The content and quality of her work influenced her peers and contributed to changing the culture of the group. As Holland, Skinner, and Valsiner (2001) write, "individuals may introduce novelty in their externalizations in ways that can potentially transform meanings and practices at a cultural level" (p. 33).

Elia may have been one of the students who most deeply felt the rupture created by Youth Radio, due to her close relation with her teacher Ray and the stability she required in school to offset the instability in her life, at that moment, at home. However, she went on to develop significant relations with other adults in the program such as her teacher Liv, myself, Milly my research assistant, and Tim. She was able to advocate for herself and seek the help she needed from the radio mentors. Through the mediation of others and her use of symbolic resources, Elia engaged in meaning-making processes that contributed to greater continuity in self and sense of personal voice: the ability to advocate for herself, to successfully communicate her understandings, and to connect and share herself with others.

Evidence of Elia's development did not end with her participation in the program. Zittoun (2010) argues that "development" is a normative concept that implies preferences for the direction of change: "development is a qualitative change that opens new ranges of possible conduct, that is, it is *generative* for further transitions" (p. 175).

Elia's development in the program appears to have opened possibilities for further change. She became a mentor in an after-school poetry program for emergent bilingual children that Tim taught the following year. From expressing no interest in arts or elective classes, Elia went on to take an art class and a film class in high school. And finally, she graduated from high school and will go to college. She and I remain good and trusting friends, *de mucha confianza*.

• CHAPTER FIVE •

Tania's Story: Constructing a Public Voice

If you don't tell people about it, how are they gunna' know and do something to change it?

—Tania

In this chapter, I explore a dimension of powerful communication related to the development of a "public voice," articulated by youth in the following terms: the importance of speaking out in public forums (such as the radio) on issues of concern to youth and their communities; representing and defending community values and cultural practices; speaking out and advocating for others; and expressing a sense of social responsibility toward younger teens and children. Using reconstructive narrative analysis of interviews with Tania (Zittoun, 2006), together with content and discourse analyses of her multimodal productions (Ivanič, 1998), I explore how cultural elements and important others mediated forms of personal and collective development that were marked as significant by Tania and other students.

Through the analysis of Tania's case, I discovered a related but new direction in developmental processes described by Zittoun (Zittoun & Grossen, 2010) and colleagues. I found that youth productions themselves—not only the cultural elements introduced and taught by adults—became symbolic resources for others. Yoli, for example, describes her collaborations with Tania as having generated new understandings: "Our feature story and digital story made me realize more what's there, not actually what it seems." The girls' work in turn became symbolic resources for others. As one student noted, the girls' digital story "changed their way of seeing things." Realizing the impact their work was having on classmates, the girls began to view their multimedia productions as tools for effecting change among youth and their communities outside of school. They would use their feature story to inform teens about sex, and younger children, adults, and the general public about the unsafe environment that exists in the Esperanza housing project for young children. I describe how participants transform cultural elements into symbolic resources through semiosis and artistic production. When these objects are put into circulation within and beyond the program, they become cultural elements that are taken up by other youth, who in turn use them for processes of creative transformation. The articulated (linked) semiotic prisms multiply in a rhizomatic fashion, linking individuals in an expanding web of transformed meanings and potential action, represented in Figure 5.1.

Tania's Trajectory in the Program

Tania began the year composing commentary and digital story about her life history. The topic of her commentary, "Every Teen Needs a Second Home," addressed the problem of violence in her own family and her felt need to have a second home when she feels unsafe. Her first digital story, composed in the fall, expressed the sense of loss she felt for her home of origin in Juárez, Mexico, to which she could no longer return due to drug cartel violence. During the second semester, when the YRRA assignments were framed within thematic units having to do with "Our School Community" (feature story) and "Our Neighborhood Communities," Tania turned her attention to the analysis of key issues in youth development: teen sex and the dangers facing girls as they transition from childhood to adolescence. In both her media productions and her interviews with me, Tania stakes a claim to an identity as an older, wiser teen or young adult giving *consejos*, or advice, to children and younger teens. These identity shifts, I will argue, reflect a dialogical process that allowed her to express (and be acknowledged by others for) core values that are consonant with her home community, creating continuity among spheres of experience among home and YRRA and, by association, school. The rest of the chapter is devoted to analyzing the semiotic processes engaged in by Tania with others in the program.

Introducing Tania

Tania is a tall, graceful, stylish, athletic young woman with an often unexpectedly glum and aloof aspect: many photos of her show her with a depressed expression, looking at the ends of her hair, her nails, or looking at others from under her eyebrows with an expression that might indicate, "stay away from me—I'm not in the mood." During the year of this study she had Ds and Fs in all of her classes. In her second semester, she dropped volleyball in favor of cheerleading. Born in Juárez, Mexico, she had been transitioned out of ESL services but was receiving extra academic support due to her failing grades. Given that she did not publically speak Spanish once during the yearlong program, I wondered whether she had been prematurely cut off from literacy and language development in her home language as a child. Tania lived in a federally subsidized housing project known for gang activity, and at the beginning of the year it was reported that she had been temporarily placed in a foster home due to problems at home.

Mirroring her larger struggles in school and at home, Tania had difficulty in the program, initially. She was viewed by staff and teachers as displaying disruptive behavior, and during the first semester she did not manage to complete her digital story about Juárez, a major class assignment that constituted 50% of her final grade. The first semester she did not attend any of the "extracurricular" activities offered as part of the Youth Radio and Radio Arts program (work sessions at the radio station, field trips to the theater), and as a consequence she did not receive a certificate of completion. Neither did she go on field trips to the radio station, theater, or the vox pops outing, but she did participate regularly in the after-school component of YRRA. In spite of this, she came to be viewed over time as an outstanding member in the program, someone whose creative work with a message of social change had a profound effect on other students. She was the only student to have two productions aired on the radio, and her digital story about her neighborhood, coauthored with Yoli, became a signature piece for public presentations of youth productions.

Tracing Tania's Appropriations of the Concept of Voice

The first transcription selected for analysis of Tania's case presents her response to a question about whether students make use of cultural elements from school/program in their everyday lives: "Do you think what you've learned in Youth Radio is connected to everyday life?" This question directly precedes the question and response discussed in Chapter 2, which queries students' understandings of the purpose of YRRA by asking, "In your opinion what is the goal of Youth Radio in school? What do your teachers hope you'll learn?" The content of Tania's responses to these two questions is addressed in the following analysis.

Transcript 5.1

1 Dana: Do you think what you've learned in Youth Radio is con-
2   nected to everyday life?
3 Tania: In some ways, just because you know Youth Radio has (..) the
4   power to make you (.) the power to make you—I don't know
5   how to say it—to share your perspective, you know, just like it
6   can help you let out your voice, and communicate with oth-
7   ers, and show people where you live, how you live, you know,
8   it can definitely shows people how, what you're made of.
9 Dana: Um, so In your opinion what is the goal of youth radio in
10   school? What do your teachers hope you'll learn?
11 Tania: Technology for one, just like basically how to use it and then
12   umm developing your voice because at first people are shy.
13   And then the radio drama as well you know people are very
14   shy but like when Federico came in he definitely got like our
15   spirits out and now everyone is like friends with everyone and
16   everybody talks with everyone when before it was just I don't
17   know you so let's keep it that way so . . .
18 Dana: So you mean like they talked in this class with each other?
19 Tania: Right.

This excerpt shows that Tania was able to articulate the personal sense she had made of the purposes of Youth Radio, which align with, but go beyond, the original purposes of the learning design. Her responses also reflect the thematic analysis of all student responses presented in Chapter 4:

(a) To help youth develop the capacity to share their perspectives (lines 6-8) (the program mission states, "To help youth represent themselves and their communities and not be misrepresented in the media");
(b) To develop expertise with communication technologies (line 11);
(c) To develop the capacity to speak out ("let out your voice") (line 6);
(d) To build the curriculum around student lives, interests, and concerns (lines 5-8);
(e) To create opportunities for identity work and performances of selves—"[S]how people where you live, how you live, you know, it can definitely shows people how, what you're made of" (lines 5-8); and
(f) To be able to communicate with others within dialogical relations: "[T]o communicate with each other" (lines 5-8, 11-17).

What I learned from Tania that was not anticipated in the program design was that to participate in the public media sphere, students needed to develop both a "public voice" and "personal voice." Chapter 4 analyzes Elia's processes of crafting a personal voice through the development of community, the appropriation of social and cultural resources made available in the program, and the construction of personal sense of socially shared meanings. In this chapter, I analyze Tania's trajectory in the program to show how the construction of personal voice evolved into an understanding of the need for developing a "public voice" as well, for participation in the larger community and public media sphere. In particular, I describe how youth productions become symbolic resources for transformation on several levels: for transformation of self; as tools for transformation taken up by other youth within and beyond the program; and transformation of the public discourse by raising awareness in the media sphere about issues of concern to immigrant youth.

Tania's Work with Cultural Elements

Tania's productions and participation in the program were inconsistent, though as mentioned, they were remarkable overall. Like Elia, Tania failed to complete a major project early on, the first digital story. However, Tania went on to gain a stellar reputation in the program and, as mentioned, was the only student to have more than one piece aired on the radio.

Table 5.1 Contrastive analysis of Tania's productions and participation in program events over the year

	Aired in Class		Aired on the radio		Aired in final public showcase		Published in chapbook		Attended one or more field trip		Work used in future years as model	
	Y	N	Y	N	Y	N	Y	N	Y	N	Y	N
Commentary: "Every Teen Deserves a Second Home"	x		x		x		~		~			x
Digital Story: "Juárez, the Home I Can't Go Home To"		x			x		~		~			x
Feature Story: "Teen Views of Sex"	x		x		x		~		~		x	
Digital Story: "Back Then"	x		x		x		~		~		x	
Published poetry in chapbook by Tim Hernandez	~		~		~		x		~		x	
Vox pop in class		x	~		~		~		~		~	

Vox pop in the streets (field trip)	~	~	~	~	x	~
Workshops at KPFW (field trips)	~	~	~	~	x	~
Field Trips to Su Teatro (field trips)	~	~	~	~	x	~
Participation in after-school component	~	~	~	~	x 15	~	~

Knowledge and Skill Acquisition

Tania stated in her exit interview that her favorite project was the feature story that she coproduced with Yoli. The manner in which she described her preference, together with additional comments made in relation to other projects, indicate that she valued cognitive resources afforded by the program that enhanced her knowledge—in this case about "what sex really means to teenagers nowadays." It is important to note, however, that Tania valued knowledge and new skills not only because they could be used in school but also, significantly, because new knowledge and skills could be used to help other teens:

> My favorite project was the feature story because I got a lot of feedback on what sex really was to teenagers nowadays, and I now know what I can say to teenagers when they think of that problem, and I can have a better (..) explanation to tell them what's right and what's wrong.

In this excerpt, Tania identified the feature story on teen sex as her favorite project because of the new knowledge she gained from interviews and background research on the topic. She had a journalist's natural curiosity for knowing and understanding social processes and events, and accessing multiple perspectives on an issue. For her digital story, she and Yoli reflected on the conditions of female children and young teens in their home community, but she did not limit herself to the immediate tasks of the school assignment: she talked to other teens about their views of the community, because she wanted access to other perspectives than her own.

Transcript 5.2

```
1   Dana:    Have you ever researched on a topic, or listened to a radio story
2            for your own pleasure, outside of class? Why? In what circum-
3            stances? What did coming back to that text give you?
4   Tania:   Um, I did do some research on my digital story about Esperanza.
5            Sometimes there's kids who just like say, "Hi" once in awhile,
6            and I ask them you know like, "What do you feel when you live
7            here? You know, and like get their feedback, and like research
```

8		on what they think about it, you know, rather than just my per-
9		spective, so
10	Dana:	Was that for the project or for your own pleasure, outside of the
11		project?
12	Tania:	It was for like both, you know? For the project and like, to know
13		what, to get a little feedback for myself.
14	Dana:	You sound like a natural journalist.
15	Tania:	[*Laughs quietly*]

This activity of interviewing youth in her neighborhood, independently of the school requirement, shows the continuity Tania was developing among the spheres of experience of school and home life through coproduced cultural elements. My acknowledgment of her journalistic interests ratified previous recognition garnered during peer critiques and public showcases of her expertise in media production. This represents a repositioning of Tania from a failing, disruptive student to the student whose work was highly regarded by the group and was broadcast on the radio. She was also aware that her work was used for presentations at educational conferences. In terms of larger educational goals, the activity also met the school and district expectations for students to foster an active attitude toward learning.

The knowledge and new skills acquired through the program were highly valued by Tania. In her exit interview she identified several domains of knowledge and skill that were important for her developing sense of self, their applicability in other academic classes, future careers, and civic action.

Table 5.2 Valued Knowledge-Skill Domains, Sources, and Social Purposes

Valued knowledge domains	Knowledge-skill source	Purpose of knowledge-skill
Knowledge about teen sex and virginity	Research and interviews with youth and adults at school, home, in the neighborhood	To inform other youth about sex and "about what's right and what's wrong"
Knowledge about conditions in her neighborhood for youth	Informal questions posed to kids in the housing project	To get other perspectives than her own
Writing	Journalist mentor Jack and poetry mentor Tim; all Youth Radio projects	To help others "bring out their voice to show how they really are"
English language skills	Jack, Liv	Can be applied in

		other classes
Technology: Audicity audio editing application	Lyle, Milly, Dana	To "correct your voice and let people know what you're actually trying to say"
Knowledge from the world outside of school	Mentors who "come from big work companies" such as Lyle (IBM), Jack from KPFW	Real-world knowledge that connects to school knowledge

In Tania's statement related to the feature story, "I now know what I can say to teenagers when they think of that problem, and I can have a better explanation to tell them what's right and what's wrong," what is notable is Tania's assertion that she values new knowledge not just for herself and her own personal sense-making, but because she can use it to help *others* make sense of the confusing meanings of sex in contemporary society. This is consistent with Tania's general use of cultural elements: to support her own knowledge and skills development to help others, which could be seen across other domains of knowledge and skills acquisition in the program. In Transcript 5.3, we see her linking new skills in writing to helping others develop their voice:

Transcript 5.3

1	Dana:	Did you discover anything that you love to do that you didn't
2		know that you loved to do before?
3	Tania:	I'd say writing, like I mean before writing was fun but now
4		I'm more engaged to it so I like it better now than I did be-
5		fore.
6	Dana:	Will you try to pursue this interest outside of class?
7	Tania:	I definitely would. Just because I know that people do need to
8		like bring out their voice and show how they really are and I
9		could definitely help people develop like their voice.

Though I did not pursue this statement with a follow-up question, it would have been interesting to know more specifically which of the multiple meanings of "voice" she is referring to here. Though Tania reiterated her previous constructions of "voice" as being related to sharing an authentic self— "how they really are" (line 7)—this is one of many constructions of voice she had proposed during the interview, including speaking voice, voice for communicating opinions and ideas, voice for representing yourself and your life, voice for engaging with others in the community, and voice for taking a stand for what you believe in. Because the context of her use of the term is writing, one might also infer that she is referring to helping others develop an "authorial voice" (Ivanič, 1998) for use in creative as well as expository writing.

Literacy/language acquisition. Tania was very interested in the opportunities for developing writing and other language domains afforded in the program. She mentioned *writing* more than once, a learning activity that was mediated by radio mentors, in particular Jack. Tania valued writing as a skill that she could use in other classes.

Transcript 5.4

```
1  Dana:   What skills or knowledge have you learned in this class in youth
2          radio that you've been able apply to your other classes? Or that
3          you think you can apply in the future?
4  Tania:  I'd say writing for like Language Arts you know Jack Reeves did
5          help with a lot of grammar, and spelling and punctuation. And
6          that's like what's necessary in Language Arts, it's like to have cor-
7          rect grammar and spelling and he did help me a lot with that so I
8          mean it does work out for a lot of the other classes just as much
9          as this class.
```

Tania defined writing broadly, both as a tool for representing self and communicating meanings—what poets, journalists, and activists do—and writing as a "skill" in sense taught in language arts and English as a second language classes, which is correct grammar, spelling, and punctuation. She values the knowledge and skills acquired in the program of both ends of the spectrum.

Writing/speaking. When asked, "Do you think Youth Radio helped you develop your language skills?" Tania responded,

> Definitely. Jack Reeves, he definitely would change our narration to something like where people could understand it with better words and better sentences and definitely it did help with grammar corrections and you know how to speak right.

Narration here refers to spoken text in youth productions. While Jack did not actually "change" their narrations, Tania indicates that Jack scaffolded her writing in helping her expand her vocabulary and improve her sentence structures and grammar. Her main concern overall is that she will be understood by others. Here Tania demonstrated her understanding of the genres taught in Youth Radio and Radio Arts by indicating that writing was used to support speaking. As coauthor Romero and I (2010) have written elsewhere regarding the practices of youth radio in the programs we have been involved with,

> In youth radio practices, writing preceded speaking, marking a contrast to historical, pedagogical and often common sense notions, where traditionally orality precedes literacy (Goody, 1968; Ong, 1982). Even though students wrote a range of written texts (drafts, note cards, scripts on pages and on screen), these served, primarily, as functional organizers, precursors for developing oral language. Although an interrelationship between oral and written language has long been acknowledged (Ferreiro, 1986; Olson, 1977, 1991; Scribner & Cole, 1981), it seems that secondary classrooms have been slow to incorporate both modalities into meaningful learning. (p. 232)

The relationship between spoken, written, and visual texts, together with one-on-one coaching from radio mentors, opened spaces for exploration and forms of communication that would not have been available to Tania and other second language learners in exclusively print-based classes.

Technology for improving "communication competence." The focus on oral language and the affordances of the audio editing and movie-making technologies was for many students a new and stimulating—though often frustrating—experience. Tania suggested that the audio-editing application Audacity gave her a sense of power over her oral language production, which is significant for a person positioned as less-than-competent in the dominant language. When asked what she had learned about technology that she found most useful, she replied:

> I'd say Audacity because that does help you, you know, correct your voice and let people know what you're actually trying to say rather than just like a mumble. You can erase that mumble and actually have the real thing.

I interpret her remarks to mean that the audio-editing software allowed her communicate her ideas. From incoherent mumble, she was able to express "the real thing," that is, her thoughts and what she had written in her script. This finding confirms previous research from our study cited above:

> [W]hen students were able to comprehend how they could modify their voice and others', even after the speaking had happened, they were afforded the possibility of taking risks and creating new, redefined representations of themselves and their oral language, vis-à-vis their peers and other speakers. Several students commented positively about the editing process, saying they enjoyed being able to "delete things you don't like" and "that if you make a mistake [speaking] you can actually erase it!" Others confirmed that they learned that "you can record and edit yourself." (Romero & Walker, 2010, p. 230)

When asked "Do you think that Youth Radio can help students communicate their ideas more effectively?" Tania stated, with echoes of Federico's words, "Definitely. They [students] can show teachers and people from the school or people from the class their idea, how they live, or what they do, or how they think specifically." To communicate fully means to listen, to be heard, and be seen—or recognized (West, 1993). To be fully human is to be in dialog with others. At another point in the interview Tania said, "I learned that if I spoke, people would understand me." This is a profoundly empowering realization. Imagine that when you spoke people did not understand you, as though you were locked in a cage with your thoughts, not able to communicate them. Not being able to communicate means not being able to participate in social meaning-making processes. As Biesta (2004) writes, "Meaning exists only in and through communication."

Tania and Yoli's Feature Story

Tania and Yoli's feature story, "Teen Views of Sex," was viewed by teachers and students as a slightly shocking, courageous, and high-quality production: it was one of two feature stories that was considered to have achieved "broadcast quality" and was aired on the radio. The topic represented a change in the kinds of topics that could be discussed in the ESL and other classrooms, other than sex education. Though many Youth Radio Oakland feature stories and commentaries chosen to model the genres focused on relationships, including secret dating and teen pregnancy, none dealt directly with teen sex and virginity. Tania and Yoli expanded the relevance and scope of the topic and in the process generated even greater interest for themselves and their youth listeners, as evidenced in multiple requests to replay the feature story in class. The piece was also highly valued by teachers and myself as researcher, and it was presented as an exemplary feature story at several educational conferences. The feature story was played as a model of the genre for future classes (2011–2013) as well. The cultural element created by Tania and Yoli was thus taken up as a resource by the program planners as a tool for the furtherance of the cultural practices of the program from one year to the next. "Teen Views of Sex," in this sense, became a "reification" (Wenger, 1998) of cultural practices of the community, a tool to represent these practices and processes of change for current and future members of community and for people outside the program. A transcription of the feature story follows.

Transcript 5.5

1	Tania:	Today, sex is a subject that is openly discussed among
2		teens. It's a subject that seems to lose its value more and
3		more as teens evolve into a new era.
4	Yoli:	I think nowadays teens want everything now. We don't
5		want to work hard for something and then have it pay

6		off in the end.
7	Tania:	Especially sex. The age of teens having sex is getting
8		younger and younger. During this process, we inter-
9		viewed a mom who shared with us her opinion on how
10		sex is viewed by teenagers nowadays.
11	Mom:	It has changed because it seems to me that most girls
12		don't have respect for themselves, for the way they act,
13		the way they dress. They lack lots of respect.
14	Tania:	We walked along Boulder High halls and asked a senior
15		and a freshman on what they thought about sex to get
16		the views of both a newcomer to high school and some-
17		one who has been through it all.
18	Tania:	What is making us teens want sex so bad? Is it that it
19		gives us a feeling of being older and experienced, or is it
20		just another oh-everyone's-doing-it type of thing?
21	Boy:	Oh my god! But, I think it's really fun.
22	Girl:	I think sex is a normal thing for teenagers (.) they should
23		know about it first.
24	Tania:	If this is how teens are viewing sex, then is it viewed the
25		same in their families? Do parents have a big impact on
26		teens deciding whether to have sex or wait?
27	Boy:	They told me to wait and that everything comes at its
28		time.
29	Girl:	My mom talked about it since I was eleven, so, um, it's
30		like I'm pretty aware.
31	Tania:	What about the pressure of high school or friends? Be-
32		ing around kids that are or are almost adults is a bit in-
33		timidating, if you ask me.
34	Tania:	Coming into high school, do you think that everybody
35		lost their virginity in high school?
36	Boy:	No, I think some people are still virgins.
37	Girl:	I don't know, but probably I would say that, like, fifty
38		percent or like
39	Tania:	Studies show that roughly only fifty percent of high
40		school students lose their virginity in high school. So,
41		about fifty percent of teens are virgins by the time they
42		reach seventeen.
43	Yoli:	Which is a good, responsible age to start having sex,
44		right? Because at seventeen you are able to deal with the
45		consequences of having sex, if there is any.

46	Girl:	Yes, a lot, like pregnancy, (.) HVI
47	Tania &	
48	Yoli:	[*laughter*]
49	Yoli:	HIV
50	All Girls:	[*laughter*]
51	Tania:	As you can see, the adult perspective is different from
52		the teenage perspective.
53	Yoli:	Knowing teens want to have sex and considered to be
54		something that is common among high school students,
55		then teens should be taught about contraceptives and to
56		be smart when it comes to sex.
57	Tania:	Life is too short to have it end so quickly.
58	Yoli:	So, don't let the pressure of sex get to you.
59	Tania:	For Youth Radio at Beckwourth High, this is Tania Ve-
60		lásquez.
61	Yoli:	And Yoli Solórzano.

Tania and Yoli make the already compelling topic of sex even more interesting by including unexpected voices: a mom's, male and female teens in the school hallway, their own perspectives, and the "official research" on teen sex. It is easy to see why this feature story was such as success in the class. It is "cool," titillating, and fun: Clips of excited laughter from teens being interviewed about sex in the school hallway produce the same effect on the youth listeners. Nevertheless, Tania and Yoli obviously take the subject seriously, providing personal opinions and *consejos* (advice) to teens about adolescent sex within a future orientation about life beyond adolescence. Giving *consejos* is a pattern seen throughout Tania's work and can be interpreted as constituting identity processes involving a growing sense of agency across several projects as the year progresses. Giving *consejos* indicates a repositioning of Tania from a girl child to a more mature teen: from a girl who, in her digital story, is represented as one of a class of people (girls from her housing project) who are subjected by older adolescents to the dangers of sex, drugs, and alcohol as they move into early teens, to a worldly teen who has the knowledge and will to help younger teens and children avoid these dangers facing teen girls.

It is interesting to note here the dynamic relation between knowledge acquisition and personal sense in Tania's case. Knowledge served both personal and social or communal purposes. On the one hand, doing background research and conducting interviews for the feature story provided new knowledge and multiple perspectives on this topic of keen interest that they had not gained elsewhere. As Yoli reported, "Sex is a thing that some kids thought eve-

ryone did by their junior. But we learned that's not true." On the other hand, knowledge garnered through the school-based feature story gained
salience for Tania when she could use her new knowledge to help other youth and children in and outside of school on their path to and through adolescence: "I now know what I can say to teenagers when they think of that problem, and I can have a better explanation to tell them what's right and what's wrong." This interest in linking school/program-based knowledge to spheres of experience outside school, together with gaining the tools to render actionable her already strong sense of social responsibility, seems to have facilitated processes of personal sense making of program projects and the cultural elements employed. It may be, too, that through her semiotic work, Tania came to realize the worth of the personal and community values—such as social responsibility—that she brought to the enterprise. As revealed in her exit interview, she was coming to realize changes in herself as well.

Personal sense. The feature story was a cultural element in the program that was taken up and transformed by Tania into a *symbolic resource* for the three domains theorized by Zittoun (2006) as being involved in processes of development: identity processes, knowledge-skill acquisition, and personal sense-making. Personal sense making involves linking objects of knowledge to situations and experiences that are familiar to the young person, as described above. Personal sense making also requires the elaboration of emotions, which can be seen in Tania's reflection in the following transcript.

Transcript 5.6

```
1   Dana:    Did projects you did in this class help you better understand
2            your emotions?
3   Tania:   In a way just because um you know how I feel about like teen
4            sex views or you know is that why it does like bring out a little
5            happiness or a little sadness or a little angriness, you know, to-
6            wards like what I'm living or how I'm living and so forth.
7            That's basically how I see it.
8   Dana:    Did it help to be able to express those feelings?
9   Tania:   It did just to like let them out you know like rather than have
10           feeling all bottled up and what you really think. You can
11           actually express your feelings and stuff.
```

According to this account, Tania did use the affordances of the program and especially her own productions to elaborate emotions. She admitted that she had a lot emotion around the issue of sex—"a little happiness or a little sadness or a little angriness" (lines 3–5)—and that the process of creating the feature story allowed her to better understand and express her emotions, while creating a reflective space for considering her life in relation to sex—"what I'm living or how I'm living." It could be said that Tania's use of cultural elements as symbolic resources in the program involved externalizing her experience of the world by naming it, which allows her to reflect upon her experience, thus changing her relationship to the world as well as to herself.

Transcript 5.7
1 Dana: In this class are you the same kind of student as you are
2   in other classes?
3 Tania: I wouldn't say I am, just completely. Just because like in
4   this class I'm not shy. In other classes I am shy. Just be-
5   cause this class has let me to adjust to, you know, being
6   myself and other classes are like here's the work do the
7   work, you know, like same schedule and this one is like,
8   you know, connect with your classmates, learn some-
9   thing new. I'm definitely more confident in this class
10   than in others.
11 Dana: I don't see you as being shy. Isn't that funny how your
12   appearances can be different than what you really feel...
13 Tania: Right, right.

The statement, "this class has let me to adjust to, you know, being myself," reveals greater continuity of self and maturation in her trajectory through adolescence, which has been difficult for her.

Identity Processes Engaged through the Feature Story

The feature story project seems to have had significant implications for Tania's identity processes, in terms of a personal sense of voice, repositioning of self in relation to others, and power that comes with knowledge. In fact, though Tania reported valuing the knowledge acquired in creating the feature story, much of the knowledge or insight gained had to do with the construction of female teen identities in regards to sexual relations.

There were a number of ways in which Tania and Yoli demonstrated enhanced agency and relational power in their feature story. Listening to the story, one is struck by the reversal of roles in terms of who gets to ask whom about sex: in this instance, it is *girls* asking boys and adults—both male and female—about sex, in ways that are not commonly heard in public spaces, a fact noted by the girls themselves. The girls thus challenge accepted gender roles, and in the process of interviewing they reposition themselves from "shy girl" (which his how Tania describes herself) to interviewer who—in the moment of the interview—holds more power than the interviewee. The following transcript is somewhat confusing, as it is not clear to whom Tania is referring as "they" in lines 7-9. I understood her at the time to be referring to the class audience, as can be seen in my response to her in line 10.

Transcript 5.8

1	Dana:	Has youth radio helped you develop more self-confidence in any
2		way?
3	Tania:	It has. Just because you know we show our feature stories and
4		people are seeing what we did specifically, what we worked for,
5		how we like developed out narration. And we play them [to the
6		class] in the end. At first it's a little shy but like in the end you
7		see how they [the interviewees] really see it and they're [inter-
8		viewees or audience?] not laughing and cracking jokes about it.
9		They're [interviewee or audience?] really taking it seriously so.
10	Dana:	So the audience helps you develop confidence?
11	Tania:	Definitely.
12	Dana:	That's interesting. I hadn't thought about that. What was it like
13		to interview people who weren't necessarily your friends for your
14		feature story? Was that difficult?
15	Tania:	At first it was just because they take you like as being always the
16		funny friend someone you can count on but when it comes to
17		serious work like you know interviewing on their perspective on
18		sex, they take it like, they'll accept it, but it's a little awkward at
19		first for them because now they see you all serious.
20	Dana:	Now you're talking about your friends, right? Right. And what
21		was it like it like to (.) Did you interview people that you didn't
22		really know?
23	Tania:	I did. With Selena it was. Or an adult, or (..)? Oh yeah. Mr.
24		Lyndberg, I think it was. He's a gym teacher here.
25	Dana:	He teaches Sex Ed? Health and Sex Ed. So what was it like to
26		interview him?
27	Tania:	At first it was like a little nerve-wracking just because <u>he is an</u>
28		<u>adult and he is a male</u> so it's like and <u>we're both girls</u> so it's like,
29		at first it was a little nervous but after you know, <u>he adjusted to</u>
30		<u>it</u> and it was like, he was [thinking], "This is for their grade," so
31		he was like, "So." He did help us out, so it definitely worked

32		out.
33	Dana:	How did you feel after you interviewed him, after going through
34		your nervousness?
35	Tania:	Afterward it was a little more comfortable and like now every
36		time I see him in the hall it's always like, "Oh hey how are you?"
37		"Good." So I think it definitely built up my confidence to talk to
38		people when I need to.
39	Dana:	And maybe developed relations with other people that you
40		didn't know? Like him? Like now you say hello and stuff like
41		that.
42	Tania:	Yeah.

In lines 27–32, Tania describes the discomfort felt on the part of both the girls and the adult male teacher, and she notes that *he* was forced to adjust to *their* agenda, reversing the existing gender and age positionings. It is interesting to note that in the interview it is she, not the male teacher, who initiates the informal, friendly greetings in the hallway. This experience built her confidence in talking to people, including those outside her usual spheres of experience.

The other identity shift signaled in Tania's interview is the *multiplication* of identities and the transition from someone who is not taken seriously, to someone who can be both lighthearted *and* someone of consequence. Before, she was seen only as "the funny friend" (line 16) or as she says at another point in the interview, "someone who is outgoing and funny and different." Now, she also wants to be seen as someone to be taken seriously, whose opinion ("voice") matters.

Transcript 5.9

1	Dana:	Can you think of some concrete examples of things that
2		you've done in this class that have helped you develop your
3		voice?
4	Tania:	I would say the teen sex views just because, like it gets, like,
5		you know, you can tell that my voice is very serious about that
6		and before I wouldn't be able to be so serious about such a
7		small thing. And now I'm more serious and I can project my
8		voice to let them know that I am being really serious about
9		the situation.

Interestingly, Tania explicitly linked this newfound sense of "seriousness," of someone to be taken seriously, to one of the emergent meanings she attributed to "voice."

The interview experience represented significant learning for Tania on several levels. Engaging in these genre practices contributed to a shift from "shy girl" to powerful interviewer of men, women, and youth. It provided opportunities for gaining valued information from multiple perspectives not available in textbooks. It helped her overcome shyness and build confidence in crossing boundaries to communicate with others outside her usual spheres of experience. Through the process, Tania developed a new sense of self, as someone who "can be successful."

Transcript 5.10

1	Dana:	Did you learn anything new about yourself in Youth Radio?
2	Tania:	Um I learned that I can be successful you know if I...
3		because I did get a little push in Youth Radio like they were
4		like, "go and interview" you know be confident in yourself
5		and you know and just what's in me and go use it outside of
6		the you know, go interview people and don't have that little
7		shyness, like you can do it you know?

Tania's notion of "success" gains clarity when contrasted with her representation of children who might not be successful: "I want my brother and my sister to become successful, rather than be like, someone on the street doing drugs and all that nonsense."

It could be said, then, that work on the feature story led to a transformation in Tania's relationship to herself, as well as to others and to objects of knowledge. She learned that if she worked hard, developed confidence and the proper communication tools, she could be "successful." These identity relocations became real through the acknowledgment of others in the class in the context of public critiques, public showcases, and the media when KPFW selected their feature story for broadcast.

Using Other Students' Creative Work as Symbolic Resources

In her interview responses, Tania constructed a self who was seeking to transform her familial relationships. She reports using other students' creative work—not those introduced by program staff as Elia does—as symbolic resources for the elaboration of emotions and transformation of self, to become a "better person." She referred to being affected by Sugita's digital story about her mother, which was indeed a very emotional representation of her love for her mother.

Transcript 5.11

```
1  Dana:    Is there anything you read, viewed, or listened to in class that
2           affected you in any way?
3  Tania:   Um, Sugita's story about her mom—it was her digital story? (.)
4           made me kinda grasp the concept of respecting moms nowadays,
5           so you know, I've decided or—I haven't really decided but [said
6           quickly] (.) It makes me like, get a better look of how I should
7           treat my mom, and that should be with respect. So her story
8           made me realize (...)
9  Dana:    Mkay.
```

The significance of Tania's remarks here must be considered against the backdrop of her commentary written in the beginning of the academic year, "Every Teen Deserves a Second Home," in which she argues for safe houses for teens who have been physically abused by parents. This comment in her exit interview seems to indicate that Tania has turned Sugita's digital story, a cultural element made available to others through class viewings and discussion, into a *symbolic resource* for the elaboration of difficult emotions surrounding her relationship with her mother. As in much of her narrative, Tania here constructs herself as a young person seeking to better herself in school, at home, and in future careers. It is interesting that what might have been interpreted as the use of a cultural element (Sugita's digital story) as a symbolic resource for emotional elaboration is treated by Tania as a *cognitive* resource: "made me kinda grasp the concept of respecting moms nowadays" (lines 3-4). Her hesitancy to commit to appropriating the concept—"I've decided or—I haven't really decided but" (lines 4-5)—shows that she's still in the process of working through this new knowledge and associated emotions made available by Sugita's digital story, which perhaps explains her distancing herself from the emotions involved and instead focusing on "the concept." The moment-to-moment working through these emotions and new understanding in the context of the interview also indicates that the interview itself may have offered a "thinking space" (Perret-Clermont, cited in Zittoun, 2008) for Tania, allowing her to take some distance from the contradictory emotions of hurt and forgiveness, and represent—or externalize—her struggle to reconcile the experience of pain with her desire to improve herself and treat her mother with respect.

Digital Story

Tania completed one of two digital story projects assigned during the year. The first digital story focused on personal topics, such as identity or family. Molly clearly establishes the purpose of the genre for this first project in her instruction:

> Well I have a presentation to kind of guide us. On Fridays we are going to do projects that utilize technology tools but the focus of the projects is for you to express um your own ideas. So you'll be telling stories or putting some ideas out there (.) it's really a chance for you to express yourself, either about things that you're learning—so telling us what you know (*sounds like she points to the phrase projected on the screen*) or (.) some personal things, maybe telling a personal story, or um sharing something that you really like (.) And so we'll get to know you—or the world will get to know you—a little bit better.

The theme of the second digital story was "Our Neighborhood Community," shifting the focus from the strictly personal to the personal-within-community. This project followed the feature story on "Our School Community." We realized afterward that this may not have been the best theme for the digital story project: due to the high mobility among these families living in poverty, some students could not write about their neighborhood because they felt no connection, knew no neighbors, and had a hard time coming up with ideas. For example, the only topic Elia could think of related to her trailer park were the feral cats that kept her up at night.

Instruction and modeling for the second digital story centered on place. Molly talked with the class about how a place symbolizes the human relations in the community. I talked again about metaphor and showed a story from the Center for Digital Storytelling (2009) website told in Spanish and English called "*El Maletín*" (The Suitcase). The students asked once more to view my digital story about my son, and Yoli talked to me afterward about how much she liked my piece, especially the way I used music. Tania and Yoli decided to work together and requested digital cameras to take home to photograph their neighborhood and elementary school, which was not close to their homes.

Work on their digital story occurred primarily after school in the Mac Lab, amid intense conversations, much laughter, and clear signals about the need for privacy and the lack of need for adult assistance—a stark contrast with Elia's efforts to seek help and develop relationships with adults through the production process. Tania and Yoli also rejected adult "advice" regarding what Liv and I considered the questionable decision to represent Mexicans (including themselves) with an offensive, stereotypical image of a Mexican peasant in a large sombrero. When Liv and I suggested that the image might be misinterpreted, Yoli insisted on keeping it, without explanation. I interpret the girls' use of this stereotypical image as similar to Federico and students' parodies of "gringo" accents: parodies of mainstream white North American stereotypes of Mexicans, which in a carnivalesque way challenges the deficit discourse about Mexicans. Mexican student in the program were clear about this stereotype and made note of the hidden curriculum of one school program as conveying the message that "Mexicans are stupid."

In their digital story, the girls continued to develop themes introduced in their feature story, such as health risks represented by sex and teen girls' respect for themselves in relation to heterosexual relations. Their multimodal composition is a reflection on the transition from innocence of childhood to the dangers of adolescence. Specifically, it is an indictment of the illicit activities carried out in full view of children by older youth and young adult males in the housing project. Table 5.3 presents a transcript of the digital story.

Table 5.3 Transcript of "Back Then," Digital Story by Tania and Yoli

Time	Narration, sound, text	Image
00:00	(Music)	photo of entrance to their housing project
00:10	(Yoli) Esperanza is where we live. It's a neighborhood that is mostly populated by Mexicans. We've lived there for a little bit more than five years.	-stereotypical image of a poor Mexican peasant in a large sombrero, taken from a 1940s black-and-white Mexican film -children playing in the neighborhood
00:20	Back when we were 10 in elementary everything seemed fine: we had playgrounds wide open fields, friends. What more can we want?	-children in classroom -different image of children together in class -playground at their real school -clip art of bucolic outdoor setting
00:29	(Yoli) Everything seemed perfect in our own little world, when everyone around us seemed like heroes the only bad people were Swiper the Fox on *Dora* or Mojo Jojo on the *Powder Puff Girls*. Life was paradise.	-photoshopped image of the world within a blue eye -cartoon images -photo of Disneyland from corporate website

00:40	(Tania) But then, came 13 when we started to grasp the concept of what real life is, what actually happens over where the crowd of older kids hang out, what you have to do to be cool.	-young teen girls standing on a stairway -young adult white males, tattooed, threatening expressions, holding cigarettes
00:52	(Tania) You hear stories of smoking, smoking cigarettes? No, weed. Kids in our neighborhood do it everywhere; the parking lot, the park, in front of their house.	-girl with a cigarette -marijuana cigarette -youth smoking pot in parking lot -youth smoking in the park -youth smoking in front of houses
01:03	(Yoli) Little kids running around with curiosity of what the cool kids do behind the trash can after school with hopes of one day being cool enough to stand there and be a part of whatever the cool kids do.	-children running near the trash can area
01:14	(Tania) Little do they know the horrible things that lie ahead for them weed cocaine alcohol and sex. It's all part of the ugly world the cool kids are living.	-photo of a marijuana pipe with smoke -photo of cocaine on a table -photo of a shelf of bottles behind a bar -photo of scantily clad adults kissing
01:23	(Yoli) I wanna be able to go back when you can run around free with no worries about homework or chores.	-children playing outdoors
01:31	(Tania) The worst you could do is call someone a name and the only thing hanging out of our mouth was lollipops and not cigarettes.	-children with lollipops -young girl smoking a cigarette
01:38	Music and credits	-happy children playing

The thematic content of this digital story shows the appropriation and reworking of themes introduced through various genres in the program dealing with the challenges of adolescence. This includes my own digital story, signaled by Yoli as meaningful to her, about my son, the loss of childhood innocence, and struggles in adolescence, similar—in some respects—to those described in the girls' digital story. However, Tania and Yoli rework given forms to create something new in this autobiographical narrative that weaves their own stories, indirectly, into the history of the children—specifically girls—in their neighborhood. Notable in this multimodal composition is also the weaving through the text, through intertextual links, of key genre features and themes introduced from different spheres of their experience: popular culture, seen in the iconic images of Disneyland representing "paradise" (perhaps parodically), and Japanese cartoon characters such as Mojo Jojo; the program, represented by recurrent themes and discourses about youth in society; their neighborhood community, the topic of their reflections; and childhood, with their particular, gender-inflected, nostalgic narrative of the past. It could be said that the semiotic work undertaken in this multimodal composition, conducted primarily after school in joint peer activity, allowed for the "articulation," or linking, of these various several spheres of experience. This semiotic work could therefore be seen as having contributed to a sense of continuity of self.

Mastering the genre. In their digital story, Tania and Yoli demonstrated full control of genre conventions of the digital story, as established in YRRA through program documents including guidelines, checklists, and rubrics, such as the one in Table 5.4.

Table 5.4 "Exceeds Expectations" Criteria from Digital Storytelling Project Rubric

Criteria	Exceeds Expectations
Title and Name /5	Title captures viewer's attention and conveys the content. Name included.
Content /35	Content of the video tells a story using details and story elements (well developed characters, setting, theme). Ideas are clearly presented and engaging.
Video/Audio Clarity and Interest /20	Audio elements and narration/interview are well edited and enhance the story and/or engage the listener.
Visual Design /20	Images enhance the story by providing additional or secondary meaning or interpretation. Images are seamlessly integrated with audio.
Time	The length is appropriate for the story content. The

/10	story is enhanced by the use of time in the story.
Credits /5	Credits are included. Information, images, and music are credited.
Submission /5	Saved in appropriate format (.mov/.wmv). Submitted and uploaded to shared class space.

Tania and Yoli demonstrate a keen sense of the social purposes of the digital story: to tell a powerful personal story that also has a social message, with the goal of affecting change in the emotional states and perspectives of viewers. Their piece displays control over the language and structural features highlighted in the digital story rubric presented in Table 5.4. They also evince dimensions of voice that not only conform to but also improve on the genre conventions taught in the program, as discussed below.

Possibilities for selfhood. Following Ivanič's (1998) framework of possibilities for selfhood made available in this sociocultural context, Tania and Yoli clearly establish an *authorial presence* in their digital story. The instruction on the digital story—like other radio genres—encouraged them to write about topics that inspired passion and to represent their realities as they see them. In their digital story they convey strength and authority both in their spoken voice and in the subject matter on topics on which they are uniquely suited to be experts. The *discoursal self* can be seen in the assertion of values, beliefs, and ideologies that reflect several possible discourses: the discourse of community activism, social responsibility toward young children, youth media (in which youth turn a critical lens on conditions of their lives and communities), and— one could argue—a feminist discourse. The critical evaluation is more about girl children than children in general, and given the choice of images, the targets of their critique are adolescent and young adult males.

The *autobiographical self* in the digital story can be seen in the composers' sense of their roots, where they come from. As noted earlier, Ivanič (1998) emphasizes that it is not so much the events that people recount that matters, but rather the way they represent these experiences to themselves and to others, which constitutes their current way of being. This digital story could be understood as a kind of self-within-community portrait. Tania did her commentary on home—a second home—and her first (incomplete) digital story was entitled "Juárez, the Home I Can't Go Home To": Home was important to her. The story begins, "Esperanza is where we're from," conforming to the digital story subgenre of *place*. It indicates a strong sense of identity as part of or located in a place, and *place* as a symbol for the social relations of the community. It could be said, given that examples discussed in whole-class instruction included a basketball court and a street corner (which the students interpreted rowdily as the gathering place of prostitutes), that the *place* in Tania and Yoli's digital story is even more specific than the neighborhood: *place* could be interpreted as the housing projects' trash can area and the portentous activities that go on there, which shows the authors' mastery of the use of metaphor for communicating deeper layers of meaning. There is also the parodic representation of their social identity as Mexicans, which some audience viewers have found difficult to interpret: The parodic and ludic element may have introduced too much complexity in the girls' performance of their identities for most audiences to understand, since the dominant genre of their piece is the serious, autobiographical narrative and societal critique. Overall, the digital story shows a strong sense of a developing and changing self.

New Understandings of Self

The identity enactments seen in this digital story, as well as the feature story, poetry, and other projects, may have culminated in transformations or "reorientations" (Hull & Zacher, 2007) of self. Zittoun (2006) and Zittoun and Grossen (2010) developed their interview protocols to examine changes in self and personal meanings made of cultural elements used in schools as well as possible new trajectories young people might entertain in terms of schooling and career futures. In what follows, I present evidence from Tania's exit interview responses of identity processes she engaged in through her semiotic work with interpersonal and cultural resources afforded by the program. In this analysis, I am interested in how participation in the program affected how she saw herself and whether others recognized her as such, and how her sense of self had shaped her participation in program learning activities. It is important to keep in mind in listening to her words that this narrative of self-transformation is constructed against the backdrop of a history of academic failure in the high school, initial non-completion of Youth Radio projects, and instructor perceptions of her as disengaged and disruptive in class at different periods of the year. In addition, Tania was struggling with difficult family dynamics and other emotionally difficult issues, as revealed in her exit interview. The reorientations of self and recognition she gained for her accomplishments are that much more striking given this context.

New understandings of self. In Transcript 5.12, Tania discusses a new side of herself that she discovered through doing multimodal composition, which was her creativity.

Transcript 5.12

1	Dana:	Do you think of yourself as a creative person?
2	Tania:	Before I didn't but now I do. Just because like looking back on
3		my stories I've realized like what words I've used or what pic-
4		tures I've used or what sentences I've used and I say like, "Wow!
5		that's very creative." And then like I've done that and so I do
6		think that I have a creative side.
7	Dana:	What was the most creative project you did in the class, or po-
8		ems, or theater or anything?
9	Tania:	I would say the digital story just because I did get a lot of good
10		feedback on that and so like including the pictures and how well
11		it went with the narration. So I definitely feel like that was the
12		good one.
13	Dana:	Was that a satisfying feeling? To use your creativity?
14	Tania:	It definitely was just to show people how creative I really am.

This excerpt shows that *acknowledgment* from others was critical for this new sense of self as a creative person (lines 5-6). In an analysis of the socially mediated nature of the meanings of art and artist identities, Zittoun and colleagues (Zittoun, Duveen, Gillespie, Ivinson, & Psaltis, 2003) argue that groups such as peers or classrooms "anchor art objects within their own hierarchically structured systems of meaning" (p. 431), and that in the process, these objects acquire values such as good, bad, weird, creative, and so on. Because artistic productions are often viewed as extensions of the individual projected into the world, being recognized as "creative" or "talented" (or lacking creativity) has strong identity implications. At the same time, when a young person is creating an artistic production such as a digital story for the first time, she or he relies on others' interpretations of the value of the object and the social identity extended to the person who created it. Tania seems to suggest this in showing some surprise at being acknowledged as a creative person, thereby discovering herself that she is a creative person, and showing the importance this valuation holds for her. The discourse in Transcript 5.12 shows how Tania begins to see herself differently and to construct a new identity as a creative person. This is accomplished both through her acceptance of the social identity extended to her by the group and through her discoveries about herself realized through semiotic work through the digital story.

The digital story thus serves two functions as a symbolic resource for Tania. On the one hand, it is a genre introduced by the program with the particular social meanings constructed within the program. I have described how my digital story—an official curricular cultural element—became a symbolic resource for Tania and Yoli. Furthermore, Tania mentions other students' digital stories that became symbolic resources for her own meaning making, as shown in Transcript 5.11, in which Sugita's digital story is identified as a cultural element that helps her rethink her relationship and behavior toward her mother. At this level, the digital story serves as a container that creates a space for working through emotion and constructing new understandings of self, objects, and others. When Tania, with Yoli, create a digital story appropriating the meanings, features, and purposes of the genre for their own artistic and compositional purposes, the object becomes a symbolic resource for working through emotion and linking a current sense of self to selves and experiences in the past. Simultaneously, their artistic production becomes a cultural element itself as it is placed in circulation for others to interpret and use for their own semiotic work.

Tania's coauthored productions were identified as having been appropriated for sense-making activities by other students in the program. In response to the questions, "Is there anything you read, viewed, or listened to in class that affected you in any way?" or "Was there a speaker, a book, a digital story, a radio story that changed your way of seeing things?" Eugenia and Sugita replied:

> Tania and Yoli, about how they live in Esperanza. That changed my opinion about drugs. My brother would be in Esperanza a lot. They spoke the truth because the children are looking at what the older kids are doing. Once I picked up my friend and I saw a 5th grader smoking. (Eugenia)

> Yeah, the digital story by Tania and Yoli, because I agree with: them it makes me think about what I shouldn't be doing in the future. (It made me think about) drugs in my neighborhood. They do drugs around children—I wonder why they do that? (Sugita)

Tania also reported being aware of the effect their digital story had on others, based on feedback they received during the public critiques in class:

Transcript 5.13
1 Dana: Do you remember the feedback, like when we showed your story
2   in class?
3 Tania: There was um, a lot of people really responded because (.) of the
4   children, and in the interviews a lot of people have said,
5   "Tania's story really affected me." I think just because, the kids
6   that look up to us nowadays; I mean, they expect more. Rather
7   than just like, they, they see what we do, and you know, maybe
8   one day they're gunna follow up to that. And as they see they

```
9          have younger brothers and sisters they say, "You know, "I need
10         to do what's right—for them." That's how I kinda put it, like, "I
11         have a little brother I have a little sister and I wanna do what's
12         best for them." So I think that's why they were like, "That's so
13         touching," because I want my brother and my sister to become
14         successful rather than to be like, someone on the street doing
15         drugs and all that nonsense.
```

These statements show clearly that Tania and Yoli's digital story became a symbolic resource for other youth making sense of their own experience, attributing new understandings. These statements also suggest that the digital story might cause change in others' behavior, leading to improved conditions for some children, which was one of Tania's stated purposes.

Social Responsibility

Within Zittoun's (2006) framework, cultural elements can be used to mediate relations with others and oneself and to mediate thinking and feeling. The question posed in the following transcript was designed to access evidence about how participants used objects to mediate relations with others. Once again Tania expands the mediated relationship beyond the *person-other* vector to include an element of social responsibility: the desire to serve others and effect change.

```
Transcript 5.14
1   Dana:   Do you ever have any desire to share your work with someone
2           close to you?
3   Tania:  I do, I wanna share it with my sister, just because you know,
4           she's outside of Esperanza every day, you know, and I'd rather she
5           be successful, rather than like just play outside all night
6           and see what I see rather than just her, what she sees, you know.
7           If she sees what I see, I mean I hope she'll understand what's real-
8           ly going on in our community.
```

In this passage, Tania expressed her belief that her artistic production has the power to show her sister what *she* (Tania) sees, in a way opening her world, or her vision, to her sister. This statement reveals a change in perspective about the ability of people to connect and communicate at a deeper level. It is a different orientation than her statements about her feelings of isolation and existential alienation at the beginning of the year, before Federico "got [their] spirits out" and people in the class started talking to each other.

Tania's desire to have others "see what I see" was not limited to her sister. She expressed the desire to use her work to influence public opinion and move people in her community to take action.

Transcript 5.15

```
1    Dana:   Do you think your own work has affected other people in the
2            same way that the work you referred to earlier affected you?
3    Tania:  I do in this case, just because, you know, a lot of people are not
4            familiar with that neighborhood and you know, they get a better
5            look of what, what's really is happening in that story. So I think
6            like, if people from my neighborhood would watch my story
7            they'd understand we need, you know, come together as a com-
8            munity and fix the problems that we have here. Because you
9            know as kids grow up they gotta experience more things and be
10           successful, and you know, so, I think if they saw it they'd under-
11           stand.
```

Thus, the feature story and digital story are viewed by Tania as resources for reflection and realizing her new identity as a capable young woman with important things to say. Tania now has a clearly articulated position on social responsibility and the need to influence public opinion for social change.

Tania's case helps distinguish activities, knowledge and skills, identity processes, relationships, and creative productions in the program that were consequential for student learning and development over time. In her exit interview, Tania identified key elements of the program that I have come to elaborate as principles of a *pedagogy of powerful communication*. She identified the purpose of the program as being the development of youth voice and pointed to the importance of community for developing voice. Significantly, Tania's work was indicated by other students as having mediated their own thinking and creative work, a key finding of the study being that youth productions—not only cultural elements introduced in the curriculum—became symbolic resources for other youth in their meaning-making processes. She articulated a strong sense of social responsibility in using her new knowledge and media productions to shape the thinking and actions of younger siblings, teens, and her neighborhood community. In this way, Tania's case exemplifies Freire's (2005) interest in externalization as the process through which people acquire tools to work on, and alter, not only themselves but also their environments "to create new settings, social destinations, personal and group trajectories, and means for producing them" (Souto-Manning & Smagorinsky, 2010, p. 44).

Constructing a Public Voice

Tania's developing awareness of her capacity and desire to use her productions and her voice to participate in public discourse, influence public opinion, and move people to action was not unique. There was a general expression in the interviews of the sense of social responsibility: the notions of "the right to speak" and the need to "speak out" were linked to the need to represent others as well as themselves, and to use newly acquired skills and knowledge to help others. Table 5.5 presents student responses to questions about the meaning of "voice," and how Youth Radio and Radio Arts could help them be more engaged in civic life and their communities.

Table 5.5 Selection of Student Responses to the Questions about the Meaning of "Voice"

> People are going to start realizing, cuz they don't know if you don't tell them. So, it's good to tell the people and to do projects about something you want like the park, so people are gunna hear and start noticing. (Elia)
>
> Youth Radio can help you in your life outside of school because you have the power to make yourself heard, to share your perspective, let out your voice, show people how you live. Like the Dream Act for my race, it puts us down. Some students want to go to college but can't. People need to know this. (Tania)
>
> ["Developing voice" to me means] sending a message to the public. Talking about what you want to tell the world, what people should know about something. (Sugita)
>
> My mother has already taught us to be involved in community service. Being in the radio program we have learned much about this. *Tienes que dar a la communidad*/You have to give to your community. Speaking in public can help so people are aware of what we need. If we don't unite, my mom always says, nothing will happen. (Delfina)
>
> Showing our digital story to someone in government would make them think.

> Starting school later—we're actually going to start school later. (Beto)
>
> We talked about what people can do to make Beckwourth a better place for youth. (Eugenia)
>
> If you don't know how to develop your voice nobody is really going to listen to you. High school shuts up a lot of kids. Being a freshman is scary. Then when they grow up they don't think they can vote, they don't think they know anything. (Sonia)
>
> This program helped us talk about what you feel, think more deeply about a certain topic, and talk about what you want to tell the world, tell people what they should know about something.

In these comments, students express a sense of agency in knowing that their voices and media productions could have an impact on public views and actions. From isolation and social alienation, passivity and invisibility, to a sense that they could participate in public discourse and even cause change, was a significant development for these students. As heard in the comments above, transforming the curriculum to allow for a focus on youths' lives and communities outside school encouraged them to "think more deeply about a certain topic," and "talk about what you want to tell the world, tell people what they should know about something," in order to set change in motion.

Beto's comment, "Starting school later—we're actually going to start school later," refers to the feature story he did with Julio and Jesus on why high schools should start later, which included background research on adolescent sleep cycles and an interview with the principal. A week after their piece was completed, a newspaper article came out on the topic; then a schoolwide meeting was organized by the principal, and later in the semester he announced that next year there would be a later start of the school day. Though the youths' feature story could not have had a direct impact on changing the school day start time, they had a sense of having contributed to—and been a part of—the public discussion on this issue of great importance to them and were delighted to see the change happen.

A changing field of action and communication. Leander (2002) writes that researchers often pay attention only to physical space and activity that is visible in that perceived space. He suggests that we also need to notice what mental conceptions and symbolic representations people have of space, which Lefebvre calls "lived space," space that is "directly lived through its associated images and symbols, and hence the space of 'inhabitants' and 'users'...it overlays physical space, making symbolic use of its objects" (Lefebvre, cited in Leander, p. 216). This conception of space and human perceptions of space in relation to activity applies to students' changing sense of the dimensions of their field of action and communication. Ray argues that this new sense of agency for participation in the public realm had a lot to do with feeling that they belonged to the larger civic community.

Transcript 5.16

1	Ray:	One of the bullet points I make [for a conference presentation
2		we did on Youth Radio and Radio Arts] is belonging to a greater
3		community, and once they do that then they feel they're impor-
4		tant, and they have a voice. Somebody else in the community is
5		saying the same thing, and all of a sudden they make a connec-
6		tion, "Wow, we must be, we must fit more, and belong more in
7		this community, if there's other people thinking like us." Like in
8		the articles, the newspaper articles they wrote on the same issues
9		they thought of before [referring to Julio, Beto, Jesus's feature
10		story on instituting a later start at school].
11		That feeling, feeling important (.) the thought was important
12		even if it comes out in the newspaper, or your book. If we're
13		important enough to write a book about us (.) It's important you
14		feel you can belong before you can have a voice. Like when I go
15		to Columbia (.) if they make me feel like I belong, like you're
16		important, you're part of us, I will stand up and say something,
17		like there should be a fee for collecting trash.
18		I think that the community has made them feel that—the Lyles,
19		the Jack Reeves, that they belong to this community.
20	Dana:	What community?
21	Ray:	Beckwourth. And our studies on community, school, their
22		neighborhood, combined with people from the community
23		coming to them and saying, like Tim lately saying, "You guys
24		have something to say." Not just teachers–teachers are supposed
25		to say that. So I think all that contributes, and now they're start-
26		ing to have their voice, they're starting to say, "Yeah, I do have
27		something to say."
28	Dana:	Sandra said something interesting to me. She said, "We start
29		looking into issues and problems in our communities and then
30		we feel like we *wanna* do something about it."
31	Ray:	Yeah, I think when you ask them to, it's saying, "you're impor-
32		tant, tell me."

Here Ray provides concrete examples of how "lived" or "perceived space" as theorized by Lefebvre can change the nature of activity and symbolic representations of fields of action, into space in which an individual feels she can take action. Ray's argument is actually closer to Wenger's (1998) social theory of participation and learning within communities of practice, but the sense of space that one occupies adds a critical dimension when activity involves media production and having your voice heard—potentially—on the airwaves.

The expanded sense of community, as Ray suggests, could be attributed, in part, to the networked learning design. Mentors and guest speakers coming in from communities of practice outside of school telling them that what they had to say was important, combined with students actually going out to media organizations, learning alongside mentors in the studios, all expanded their perceived space of action through a (hypothesized) sense of belonging to the larger civic community. As Elia stated,

> It was a really good class . . . how you took us to the radio station, I didn't even know there was a radio station!; guest speakers—Sonia and Luis; you brought people to help, we met Lyle and we chilled, Reeves was a writer, especially Tim.

There was also imaginative work undertaken to expand the students' sense of perceived space and fields of action. In class we rehearsed doing vox pops (Voice of the People interviews) in the streets, as Eugenia mentioned in her comment in Table 5.5, "We talked about what people can do to make Beckwourth a better place for youth." In class, we asked them to imagine what they would do if they were the mayor of Beckwourth. Their comments might have surprised city officials, had they listened:

Transcript 5.17
If I were mayor of Beckwourth . . .
    Student 1: I would make downtown more secure [safer]
    Student 2: I would make it legal for Mexican youth to drive
    Student 3: I would provide better bus services at night
    Student 4: I would make a technology center
    Student 5: I would let people sell food in the streets
    Student 6: I would create more programs to help kids get off drugs
    Student 7: I would make bus fares cheaper
    Student 8: I would give homeless people a place to live
    Student 9: I would make it possible to work at a young age
    Student 10: I would make nightclubs for young people
    Student 11: I would make a free smoke-free arcade for youth

Student 12: I would create a center called Kids' Hope that would provide a fun center, field trip center, and tech center

Imaginative work also took place through frequent talk of radio audiences, including radio mentor Kareem's mention that "you never know who might be listening," and "there may be millions of people listening all over the world" (through Internet radio).

The development of a sense of public voice was promoted through engagement in media and literary practices that students saw real practitioners and artists doing. Liv commented that going out into the community on field trips and assignments (vox pops on the street) made visible the "real-life application" and planted the idea that "they are part of a larger community even though they are so disenfranchised." Engaging in some of these professional practices, such as interviewing people with recording equipment outside the classroom and the school, in the streets and in their communities, using the audio board at the radio station, being interviewed on the air, all contributed to expanding their vision not only of *how* one does radio but also *where* radio and related literacy practices are engaged, and the perceived spaces and agentive potential of this activity. Going to the radio station and being on the radio news show was an element of the program that students identified as being important for their sense of confidence, voice, and agency.

Table 5.6 Going to the Radio Station

How can developing voice be important in your life outside of school?	*Puedo hablar major* [I can speak better], cuz I was shy. *Yo sé que mi nombre no esta allí y todo eso, pero me dió mas confianza hablando en la radio.*/[I know that my name was not mentioned on the radio and everything, but it gave me more confidence talking on the radio]. (Delfina)
Can you think of some concrete examples of things you have done in this class that have helped you develop your voice?	Going to the radio station, being on Daily Magazine; writing my commentary and having it be on the radio.

Finally, going to the radio and being interviewed on the air helped students solidify the meanings and consequentiality of developing a "public voice" for participation in the public media sphere. The following is a transcription of a section of a live radio interview by Colleen—one of KPFW's news directors—

with Liv, Sonia, and Dipashri, and a youth mentor—Teresa—who regularly attended the Youth Radio class.

Transcript 5.18

1	Colleen:	What does it mean for you to be able to have access to
2		radio and the media? To be able to talk about these issues
3		like immigration, that really are so close to your heart,
4		your communities and your friends.
5	Teresa:	It's good. It's a good way of getting people's voices heard.
6		Because I not only speak for me but for a lot of other stu-
7		dents. It's just a great opportunity being able to get heard,
8		getting our voices out there.
9	Sonia:	I think the same thing as Teresa. It is true. You can get
10		your voices out, you can be heard. If you can be heard by
11		other people then you can be heard here, and you can ex-
12		press your-self.

These statements once again underscore the theme of social responsibility, a value and felt need on the part of these youth that the program helped develop. "Getting people's voices heard" for Teresa, as well as Tania, Elia, and Delfina, means that when one speaks in the public media sphere, one speaks not just for the oneself but for others who voices are not heard, who do not have the access.

Spreading Change: A Rhizomatic Analysis

The viewpoints expressed by students in interviews at the end of the year were notable for the depth of insight they showed about their understanding of the purposes of our enterprise in Youth Radio and Radio Arts. They also showed that they had used the opportunities afforded in the program to examine their learning not only in the program but also in school and life outside of school. Some of the students even articulated deep reflexive positions on their development as adolescents moving through transitions from childhood to adulthood, revealing a new sense of continuity across time, past, present, and future. It could be said that the meaning making and identity work undertaken through dialogue and the use and creation of cultural elements in poetry, drama, digital storytelling, and radio production created spaces for containing and transforming feelings, identities, and exploring possible experiences (Zittoun, 2008). These spaces for reflection and elaboration of emotion may have helped students evolve greater self-reflexivity about their learning and development through participation in the program. Against a backdrop of her low performance in school, which she attributes to comprehension problems in English, Delfina describes the growth and learning she experienced in Youth Radio. Code-switching between Spanish and English, she describes a sort of "epiphany" she had during an interview at the radio station with talk-show host Kareem:

Transcript 5.19 [CS = codeswitch]

1	Dana:	Was there a speaker, a book,	Was there a speaker, a book,
2		a digital story, a radio story	a digital story, a radio story
3		that changed your way of see-	that changed your way of see-
4		ing things?	ing things?
5	Delfina:	Me, uh yeah, [excitement in	Me, uh yeah, [excitement in
6		her voice]	her voice]
7		Me hizo como crecer mas	it made me grow more [CS
8		[CS>Sp]	>Sp]
9		Like como antes as veces, este,	Like before, sometimes, um
10		[CS>Eng>Sp]	[CS Eng>Sp>Eng]
11		todavia estaba muy rebelde y	I was still very rebellious and
12		todo eso.	everything.
13		Pero estando en el programa	But being in the program
14		me ayudo a	helped me to
15		Um, I don' know (.)	Um, I don' know (.)
16		[CS>Eng]	[CS>Eng]
17		A pensar ya grande	To think more like an adult
18			[CS>Sp]
19		Like, a actuar ya bien	Like, it's time to act more
20		[CS>Eng>Sp]	correctly, like an adult
21		Como cuando fuimos a la radio	Like when we went to the
22		station? [CS>Eng]	radio station? [CS>Eng]
23		Cuando hablamos de todo estos	when we talked about all
24		topicos	those topics [CS>Sp]
25		I don' know [CS>Eng]	I don' know [CS>Eng]
26		Me hizo pensar	it made me think [CS>Sp]
27		Que no me, no me ayuda en	that it does not, it doesn't
28		nada	help me in any way
29		Estar actuando como (.)	to be acting like (.)
30		Como, nina Chiquita	like a little girl
31		Como los ninos de alli	like the boys in the class

32		Y este, yo pienso que eso	...and well, I think that
33		Y lo que me ha ayudado el pro-	and what the program has
34		grama	helped me with
35		Es ver cosas diferentes	is to see things differently
36		Así es.	That's how it is.
37	Dana:	Eso me da mucho placer escu-	For me, that is a pleasure to
38		char [laughs quietly]	hear [laughs quietly]
39	Delfina:	[Laughs]	[Laughs]

The self-transformation represented in Delfina's narrative is striking: "It [the program] helped me grow"; "Being in the program helped me think more like an adult"; "When we went to the radio station and we talked about all those topics...made me think that it does not help me in any way to be acting like a little girl (like the boys do[!])." She represents a significant identity shift from being a "little girl" to someone "who thinks more like an adult." During the radio interview, Delfina, in spite of her shyness and lack of English fluency, spoke powerfully and convincingly: as Ray would have said, she "stepped-up and spoke out." She spoke from the heart about key issues of concern to her and her peers, such as deportation, living in fear of being separated from her family, of her desire to "be someone" and continue her education in spite of the obstacles that have been erected to the higher education of undocumented youth. Speaking to the public in that interview about issues she and her peers struggled with, including the effect on young children in her neighborhood of youth drug use, made her feel that acting out and acting "*como niña chiquita*"–like a little girl–was no longer a useful role to play. According to Delfina, it was time for her to assume responsibility as a person who could speak for her community and speak to these issues. In that moment she learned that she could speak and that people were listening, and that coming to voice carried certain responsibilities. Later in the interview, Delfina remarks:

> This program has helped me a lot with this (switches to Spanish—what follows is translated). Well, like before . . . . Now we talk about themes that are more central, more personal (*más a dentro*). I don't know, it helps me more, like I understand better; now I see how others act. I want to . . . . Like me and Elia, we want to show them (the young children). We want to act well so that they follow our example. I want the best for them (the children) too, cause (..) sometimes, this thing they talked about on the radio (with Kareem), marijuana. I don't want for them to go through this because of bad influences.

Delfina, like Tania, expresses a transformation in her understanding, in critical consciousness, and potentially her actions, through new knowledge and insight gained from other youths' media productions. She and Elia want to "act well" to become better role models for children in her neighborhood. In this statement, Delfina signals three important findings from this study that I have discussed in this chapter: (a) what youth learned from each other changed their way of "seeing" and potentially their behavior; (b) students aspired to use their productions to influence other youth and younger children, and (c) the desire to use their productions as tools for social action builds on these immigrant youths deep-rooted sense of social responsibility, especially toward younger children and other teens in their communities.

This analysis suggests that program activities, and youth productions in particular, become cultural resources for transformation on several levels: for transformation of self; as tools for transformation taken up by other youth within and beyond the program; and transformation of the public discourse, by raising awareness in the media sphere about issues of concern to immigrant youth. These findings led me to propose a rhizomatic analysis (Leander & Rowe, 2006) of process of change and transformation through youth productions that contribute to changing the cultural practices of the collective, as shown in Figure 5.1

Figure 5.1

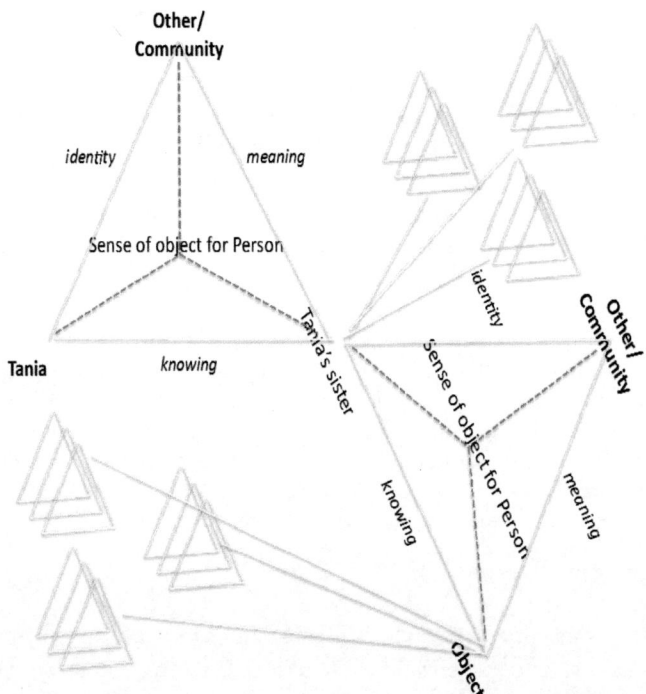

Tania's coauthored digital story mediated interactions, thinking, feeling, and possibly action among other youth in the program and children beyond. This diagram thus represents how processes of change and development achieved through the individual's use of symbolic resources can have multiplying effects with the potential to effect collective change within the multiple communities in which the cultural element is circulated, in this case the Youth Radio and Radio Arts class, Tania's neighborhood, and the radio audiences of KPFW.

• CHAPTER SIX •

Toward a Pedagogy of Powerful Communication

The realities of the work place and social life today require new understandings of language and literacy teaching. This study suggest that to break the cycle of remedial ESL instruction that reproduces the marginalization of poor and immigrant students, we must shift our attention from language skills and exercises in communicative competence to creating the conditions for a *pedagogy of powerful communication*. This pedagogy prepares students to participate in their multiple spheres of experience (school, work, online communities), with agentive identities and powerful language to accomplish personal, social, and civic goals.

As the participants in this study showed, powerful communication addresses the multiple dimensions of being human: knowing oneself, expressing feelings and ideas, sharing yourself with others, making yourself understood by others, participating as a member of a group, representing your ideas and emotions in multiple modalities and genres, shaping life in your local community, and gaining access to public media sphere to create new communities and participate in public discourse. Many of these dimensions of human activity are overlooked in the education of multilingual learners in U.S. schools.

In this concluding chapter I summarize findings from this research that indicate directions for a pedagogy of powerful communication. The framework for this pedagogy was derived primarily from the perspectives of youth on aspects of the program that supported learning and transformation: transformations in new understandings of self, self in relation to others, and self in relation to possibilities for new forms of self-representation and action in the public arena, including their home communities. To reconstruct these youth perspectives I have adopted a methodological and theoretical framework that examines conditions that facilitate or constrain the uses of social and semiotic resources for meaning making, learning, and development. I contextualize these insights offered by students in an analysis of continuity and change over time through collective activity, focusing on the cultural resources that were made available in the setting (Putney, Green, Dixon, Durán, & Yeager, 2000) and the conditions that facilitated or constrained student appropriation of these resources for personal sense making (Zittoun, 2006). Combining Zittoun's semiotic prism analysis with the interactional ethnographic analysis provides both a perspective on the "proper contexts for learning" and what individuals do with the affordances of the context.

In undertaking this study, I was particularly interested in the question of how educators can make learning meaningful and promote youth development to combat long-term trends of alienation, nonparticipation, and academic underachievement. Wenger (1998), for example, has theorized that identities of long-term nonparticipation, such as academic disengagement, develop when individuals feel powerless to negotiate meanings within communities to which they belong. Sociocultural psychologist Tania Zittoun and colleagues (Zittoun, 2006, 2008; Zittoun & Grossen, 2013) have shown that for learning to take place and new learner identities to emerge, people must elaborate a personal sense and emotional responses to new situations and the socially constructed meanings of a given context. When a person is not able to make sense of a task she is required to do or the situation she finds herself in, or she finds herself confronting conflicting identities, her thinking abilities may be inhibited.

People make personal sense through semiotic work that involves cultural elements (such as the digital stories presented as curricular texts) and people (such as the mentors). The case studies presented here in many ways confirm the theoretical insights of these neo-Vygotskian researchers regarding the ways adolescents transform cultural elements into symbolic resources—as tools for semiotic work—through the mediation of significant others, close or distant. Elia, for example, identifies Tim as someone whose discourse and poetry opened new doors for her, to her own creativity, to trying out new ways of seeing, speaking, and being. In this way Tim mediated Elia's identity processes of constructing and mobilizing representations of herself in the past, and of possible selves in a future (Zittoun, 2004). Elia expresses a sense of greater agency to change herself, in overcoming presentation anxiety, for example, and to make more meaning of the world and her place in it. In the processes of making personal sense through semiotic work in various projects and relationships, Elia is able to also construct a sense of continuity of self across spheres of experience. The program became meaningful for her when her lived experience outside of school became relevant to inquiry and dialogue in the classroom, through the sharing of personal stories and the elaboration of emotion and experience through digital stories, radio productions, and poetry.

Building Community Is a Prerequisite for Constructing Personal Voice

To support the development of powerful communication, educators must create the conditions for opening these channels. This means helping students from non-dominant groups overcome alienation and isolation, which contributes to their silencing and invisibility. For communication to happen, there must be trust—*confianza*—and a developing sense of community, a sense of belonging. This does not mean that everyone is equally invested in the "shared enterprise," as Wenger (1998) suggests, but it does mean that there must be a sense of a shared, safe space where learners can feel visible and audible, feel that their humanity is recognized (West, 1994). This is the minimal condition for dialogical interaction to occur, and for intersubjective understandings to emerge among members of a community (Greene, 1982). As Elia, Beto, Dipashri, and Tania reported, the sense of trust that developed in the class allowed them to enter into dialogue, to share themselves through personal stories, to speak and feel that they were understood.

Creating a protected space for communication in Youth Radio and Radio Arts involved bringing youth life worlds into the classroom. What allows students to make meaning is allowing the person to bring to the learning situation her ways of making meaning: her memories, desires, imagination, knowledge, languages, embodied experiences, and representational repertoire. In Chapter 3 we saw how Federico built symbolic bridges to student life worlds through language and cultural memory. Bloome, Carter, Christian, Otto, and Shuart-Faris (2005) argue that the ways people make intertextual links can bring different worlds into a classroom. Federico's and Eugenia's uses of Spanish language, prosody, postures, and gestures brought the world of Mexico into the classroom space. In his interactions with students during radio improv, Federico shifted in and out of a conversational style that reenacted discursive practices carried out in Mexico, activating subjective resonances of "cultural memory" (Kramsch & Whiteside, 2008). The use of and indexing of multiple linguistic codes served to validate Spanish as an appropriate form of communication, allowing participants to experience Spanish and Spanish speakers from a nondeficit perspective.

The affective and subjective dimensions of language. The affective and subjective dimensions of language must be taken into consideration both in terms of the construction of meanings in the present moment and for personal meanings that are necessary for learning over time. Hybrid discourse practices engaged in the program established affective openings for students who, in a school such as this, are expected to leave their linguistic repertoires and meaning-making resources at the door. These hybrid discourse practices—the use of Spanish and Spanish-English code-switching—also contributed to the creation of shared meanings that, according to Zittoun (2010), is a necessary first step toward the construction of personal sense. Findings from this study confirm other research that has found that reductive pedagogies that exclude the linguistic resources of students can limit the academic development of multilingual learners (González & Moll, 2002; Gutierrez, 2001) Analysis of classroom interactions revealed, however, that the linguistic and cultural repertoires of three students and one teacher who did not speak Spanish were consistently excluded, which raises questions about how to create inclusive environments in multilingual settings where the majority speak one nondominant language. The temptation to engage in resistance to the symbolic violence that Spanish-speakers experience on a daily basis in our region of the country is great but must be confronted.

Embodied play, improvisation, and literary arts. Language play, improvisation, using the imagination, and the expressive body are other forms of engagement that enable emotional and interpersonal attunement (Zittoun, 2006). As Tania said, "when Federico came in he definitely got like our spirits out and now everyone is like friends with everyone and everybody talks with everyone." Play can change people's relationship to real-life issues; it can open up imaginary worlds and possibilities for other selves. Improvisation can create spaces outside adult control, and at the same time it challenges young people to take risks and can help them overcome fears and inhibitions. Much of this work in radio improv was anchored in the body, contrary to what most often happens in school. Not all students felt comfortable moving out of their desks and "into their bodies." Nevertheless, culturally specific forms of movement, dance, and language allowed students' life worlds to enter the classroom and enlivened the space, providing opportunities for most students to participate in ways not usually available to them, and for some students to "shine," as Liv said.

The Radio Arts, represented by Tim and Federico, proved particularly productive for language development and the recognition of student linguistic repertoires. These two artists made visible how they play with language in theater and poetry, and they provided structured opportunities for students to do the same—to turn language upside down and inside out, to free language from its prison and envision more invigorated and engaging modes of deployment. Students appreciated these openings for creative expression through poetry and radio improv, and teachers reported that work with these mentors allowed them to see aspects of their students that they rarely had a chance to appreciate. When Tim read the following poem, there were gasps and exclamations of "Wow!" "Beto wrote that?!" when we learned who the author was:

> We are emptiness
> When stage snitches blue at night,
> Deer mustard, fat and yummy
> Deer night, duck mice
> Sick seabirds, wolf, sick deer,
> Beethoven. Lights die he
> Wrote at night, ran fast
> Under straight frequency, blackened
> Hi happy night! Hateful, so I
> Night August in aged deer,
> Under drag night aliens
> Under web and wagons,
> And greenhouses
> Umbrella, sea boat,
> New drill.

We were all surprised that Beto, who rarely spoke in class, has such a rich linguistic repertoire. For Beto, the group acknowledgment of his artistry may have been consequential. The summer after the program he chose to participate with Elia in a university poetry writing summer program with adults. Though he did not participate beyond the first day, his interest indicates that the seed had been planted, that he was willing to cross the boundary into the university space to learn something new in the midst of strangers, to learn more about writing.

Opportunities to develop expressive language in high school come rarely for students who have to take ESL classes instead of electives. Teaching expressive ways with words through the literary and performing arts component can create an alternative space for development, in which young people can refigure their roles as poets, writers, and performers with talent and a larger communicative repertoire of which even they themselves are unaware. Liv felt that Tim was an inspiring, motivating mentor and showed students that writing can be powerful, "if you know how to use language." For Elia, Tim changed the way she saw her world: "Cuz he thinks in a different way. I like how he expresses himself, [in] a unique way . . . Timmy showed us, you know, like to put more meanings to things you see in life." Zittoun (2006) suggests that art and artists matter for young people constructing present and future identities and coherent systems of meaning: "[D]evelopmental transitions are facilitated by sociocultural contexts that show a higher degree of tolerance of young people's explorations of alternative or artistic life styles" (p. 14).

Social and Academic Language Development

Genre-based pedagogies can support the development of powerful communication. Through the genre pedagogy employed in Youth Radio and Radio Arts, students learned the social, compositional, and performative requirements of radio and literary genres, which they recognized could be applied in other classes and content areas. A focus on genre helps students understand not only the features and forms of language required but also the social purposes and possibilities for personhood available through particular genres. The intent of the planned curriculum for the youth commentary genre, for example, was to reframe "language" as being used to critically question and investigate issues of concern to youth themselves; construct a persuasive argument supported by personal or research evidence; communicate effectively to a general public outside of school; and use communication technology to amplify one's voice and broadcast one's perspective, thus contributing to the youths' participation in the public discourse.

Language and concept development is enhanced when conversation, dialogue, and critical inquiry are supported across learning activities in varied participation structures (Gutierrez, 2008). In Youth Radio and Radio Arts these participation structures included teacher-led whole-class discussion, one-on-one instructional conversations, peer and public (class) critiques, story-pitching circles, improv ensembles, paired interviews, and coproduction. This study suggests that instructional conversations (Tharp, 1991) and one-on-one coaching (Clark & Fry, 1992) were particularly helpful in elaborating ideas and rich language for radio and digital stories. Several students mentioned the importance of instructional conversations with writing coach Jack and radio mentor Lyle, who helped them to "speak better" (*hablar major*) and write more clearly with better spelling and grammar. Tania even stated that after her year in the program she considered herself an expert in writing and could now teach writing to other teens.

The emphasis on oral language development, something that middle schools and high schools tend to overlook, appears to have been especially appreciated by these students working in a second language. The teachers recognized the importance of oral language development as well. Liv observed,

> We started with their strengths and showed them a lot of different ways where they could talk about their experiences. Then we were able to support them in writing about their experience, with the exception of reading. They really fine-tuned their oral skills, in terms of public speaking, being taped, having to do and redo, enunciate. We spent an awful lot of time fine tuning their oral skills. Doing something that was meaningful gave them the motivation to do that. We did a lot of listening: a variety of different people, listen in a critical and reflective way and give feedback.

Liv noted that sharing and developing ideas in small groups, such as when students pitched their stories, allowed them to explore ideas while rehearsing the language needed for expressing the idea. Conversations with a radio mentor surrounded by a supportive circle of peers gave them "practice in a safe environment, with opportunities for feedback," and was "a really scaffolded way to use their academic voice, especially when students were unclear about the outcomes expected of their writing and production." Liv concluded that the program met the goals of her "Academic Literacy" class, because students were learning "academic skills versus study skills." Both Ray and Liv felt that academic learning was significant, though they suggested that the following year we incorporate more reading, which we did. In a conference presentation Ray stated to the audience that in Youth Radio and Radio Arts students synthesized information from a variety of sources; used technology to communicate original perspectives; and presented their ideas clearly in ways that others could understand—"In other words, they communicated."

In Chapter 4, I described student perceptions of the applicability of skills and knowledge gained in Youth Radio in other classes and future careers. Tania indicated that journalist mentor Jack scaffolded her writing, helping her expand her vocabulary and improve her sentence structure and grammar. Her key discovery and learning outcome was that she could be understood by others. "I learned that if I spoke, people would understand me." In their interviews students also mention "developing voice," with its multiple meanings, as something they could use in other classes and in the future: for class presentations, job interviews, and work that requires people to talk and "not be scared": as one student said, "Learning how to speak right, going into an interview, how to present your voice, show who you are." Liv's perspective on this question was that public speaking, word processing, managing digital files, writing-editing-revising, and listening and giving feedback were all skills learned in YRRA that could be applied in other classes. Among the most important skills gained, according to Liv, was perseverance: not just being content with getting the work done, but wanting to do a good job because multiple audiences would be hearing or viewing their productions.

Communication technologies for communicating meaning and influencing public opinion. The focus on oral language and the affordances of the audio editing and movie-making technologies was for some students a new and stimulating—though often frustrating—experience. Tania and Elia both suggested that Audacity gave them a sense of agency over their oral language production; this is significant for a young person positioned as less-than-competent in the dominant language of school and society. When asked what she had learned about technology that she found most useful, Tania replied, "I'd say Audacity because that does help you, you know, correct your voice and let people know what you're actually trying to say rather than just like a mumble. You can erase that mumble and actually have the real thing." Audio-editing software allowed her communicate her ideas: from incoherent mumble she was able to express her thoughts and what she had written in her script. This finding confirms previous research in which students identified audio editing as an empowering and enjoyable process (Romero & Walker, 2010). In addition to the audio editing, the recording process encouraged multiple "takes" and opportunities to practice, which a number of researchers argue is critical for second language learners. McDermott (2006) found that learning depends on the quality of social relations that give participants enough practice in community activities to become good at what they do. Heath (2004) writes, "Writers and dancers, like all artists . . . into a future that is bodily and mentally engaged in casting forward in time, and they practice, practice, practice to build habits both mental and physical" (p. 339). Elia in Transcript 5.4 provides an insightful example of this:

> [My English improved by] talking a lot, you know? Like recording your voice. You practice and practice and read like three times, or many times the things that you were gunna say? . . . Like once you have it done you feel good about it, [recording] by yourself and everything. Cuz like the first recording I did was really BAD. But the second got kind of better, and then the third was better, and the fourth, maybe it was *la vencida*, you know? It was *la buena!* [the winner] (*laughs out loud*).

Opportunities to practice and rehearse language helped reduce Elia's "extreme presentation anxiety," and she reported being able to speak with confidence in this class: "I didn't have low self-esteem, I felt confident about myself." She also reported that her improved oral language production would help her in other classes.

Multimodal storytelling provided opportunities for students to represent their meanings and understandings in modes of communication that went beyond spoken or written language. In addition to the benefits for multilingual learners of engaging multiple senses and modalities beyond reading and writing, of recruiting a broader range of representational repertoires, and the novelty of using image, music, and voice-over for a "class" assignment, I believe that digital stories were of particular interest to these youth for allowing identity explorations and constructions as modeled in the examples from the CDS website. What appears to have been also salient for them in this genre was the chance to mix and mash multiple discourses (popular culture, youth culture, Mexican culture, community activism), to express and be acknowledged for their creativity, and to use this powerful medium to influence other youth and communities, as Tania would do.

What we came to recognize, however, was that it was not the technology itself that mattered most to students: it was the social and personal purposes of technology for exploring identities, emotion, ideas, and the contradictions in society, and communicating their perspectives and constructing identities, that mattered most to them. Beto felt that Audacity and iMovie were useful to him because they allowed him "to show my ideas to the world." For Cipriana, the digital story was a way for her to poignantly represent her abandoned life's dream of becoming a dancer in a magical piece entitled "Dancing through Life."

Constructing Personal and Public Voice for Powerful Communication

In this book I argue that a *pedagogy of powerful communication* requires attention to two key dimensions of communication: personal voice and public voice. Chapter 4 discusses findings related to personal voice. In Chapter 5 I describe findings related to the development of a "public voice," articulated by youth in the following terms: the importance of speaking out in public forums (such as the radio) on issues of concern to youth and their communities; representing and defending community values and cultural practices; speaking out and advocating for others; and expressing a sense of social responsibility toward younger teens and children.

An interesting finding from this study was the way youth's productions, more than curricular cultural elements, became symbolic resources for other youth in their elaboration of emotion, identities, and personal sense. For Tania, it was Sugita's digital story about her mother that made her grasp "the concept of respecting moms nowadays" and begin to change her thinking about her relationship with her own mother. Other students mentioned that it was Tania and Yoli's digital story that changed their way of thinking about drug use and how they needed to protect young children from the malignant examples of older youth. Tania expressed awareness that her coproduced work was affecting others. As this realization grew, she began to view their digital story and their feature story about teen views of sex, as tools for effecting change among children, youth, and their home communities. Tania said that she would use their feature story to inform teens about sex and younger children and adults in the community and general public about the unsafe environment that exists in her housing project for young children. Tania's case study allowed me to describe the process by which youth productions were put into circulation within and beyond the program, and how they became cultural elements that were then taken up by other youth, who in turn used them for processes of creative transformation. The articulated semiotic prisms multiply in a rhizomatic fashion, linking individuals in an expanding web of transformed meanings and potential action.

Tania's awareness of her capacity to use her productions as tools to influence public opinion and move people to action was not unique. That all students interviewed appeared to have made personal sense of the program and their own learning can be perhaps attributed to the transformation by youth of program resources for their own purposes, and the flexibility of the program in responding to their interests. These immigrant youth brought to the program an already strong sense of social responsibility and a related set of cultural practices. Students enlarged the notion of voice and communication—the right to speak and advocate for oneself—as introduced originally by Federico, to encompass others as well. When Teresa and Sonia spoke with the radio host about what it meant for them to have their voices heard on the air, the girls responded that it was important for them personally to have their voices heard, but that they represented others like them as well. Tania and other students explained that they valued newly acquired communication skills and knowledge because it would allow them to help younger siblings and other youth, as well as to make visible to adults the dangers that existed for young children in their neighborhoods.

In the same way that a sense of personal voice depended on the construction of a classroom community, the notion "public voice" depended on an expanding community that began with youth members and extended outward to youths' home communities, and through the learning network to the larger civic community and public media sphere. Though the students did not directly comment on this larger conception of community in these terms, the teachers did. Both Ray and Liv felt it was consequential for student learning that professionals from outside the school valued youth perspectives and opinions. Working with mentors from community and participating in public community settings such as the radio station made them feel, according to Ray, like they belonged to the larger civic community. And feeling they belonged to the larger community gave them a sense of agency to participate in this large sphere of action. Students themselves remarked that doing workshops at the radio station and being interviewed on the air was, as Teresa said, "a great opportunity, being able to get heard, getting our voices out there." These experiences, I argue, helped students (and teachers) expand their perceived space of action through a sense of belonging to the larger civic community, and contributed to constructions of an agentive "public voice."

This book argues for a revisioning of second language education that moves away from remedial instruction and deficient notions of communication, toward a *pedagogy of powerful communication* that develops critical multiliteracies and promotes youth engagement with media and the arts across multiple contexts. The principles of this pedagogy were distilled from results of a year-long participatory study of a Youth Radio and Radio Arts program. As such, this pedagogy is understood in terms of local complexities and possibilities rather than a totalizing theory or method (Pennycook, 1989; Norton, 2004). This study's contribution is that it offers insights from teachers and youth themselves about what young people need in order to engage meaningfully in social, academic, and civic life, and to have a voice in the public media sphere.

Bibliography

Agar, M. (2006). Culture: Can you take it anywhere? *International Journal of Qualitative Methods, 5*(2).

Anderson, D. D. (2008). The elementary persuasive letter: Two cases of situated competence, strategy, and agency *Research in the Teaching of English, 42*(3), 270-315.

Arendt, H. (1958). *The human condition.* Chicago: University of Chicago Press.

Baker, D. (2001). *Artists in the making: An ethnographic investigation of literate practices as disciplinary processes in a high school advanced placement studio art classroom.* Dissertation. (3024404). University of California Santa Barbara.

Bakhtin, M. (1986). *Speech genres and other late essays.* Austin: University of Texas Press.

Barton, D., Hamilton, M., & Ivanič, R. (Eds.). (2000). *Situated literacies: Reading and writing in context.* London: Routledge.

Bernstein, B. (2000). *Pedagogy, symbolic control and identity.Theory, research, critique.* Oxford, UK: Rowman & Littlefield Publishers.

Biesta, G. (2004). "Mind the gap!": Communication and the educational relation. In C. Bingham & A. M. Sidorkin (Eds.), *No education without relation* (pp. 11-22). New York: Peter Lang.

Birdwhistell, R. L. (1977). Some discussion of ethnography, theory, and, method. In J. Brockman (Ed.), *About Bateson: Essays on Gregory Bateson.* New York: John Brockman Associates.

Bloome, D., Carter, S. P., Christian, B. M., Otto, S., & Shuart-Faris, N. (2005). *Discourse analysis and the study of classroom language and literacy events: A microethnographic perspective.* Mahwah, NJ: Lawrence Erlbaum.

Camangian, P. (2010). Starting with self: Teaching autoethnography to foster critically caring literacies *Research in the Teaching of English, 45*(2), 179-203.

Campbell, P., Hoey, L., & Perlman, L. (2001). *Sticking with my dreams: Defining and refining youth media in the 21st century.* Groton, MA: Campbell Kibler Associates.

Canagarajah, A. S. (2013). *Translingual practice: Global Englishes and cosmopolitcan relations.* New York: Routledge.

Castanheira, M. L., Crawford, T., Dixon, C., & Green, J. (2001). Interactional ethnography: An approach to studying the social construction of literate practices. *Linguistics and Education, 11*(4), 353-400.

CCC. (1974). Students' right to their own language. . *College Composition and Communication,* XXV. http://www.ncte.org/library/NCTEFiles/Groups/CCCC/NewSRTOL.pdf

CenterforDigitalStorytelling. (2009). Center for Digital Storytelling. Retrieved July 10, 2010, from http://www.storycenter.org/index1.html

Chávez, V., & Soep, E. (2005). Youth radio and the pedagogy of collegiality. *Harvard Educational Review, 75*(4), 409-434.

Clark, R. P., & Fry, D. (1992). *Coaching writers: Editors and reporters working together.* New York: St. Martin's Press.

Cole, M. (1996). *Cultural psychology: A once and future discipline.* Cambridge, MA: Harvard University Press.

Collins, E., & Green, J. (1992). Learning in classroom settings: Making or breaking a culture. In H. Marshall (Ed.), *Redefining student learning: Roots of educational change* (pp. 59-85). Norwood, NJ: Ablex.

Cummins, J. (2000). *Language, power and pedagogy: Bilingual children in the crossfire.* Buffalo, NY: Multilingual Matters.

Dagron, A. G. (2001). *Making waves: Stories of participatory communication for social change.* (p. 246). New York: The Rockefeller Foundation.

Darder, A. (2010). Schooling Bodies: Critical pedagogy and urban youth. In S. R. Steinberg (Ed.), *19 Urban questions: Teaching in the city* (2nd ed., pp. xiii-xxiii). New York: Peter Lang.

Del Castillo, R. (2002). *Tales from a Michoacano.* Denver, CO: Auraria Graphics Inc.

Dwyer, D. (2010). Defying cops and clan, immigrants trek 1,500 miles to Washington. Retrieved August 20, 2010, from http://abcnews.go.com/Politics/illegal-immigrants-seek-reform-1500-mile-trek-dc/story?id=10499173

Edwards, A., & Mutton, T. (2007). Looking forward: Rethinking professional learning through partnership arrangements in Initial Teacher Education. *Oxford Review of Education, 33*(4), 503-519.

Eisenhart, M., & Finkel, E. (1998). *Women's science: Learning and succeeding from the margins.* Chicago: University of Chicago Press.

Evaldsson, A.-C., & Corsaro, W. A. (1998). Play and games in the peer cultures of preschool and preadolescent children: An interpretative approach. *Childhood, 5*(4), 377-402. doi: 10.1177/0907568298005004003

Fisherkeller, J. (Ed.). (2011). *International perspectives on youth media: Cultures of production and education.* New York: Peter Lang.

Freed, M. (2010). The personal side of the Dream Act. Retrieved August 21, 2010, from http://youthcast.org/?p=1589

Freire, P. (1970/2000). *Pedagogy of the oppressed.* New York: Continuum.

Freire, P. (1995). *Pedagogy of hope. Reliving pedagogy of the oppressed* New York: Continuum.

Freire, P. (2005). *Education for critical consciousness.* New York: Continuum.

Friedberg, J. (Producer). (2007, December 12, 2009). Un poquito de tanta verdad. [documentary] Retrieved from http://difusionrebelde.blogspot.com/2011/01/documental-un-poquito-de-tanta-verdad.html

Gee, J. P. (2003). *What video games have to teach us about learning and literacy*. New York: Palgrave/Macmillan.

Gee, J. P., Hull, G., & Lankshear, C. (1996). *The new work order: Behind the language of the new capitalism*. Boulder, CO: Westview Press.

Gilligan, C. (1993). Joining the resistance: Psychology, politics, girls, and women. In M. Fine & L. Weis (Eds.), *Beyond silenced voices: Class, race, and gender in United States schools* (pp. 143–168). Albany: State University of New York Press.

Goldenberg, C. N. (1992). Instructional conversations: Promoting comprehension through discussion. *The Reading Teacher, 46*(4), 316–326.

González, N. (2001). *I am my language: Discourses of women & children in the borderlands*. Tucson: University of Arizona Press.

González, N., & Moll, L. C. (2002). Cruzando el puente: Harnessing funds of knowledge in the Puente Project. *Journal of Educational Policy, 16*(4), 623–641.

González, N., Moll, L. C., & Amanti, C. (Eds.). (2005). *Funds of knowledge: Theorizing practices in households, communities, and classrooms*. Mahwah, NJ: Lawrence Erlbaum.

Goodman, S. (2003). *Teaching youth media: A critical guide to literacy, video production, and social change*. New York: Teachers College Press.

Green, J., & Wallat, C. (Eds.). (1981). *Ethnography and langugage in educational settings*. Norwood, NJ: Ablex Publishers.

Greene, M. (1982a). Literacy for what? *Phi Delta Kappan*, January, 326–329.

Greene, M. (1982b). Public education and the public space. *Educational Researcher* (June–July), 4–9.

Grossen, M., Zittoun, T., & Ros, J. (2012). Boundary crossing events and potential appropriation space in philosophy, literature and general knowledge. In E. Hjörne, G. van der Aalsvoort, & G. d. Abreu (Eds.), *Learning, social interaction and diversity: Exploring school practices* (pp. 15–33). Boston: Sense Publishers.

Guile, D., & Young, M. (2003). Transfer and transition in vocational education. In T. Tuomi-Grohn, Y. Engeström, & M. Young (Eds.), *Between school and work: New perspectives on transfer and boundary-crossing* (pp. 63–84). Oxford, UK: Elsevier Science.

Gutierrez, K. (2001). What's new in English language arts: Challenging policies and practices, y qué? *Language arts, 78*(6), 564–569.

Gutierrez, K. (2005). *Intersubjectivity and grammar in the third space. Sylvia Scribner Award acceptance speech*. Paper presented at the Annual Meeeting of the American Educational Research Association, April 7–11, Montreal, Canada.

Gutierrez, K. (2008). Developing a sociocritical literacy in the third space. *Reading Research Quarterly, 43*(2), 148–164.

Gutiérrez, K., Baquedano-Lopez, P., & Asato, J. (2001). English for the children: The new literacy of the old world order. *Bilingual Review Journal, 24*(1 & 2), 87–112.

Gutierrez, K., & Rogoff, B. (2003). Cultural ways of learning: Individual traits or repertoires of practice. *Educational researcher, 32*(5), 19–25. doi: 10.3102/0013189X032005019

Hargittai, E. (2002). Second-level digital divide: Differences in peoples online skills. *First Monday, 7*(4). http://firstmonday.org/ojs/index.php/fm/article/view/942/864for.

Heath, S. B. (2004). Learning language and strategic thinking through the arts. *Reading Research Quarterly, 39*(3), 338-344.

Heath, S., & Smyth, L. (1999). *Artshow: Youth and community development.* Washington, DC: Partners for Livable Communities.

Hill, M. L. (2009). *Beats, rhymes and classroom life: Hip-hop pedagogy and the politics of identity.* New York: Teachers College Press.

Holland, D., Eisenhart, M., & Conell, R. W. (1990). *Educated in romance: Women, achievement, and college culture.* Chicago: University of Chicago Press.

Holland, D., Skinner, D., & Valsiner, J. (2001). Discerning the dialogical self: A theoretical and methodological examination of a Nepali adolescent's narrative. *Forum Qualitative Sozialforschung / Forum: Qualitative Social Research, 2*(3), 18-35.

Horner, B., Lu, M.-Z., & Royster, J. (2011). Language difference in writing: Toward a translingual approach. *College English, 73*(3), 303-321.

Hull, G., & Schultz, K. (Eds.). (2004). *School's out: Bridging out-of-school literacies with classroom practice.* New York: Teachers College Press.

Hull, G., & Zacher, J. (2007). Enacting identities: An ethnography of a job training program. *Identity: An International Journal of Theory and Research, 7*(1), 71-102.

Hyland, K. (2007). Genre pedagogy: Language, literacy, and L2 writing instruction. *Journal of Second Language Writing, 16,* 148-164.

Hymes, D. (1974). *Foundations in sociolinguistics: An ethnographic approach.* Philadelphia: University of Pennsylvania Press.

ISTE. (2009). International Society for Technology in Education. Retrieved August 10, 2010, from http://www.iste.org/Content/NavigationMenu/NETS/ForStudents/NETS_for_Students.htm

Ivanič, R. (1998). *Writing and identity: The discoursal construction of identity in academic writing.* Philadelphia, PA: John Benjamins.

Keenan, S., & Fisherkeller, J. (2008). Making meaning of media education: Professional development among youth media practitioners *Youth Media Reporter, 2*(2), 165-187.

Kinloch, V. (Ed.). (2010). *Urban literacies: Critical perspectives on language, learning, and community.* New York: Teachers College Press.

Kramsch, C., & Whiteside, A. (2008). Language ecology in multilingual settings. Towards a theory of symbolic competence. *Applied Linguistics, 29*(4), 645-671.

Kress, G. (2000). Design and transformation: New theories of meaning In B. Cope & M. Kalantzis (Eds.), *Multiliteracies: Literacy learning and the design of social futures* (pp. 153-161). London: Routledge.

Lam, E. W. (2006). Reinvisioning language, literacy, and the immigrant subject in new mediascapes. *Pedagogies: An International Journal, 1*(3), 171-195.

Lankshear, C., Peters, M., & Knobel, M. (1996). Critical pedagogy and cyberspace. In M. Peters (Ed.), *Counternarratives: Cultural studies and critical pedagogies in postmodern spaces* (pp. 149-188). New York: Routledge.

Lave, J., & Wenger, E. (1991). *Situated learning: Legitimate peripheral participation.* New York: Cambridge University Press.

Leander, K. (2002). Polycontextual construction zones: Mapping the expansion of schooled space and identity. *Mind, Culture and Activity, 9*(3), 211-237.

Leander, K. (2003). Writing new travelers' tales on New Literacyscapes. *Reading Research Quarterly, 38*(3), 392-397.

Leander, K., & Rowe, D. W. (2006). Mapping literacy spaces in motion: A rhizomatic analysis of a classroom literacy performance. *Reading Research Quarterly, 41*(4), 428-460.

Lefstein, A. (2008). Changing classroom practice through the English national literacy strategy: A micro-interactional perspective. *American Educational Research Journal, 45*(3), 701-737.

Lemke, J. (2002). Becoming the village: Education across lives. In G. Wells & G. Claxton (Eds.), *Learning for life in the 21st century: Sociocultural perspectives on the future of education* (pp. 34-45). Oxford, UK: Blackwell.

Lemke, J. (1995). *Textual politics: Discourse and social dynamics*. Bristol, PA: Taylor & Francis.

Lemke, J. (2005). Multimedia genres and traversals. *Folia Linguistica, 39*(1/2), 45-56.

Leung, C. (2005). Convivial communication: Recontextualizing communicative competence. *International Journal of Applied Linguistics, 15*(2), 119-144.

Limón, J. (1994). *Dancing with the devil: Society and cultural poetics in Mexican-American south Texas*. Madison: University of Wisconsin Press.

Mahiri, J. (2004). *What they don't learn in school: Literacy in the lives of urban youth*. New York: Peter Lang.

Manyak, P. C. (2002). "Welcome to Salón 110": The consequences of hybrid literacy practices in a first grade English immersion class. *Bilingual Research Journal, 26*, 421-442.

Martin-Beltrán, M. (2010). Positioning proficiency: How students and teachers (de)construct language proficiency at school. *Linguistics and Education, 21*, 257-281. doi: 10.1016/j.linged.2010.09.002

McDermott, R., Goldman, S., & Varenne, H. (2006). The cultural work of learning disabilities. *Educational Researcher, 35*(6), 12-17. doi: 10.3102/0013189X035006012.

McDermott, R., Gospodinoff, K., & Aron, J. (1978). Criteria for an ethnographically adequate description of concerted activities and other contexts. *Semiotics, 24*, 246-275.

Mills, K. A. (2011). *The multiliteracies classroom*. Tonawanda, NY: Multilingual Matters.

Moll, L. C., Amanti, C., Neff, D., & González, N. (1992). Funds of knowledge for teaching: Using a qualitative approach to connect homes and classrooms. *Theory into Practice, 31*(2), 132-141.

Moran, S. (2010). Commitment and creativity: Transforming experience into art. In C. Connery, V. John-Steiner, & A. Marjanovic-Shane (Eds.), *Vygotsky and creativity: A cultural-historical approach to play, meaning making, and the arts* (pp. 141-162). New York: Peter Lang.

Morrell, E., & Duncan-Andrade, J. (2006). Popular culture and critical media pedagogy in secondary literacy classrooms. *International Journal of Learning, 12*, 273-280.

Nancy, J.-L. (1988). *The experience of freedom*. Paris, France: Editions Galilée.

NCA. (2001). *Communication: Ubiquitous, complex, consequential*. Washington, DC: National Communications Association.

NCSS. (2010). National curriculum standards for social studies

NCTE. (2008). The NCTE definition of 21st century literacies. Retrieved August 10, 2010, from http://www.ncte.org/positions/statements/21stcentdefinition

NCTE. (2007). Multimodal literacies. Retrieved January 10, 2007, from http://www.ncte.org/about/over/positions/category/media/123213.htm

NCTE/IRA. (2012). NCTE / IRA standards for the English language arts

Nespor, J. (1997). *Tangled up in school: Politics, space, bodies, and signs in the educational process.* Mahwah, NJ: Lawrence Erlbaum.

Nieto, S. (2002). *Language, culture, and teaching: Critical perspectives for a new century.* Mahwah, NJ: Lawrence Erlbaum.

Norton, B., & Toohey, K. (Eds.). (2004). *Critical pedagogies and language learning.* New York: Cambridge University Press.

Nunez, E. M. (2010). Students risk dreams—and deportation—in walk for recognition. Retrieved August 21, 2010, from http://www.cnn.com/2010/US/03/22/dream.act.education/

Pennycook, A. (1989). The concept of method, interested knowledge, and the politics of language teaching. *TESOL Quarterly, 23*(4), 589-618.

Putney, L., Green, J., Dixon, C., Durán, R., & Yeager, B. (2000). Consequential progressions: Exploring collective-individual development in a bilingual classroom. In C. Lee & P. Smagorinsky (Eds.), *Vygotskian perspectives on literacy research* (pp. 86-126). Cambridge, UK: Cambridge University Press.

Rex, L. A., & McEachen, D. (1999). "If anything is odd, inappropriate, confusing, or boring, it's probably important": The emergence of inclusive academic literacy through English classroom discussion practices. *Research in the Teaching of English, 34,* 65-129.

Romero, D., & Walker, D. (2010). Pushing the boundaries of writing: The consequentiality of visualizing voice in bilingual youth radio. In C. Bazerman, R. Krut, K. Lunsford, S. McLeod, S. Null, P. Rogers, & A. Stansell (Eds.), *Traditions of writing research* (pp. 224-236). London: Routledge.

Rosaldo, R. (1989). *Culture & truth: The remaking of social analysis.* Boston, MA: Beacon Press.

Schiffrin, D. (1994). The textual and contextual basis of discourse. *Semiotica, 102*(1/2), 101-101, 124.

Soep, E., & Chávez, V. (2010). *Drop that knowledge: Youth radio stories.* Berkeley: University of California Press.

Souto-Manning, M., & Smagorinsky, P. (2010). Freire, Vygotsky, and social justice theories in English education. In S. J. Miller & D. Kirkland (Eds.), *Change matters: Critical essays on moving social justice research from theory to policy* (pp. 41-51). New York: Peter Lang.

Spradley, J. (1979). *The ethnographic interview.* New York: Harcourt Brace Jovanovich College Publishers.

Stanton-Salazar, R. D. (1997). A social capital framework for understanding the socialization of racial minority children and youths. *Harvard Educational Review, 67*(1), 1-40.

Stein, P. (2004). Representation, rights, and resources: Multimodal pedagogies in the language and literacy classroom. In B. Norton & K. Toohey (Eds.), *Critical pedagogies and language learning* (pp. 95-115). New York: Cambridge University Press.

Street, B. V. (2003). What's "new" in New Literacy Studies?: Critical approaches to literacy in theory and practice. *Current Issues in Comparative Education, 5*(2), 77-91.

Suárez-Orozco, C., & Suárez-Orozco, M. (2001). *Children of immigration.* Cambridge, MA: Harvard University Press.

Suárez-Orozco, C., Yoshikawa, Y., Teranishi, R., & Suárez-Orozco, M. (2011). Growing up in the shadows: The developmental implications of unauthorized status. *Harvard Educational Review, 81*(3), 438-472.

Sue, D. W., Capodilupo, C. M., Torino, G., Bucceri, J., Holder, A. M. B., Nadal, K. L., & Esquilin, M. (2007). Racial microaggressions in everyday life: Implications for clinical practice. *American Psychologist, 62*(4), 271-286.

Tannen, D., Kendall, S., & Gordon, C. (Eds.). (2007). *Family talk: Discourse and identity in four American families.* New York: Oxford University Press.

TESOL. (2009). *Standards for the recognition of initial TESOL programs in P-12 ESL teacher education.* Alexandria, VA: TESOL.

Tharp, R., & Gallimore, R. (1991). The instructional conversation: Teaching and learning in social activity. *NCRCDSLL Research Reports.* Berkeley: Center for Research on Education, Diversity and Excellence, University of California, Berkeley.

Toohey, K. (2000). *Learning English in school: Identity, social relations and classroom practice.* Clevedon, UK: Multilingual Matters.

Valencia, R. (Ed.). (2002). *Chicano school failure and success: Past, present, and future.* New York: Routledge.

Valenzuela, A. (1999). *Subtractive schooling: U.S.-Mexican youth and the politics of caring.* Albany: State University of New York Press.

Vásquez, O. (2003). *La clase mágica: Imagining optimal possibilities in a bilingual commuity of learners.* Mahwah, NJ: Lawrence Erlbaum.

Vygotsky, L. S. (1978). *Mind in society: The development of higher psychological processes.* Cambridge, MA: Harvard University Press.

Walker, D. (2003). *Constructing artistic, literate, and social identities after school: Community cultural resources in support of Latino youth.* (Ph.D. Dissertation manuscript). University of Colorado Boulder.

Walker, D. (2009). Examining the intersection of popular culture in youth-radio after school. *Youth Media Reporter, 2*(1), 201-220.

Walker, D., & Romero, D. (2008). When "literacy is a bennie": Researching contested literacies in bilingual youth radio. *Ethnography and Education: An International Perspective, 3*(3), 283-296

Wells, G. (2007). The mediating role of discoursing in activity. *Mind, Culture, and Activity, 14*(3), 160-177.

Wenger, E. (1998). *Communities of practice: Learning, meaning, and identity.* Cambridge, UK: Cambridge University Press.

Wertsch, J. V. (1991). *Voices of the mind: A sociocultural approach to mediated action.* Cambridge, MA: Harvard University Press.

West, C. (1993). *Race matters.* Boston: Beacon Press.

WIDA. (2007). *Understanding the WIDA English Language Proficiency Standards.* Retrieved August 24, 2009, from http://www.wida.us

WIDA. (2012). *2012 Amplification of the English language development standards.* Madison: Board of Regents University of Wisconsin System.

YouthMediaInternational. (2010). Youth Radio from http://www.youthradio.org/

Zittoun, T. (2004). Competencies for developmental transitions: The case of choice of first names. *Culture and Psychology, 10*(2), 131-161. doi: 10.1177/1354067X04040926

Zittoun, T. (2006). *Transitions: Development through symbolic resources.* Greenwich, CT: Information Age Publishing.

Zittoun, T. (2008). Learning through transitions: The role of institutions. *European Journal of Psychology of Education, 23*(2), 165-181.

Zittoun, T. (2010). How does an object become symbolic?: Rooting semiotic artifacts in dynamic shared experiences. In B. Wagoner (Ed.), *Symbolic transformation: The mind in movement through culture and society* (pp. 173-192). New York: Routledge.

Zittoun, T., Duveen, G., Gillespie, A., Ivinson, G., & Psaltis, C. (2003). The use of symbolic resources in developmental transitions. *Culture and Psychology, 9*(4), 415-448.

Zittoun, T., & Grossen, M. (2010). L'actualisation d'intentions didactiques en classe de littérature, philosophie et culture générale: Un essai d'analyse transversale. Neuchatel, Switzerland: Université de Neuchatel.

Zittoun, T., & Grossen, M. (2013). Cultural elements as means of constructing the continuity of the self across various spheres of experience. In M. B. Ligorio & M. César (Eds.), *Interplays between dialogical learning and dialogical self* (pp. 99-126). Charlotte, NC: Information Age.

Index

A

acknowledgment, 122, 152
Amanti, C., 3, 13
Anderson, D.D., 29
Arendt, H., 3, 89, 90
Aron, J., 23
art and artist identities, 152, 171-72
Asato, J., 47
Audacity, 30, 37, 38, 119, 136, 172, 175
authorial presence, 40
autobiographical self, 41

B

Baker, D., 51
Bakhtin, M., 95, 96
banking education, 113
Baquedano-Lopez, P., 47
Barton, D., 7
Bernstein, B., 3
Biesta, G., 137
bilingual learners. *See* multilingual learners
Birdwhistell, R.L., 76
Bloome, D., 9, 10, 19, 22, 44, 47, 48, 54, 77, 169
Boal, A., 27, 28, 76
Border Story, A., 29
Bourdieu, P., 76

C

Camangian, P., 89, 91
Campbell, P., 8
Canagarajah, A.S., 7
Carter, S.P., 9, 19, 169
Castanheira, M.L., 9, 16, 43, 50, 51, 96

Center for Digital Storytelling, 20, 23, 26, 146
chapbook, 27
Chávez, V., 7, 8, 19, 29
Christian, B.M., 9, 19, 169
Clark, R.P., 35, 172
code switching, 162, 170
cognitive resources, 145
Colburn, M., 14
Cole, M., 13
Collins, E., 44
communication, 3-6, 79-81, 85, 100
    language and literacy education, 6-8
    technologies, 118-20, 174
    Youth Radio and Radio Arts and, 50
communication competence, 22, 102, 136
Communicative Language Teaching, 3, 6
community, 169176
    building, 87-88, 91-95
    expanded sense of, 159
    field trips and, 94-95
    food and, 93-94
    importance of, 88
    of practice, 159
community funds of knowledge, 33
community-based arts education, 19
community-linked learning design, 11-15
community literacies, 7
community radio, 1
Conell, R.W., 107
confianza, 69, 90, 169
consejos, 81, 96, 97, 109, 128, 139
content analysis, 127
Corsaro, W.A., 82
Crawford, T., 9, 43, 51, 96
critical language teaching, 19
critical literacy, 8

cultural elements, 86, 87, 109, 111, 112,
    131-32, 141, 154, 168
  personal development and, 127
  student use of, 129
cultural memory, 169
Culturally and Linguistically Diverse
    Education (CDL), 4
culture of romance, 107
culture of silence, 48
Cummins, J., 77

D

Darder, A., 76
Deferred Action for Childhood Arrivals, 2
Del Castillo, R., 69
delay, 95
development, 126
Dewey, John, 1, 3
Diaz, J., 5
digital divide, 7
digital stories/storytelling, 20, 25, 26, 27,
    109, 110, 111, 132, 146-51, 175
  authorial presence in, 150
  autobiographical self in, 150
  as a cultural element, 153
  as a symbolic resource, 152-53
discoursal self, 41
discourse analysis, 127
Dixon, C., 9, 43, 51, 96, 168
Duncan-Andrade, J., 7
Durán, R., 9, 168
Duveen, G., 122, 152

E

echando relajo, 69
ecological learning design, 3
economies of meaning, 11, 12
education, 3-6
Edwards, A., 13
Eisenhart, M., 12, 107
embodied play, 170
emotional resonances, 72
English as a Second Language (ESL), 4, 44
Evaldsson, A.-C., 82
exquisite corpse, 27
externalization, 155

F

feature stories, 20
Federico, 17, 27, 67-70, 72-75, 87, 147,
    169, 170, 176
  body speech, 71-72
  communication and, 79-81
  improvisational theater and, 74
  language play with, 69-70, 82
  personal voice and, 95-101
  voice and, 75-79
field of relations, 11
Finkel, E., 12
Fisherkeller, J., 8
frame clashes, 54, 65, 79
Friedberg, J., 1
Freire, P., 3, 6, 24, 48, 76, 90, 113, 155
Fry, D., 35, 172
Fuentes, Federico Garcia. *See* Federico

G

Gee, J.P., 7
genre-based pedagogies, 172
Gillespie, A., 122, 152
Gilligan, C., 101
Goldenberg, C.N., 36
González, N., 3
Goodman, S., 8
González, N., 13, 72, 170
Gordon, C., 72
Gospodinoff, K., 23
Green, J., 9, 43, 44, 51, 96, 168
Greene, M., 3, 169
Grossen, M., 10, 11, 26, 82, 85, 110, 111,
    113, 127, 151, 168
Guile, D., 12
Gutierrez, K., 12, 13, 47, 170, 172

H

Habermas, J., 3, 69
Hall, Sir Peter, 28
Hamilton, M., 7
Handy, L., 55
Heath, S., 19, 70, 118, 174
Hernandez, TZ (Tim), 14, 27, 74, 170, 171
Herrera, J.F., 27

Hill, M.L., 89
Hoey, L., 8
Holland, D., 107, 126
hook, 25
Horner, B., 4
Hull, G., 7, 151
human speech play, 69
hybrid discourse practices, 170
hybrid language practices, 59
Hyland, K., 21, 22
Hymes, D., 3, 4

I

identity
    multiplication of, 143
    processes, 121–22, 140
    repositioning, 122
    work, 161
image+sound wave, 38
iMovie, 175
improvisation, 170
intercontextual links, 64
instructional conversations, 36, 172
interactional ethnography, 9–11, 52, 53, 168
International Society for Technology in Education, 26
intertextual links, 64
internalization, 87
Ivanič, R., 7, 19, 24, 38, 40, 41, 127, 150
Ivinson, G., 122, 152

J

John-Steiner, V., 51

K

Keenan, S., 8
Kendall, S., 72
Knobel, M., 11
knowing, 3
knowledge-skill acquisition, 140
Kramsch, C., 71
Kress, G., 25

L

La Carpa, 28, 72
language
    affective dimensions of, 170
    barrier, 105
    competencies, 34
    development, 116–20, 172–75
    domains, 35
    features, 35
    ideologies, 66
    memory, 169
    subjective dimensions of, 170
Lankshear, C., 7, 11
Lave, J., 12
Leander, K., 13, 157, 158
lede, 25
Lefstein, A., 44
Lemke, J., 11, 22, 24
Leung, C., 3
liberation, 76
Limón, J., 69
linguistically handicapped, 69
literary arts, 170
literacyscapes, 13
lived space, 157, 159
Lu, M.-Z., 4

M

Mahiri, J., 7
Manyak, P.C., 47
Marcuse, H., 69
Martin-Beltrán, M., 66
McDermott, R., 23, 174
McEachen, D., 36
meaning, 137
meaning-making processes, 109, 161
Mills, K.A., 8
Mistranslations, 27
Moll, L.C., 3, 13, 170
Molotov, 29
Moran, S., 125
Morrell, E., 7
multiliteracies, 6, 19
multilingual discourse practices, 71
multilingual learners, 47

advances in language development, 118
communication technologies and, 118–20
exclusionary practices toward, 60, 167
failure to teach, 2
instructional conversations and, 38
perceptions of, 47–48
stereotyping, 49
multimodal composition, 87, 113
multimodal storytelling, 174
Mutton, D., 13

N

Nancy, J.-L., 89
National Communications Association (NCA), 5
National Council of Teachers of English (NCTE), 4, 5
Neff, D., 13
networked learning design (NLD), 11
new language, 93
New Literacies, 7
New London Group, 6, 19
new media technologies, 7
Nespor, J., 11
Nieto, S., 2, 91
No Child Left Behind, 2
Norton, B., 19, 177

O

Obama, B., 2, 3
object, 86
observable curriculum, 9, 16, 51, 52
one-on-one coaching, 172
other, 86, 112
Otto, S., 9, 19, 169

P

paralinguistic discursive practice, 66
participatory communication, 5
pedagogical situation, 22
pedagogy of powerful communication, 167, 175, 177
defined, 9
principles of, 51
social responsibility and, 155
Pennycook, A., 177
perceived space, 159
Perlman, L., 8
person, 86
person-object relationship, 111, 112
person-other relationship, 112
personal sense/sense making, 86, 122–23, 123–26, 140
personal voice, 85–87, 130, 131
community and, 169–72
constructing, 175–77
student constructions of, 101–4
Also see voice
personal-within-community, 146
Peters, M., 11
place, 150, 151
poetry genre, 27
popular culture, 7
possibilities of selfhood, 19, 38, 40
Psaltis, C., 122, 152
public realm, 90
public voice, 87, 130, 131
construction of, 95–101, 127–28, 156–61, 175–77
Federico and, 96–101
Putney, L., 9, 17, 53, 82, 83, 168

R

racial micro-aggressions, 49
radio improv, 27
reconstructive narrative analysis, 127
remedial ESL instruction, 22
representation, 36
respeto, 69
Rex, L.A., 36
Rodriquez, L., 88
Rogoff, B., 12
Romero, D., 3, 36, 54, 135, 174
Ros, J., 10
Rosaldo, R., 69
Royster, J., 4

S

safe spaces, 91
self, new understanding of, 151–54
self-advocacy, 97, 99, 100, 101
self-representation, 60, 168
self-within-community, 150
semiotic
    devices, 86
    domains, 7
    prism, 43, 85, 86, 103, 109, 123, 168, 176
sense-making activities, 153
Shuart-Faris, N., 9, 19, 169
silence, 48–49
Skinner, D., 126
Smagorinsky, P., 156
Smyth, L., 19
social
    media, 7
    responsibility, 154–56
    theory of participation, 159
sociocultural psychology, 9, 10, 122
Soep, E., 7, 8, 19, 29
Soto, G., 5
Souto-Manning, M., 156
spaces of enclosure, 11
spatial distribution, 77
speaking out, 100, 101, 163
Spradley, J., 52
Stanton-Salazar, R. D., 13
Stein, P., 25
Street, B.V., 7
Suárez-Orozco, C., 2, 107
Suárez-Orozco, M., 2, 107
Sue, D.W., 49
symbolic
    resources, 108–16, 121, 140, 141, 144–45, 168
    violence, 113

T

tag, 25
Tannen, D., 72
Teaching English as a Second or Other Language (TESOL), 4, 5
Teatro Campesino, 28
Teranishi, R., 2, 107
texts, 6
Tharp, R., 36, 172
Theater of the Oppressed, 28
thematic coherence, 54
thinking and feeling space, 112
Toohey, K., 19, 76

U

unsilencing, 46

V

Valdez, L., 28
Valencia, R., 2
Valenzuela, A., 2, 12
Valsiner, J., 126
valued knowledge domains, 133
Vásquez, O., 13
Villaseñor, V., 88
voice, 46, 50, 75–79, 85, 97, 100, 134, 135
    developing, 173
    student constructions of, 101
    student use of, 113
voice waves, 37
vox pops, 20, 24, 159, 160
Vygotsky, L., 74, 86, 123, 125

W

Walker, A., 5
Walker, D., 3, 36, 54, 70, 92, 135, 174
Wallat, C., 9
Wenger, E., 11, 12, 123, 137, 159, 168, 169
Wertsch, J.V., 10
West, C., 137, 169
Whiteside, A., 71
World-Class Instructional Design & Assessment (WIDA), 4

Y

Yeager, B., 9, 168
Yoshikawa, Y., 2, 107
Young, M., 12
youth commentaries, 20, 23–24, 28–30

context and process of producing, 30-43
cultural mediation, 55
final rubric for, 39
instructional texts and, 31-32
interactional formats and, 33-34
language and, 33-34
youth media
school based, 8
Youth Media International, 20, 29, 38
youth radio, 2, 8
Youth Radio and Radio Arts, 3, 6, 8, 9
civic life and, 156-57
collaborative tension in, 64-65
constructing student identities, 57
context of program implementation, 43-44
cultural elements, 131-32
cultural memory and, 70-72
curriculum of, 51, 52
description of first day of, 53-63
elements of change and continuity, 63-65
development of voice, 65-67
digital stories, 146-51
ESL students and, 47
exit interview protocol, 85-86
exit interviews, 114
feature story description, 137-41
as a field of relations, 13
five Ws, 62-63
frame clashes, 65
as a genre-based pedagogy, 21-24
goals of, 12
identity processes and, 121-22, 141-44
intragroup tensions, 89
language and, 70-72
literacy/language acquisitions, 135-36
mentoring and, 35, 171, 173
as a networked learning design, 11, 22
Our Neighborhood Communities, 128
Our School Community, 128
overview of genres taught in, 24-28
overview of program design, 20-21
personal voice in, 125
purpose of, 19
rhizomatic analysis of, 164
second language development and, 116-20
sharing self in, 89-91
social responsibility and, 154-56
student confidence and, 103
student perceptions of, 114-16
study of, 9-11, 11-15, 15-16, 164
traditional school-based literacy practices and, 40
writing and, 119-20
youth commentary and, 28-30
Youth Radio Oakland, 29, 32, 41

Z

Zacher, J., 151
Zittoun, T., 9, 10, 11, 17, 26, 43, 44, 74, 82, 85, 86, 87, 104, 107, 109, 110, 111, 112, 113, 112, 122, 123, 125, 126, 127, 140, 151, 152, 154, 161, 168, 170, 171

CRITICAL ISSUES
FOR LEARNING AND TEACHING

Shirley R. Steinberg & Pepi Leistyna
General Editors

Minding the Media is a book series specifically designed to address the needs of students and teachers in watching, comprehending, and using media. Books in the series use a wide range of educational settings to raise consciousness about media relations and realities and promote critical, creative alternatives to contemporary mainstream practices. *Minding the Media* seeks theoretical, technical, and practitioner perspectives as they relate to critical pedagogy and public education. Authors are invited to contribute volumes of up to 85,000 words to this series. Possible areas of interest as they connect to learning and teaching include:

- critical media literacy
- popular culture
- video games
- animation
- music
- media activism
- democratizing information systems
- using alternative media
- using the Web/internet
- interactive technologies
- blogs
- multi-media in the classroom
- media representations of race, class, gender, sexuality, disability, etc.
- media/communications studies methodologies
- semiotics
- watchdog journalism/investigative journalism
- visual culture: theater, art, photography
- radio, TV, newspapers, zines, film, documentary film, comic books
- public relations
- globalization and the media
- consumption/consumer culture
- advertising
- censorship
- audience reception

For additional information about this series or for the submission of manuscripts, please contact:
  Shirley R. Steinberg and Pepi Leistyna,
  msgramsci@aol.com | Pepi.Leistyna@umb.edu

To order other books in this series, please contact our Customer Service Department:
  (800) 770-LANG (within the U.S.)
  (212) 647-7706 (outside the U.S.)
  (212) 647-7707 FAX

Or browse online by series:
  www.peterlang.com